Sally Gold was born into a state orphanage then foster care. She was adopted at the young age of eight then raised in Los Angeles and is a proud graduate of UCLA.

For over three decades, Sally served in the FBI and counterintelligence, completing missions in places like Washington D.C., Israel, Iraq, and Syria. Along the way, she navigated the challenges of being a single mother to two wonderful sons.

In the System is a story of sacrifice and resilience resulting in finding one's own path to self-acceptance in a world few get to see.

Through her writing, Sally shares her journey of survival, encouraging others to overcome adversity despite its various forms.

In the
SYSTEM

Life as an Operative

Sally Gold

ALKIRA
PUBLISHING

In the System
Sally Gold
Copyright © 2025
Published by Alkira Publishing, Australia
ABN: 32736122056
http://www.alkirapublishing.com

All rights reserved. No part of this publication may be reproduced, stored in a retrieval system or transmitted in any form or by any means electronic, mechanical, audio, visual or otherwise, without prior permission of the copyright owner. Nor can it be circulated in any form of binding or cover other than that in which it is published and without similar conditions including this condition being imposed on the subsequent purchaser.

ISBN: 978-1-922329-79-0

Any reflections, descriptions or statements about real characters or events in this book are my personal view based on my own experiences. Names have been changed to protect living persons.

*To my sons, Eric and Evan.
You are my sunshine.*

Acknowledgment

Writing a book is not a sole effort. There were numerous people who lent their opinions, suggestions and devoted time in pursuit to have this story published. I am very grateful for Kristie Hubbard, Sherman Law, and Eric Snyder. Each encourgaed me to write believing my story was worthy of sharing with the world. The first two editors, Lamont Antieau and Donna Peacock, who shaped the dialogue, and publisher-editor Tahlia Newland.

A huge thank you to Jessica Kondracki who twice painstakingly proofread the manuscript making valuable suggestions along the way. I could not have done this without her and will be forever grateful.

I would not be who I am without the love and encouragement I received from my mother, Carolyn. Thank you for instilling in me a passion for reading and the duty to help others.

Contents

1 Caught	1
2 Elizabeth	5
3 Loretta: Welcome to Foster Care	9
4 And Back Again	20
5 Adoption	23
6 "Oreo"	27
7 High School: Many Ways of Learning	33
8 Moshe	39
9 Blue Blazers	45
10 What Kind of Internship is This?	54
11 At the Kibbutz	60
12 Moshe's Family	72
13 Israeli Defense Force Army Base	86
14 Josh	105
15 Official and Undercover	131
16 First Arrest: J. Fedders	148
17 Daniel	171
18 The Wedding	178
19 Green River	182
20 The Sinai Desert and the Bedouins	190
21 Yemen Secrets	217
22 Campbell's Story	234

23 A Mother's Son	260
24 Arghandad District: Testing of a Team	269
25 A New Assignment: A New Team	273
26 Ramadi: The Mission	289
27 Family	324
28 Fallujah: Back in the Action	335
29 Damascus	350
30 Duma	352
31 Flight	363
A Note from the Author	385

1

Caught

*Damascus, Syria,
2011*

People crowd against each other, walking swiftly through the stifling, dank, smelly streets of Damascus. The air is heavy. Here, 100 degrees is considered cool, but today it is over 110. Donkeys are pulling carts carrying anything that can be sold, and children run up to anyone who looks like a foreigner and ask for money, their little hands and faces caked with dirt. It's a constant challenge to keep from being lured by their cleverness. As one child engages the mark, another carefully inserts his tiny fingers into that person's pockets and bags, stealing everything he touches. Cars swerve from one side of the street to the other, barely managing to avoid the donkeys and their carts and the pedestrians in their paths. Bicycles start to fill the already busy street as workers end their day shifts and leave their workplaces behind. When prayer time gets closer, many of the people swiften their pace—some even shoving one another—to take their place at the Umayyad Mosque, considered to be one of the holiest sites in the Islamic world.

I am part of a special operations team with the US government. There are four of us on the team—Whit, Big Mike, J.B. and me—and we are responsible for fixing the mistakes made by earlier teams. Within our division, they call us "The Janitors."

Over the last forty-eight hours, the team has been practicing our timing and fine-tuning a plan designed by our teammate Whit. The plan begins with our leaving our apartment for a parking structure across the street, where we will prepare our weapons, wait for our target to come into view on his way to the mosque, take the shot, and then get to our car on the second floor of the structure and leave this dirty city behind. The previous team took too long in their attempt to meet the same objective. They were spotted by the target's security crew and ended up leaving Damascus in burial shrouds.

Today is the day we complete our mission. Before leaving the apartment to take his place on the fourth floor of the garage, which we found to have the best view of the street below, Whit instructed me to meet him at our car at 16:14. The time now is 16:10, close to evening prayer time.

I go out the door and into the congested city street. I gather my skirt, keeping the cotton fabric below my knees but above my ankles so I can walk faster, hoping no one will notice and object that part of my legs are uncovered. Because timing is crucial, each time I've performed this part of the plan I've tried to shave precious seconds off my previous time. On this day, I record my fastest time: four minutes, two seconds! Looking around, I see only a few cars scattered throughout the garage. I feel confident that no one has followed me. The time is 16:14:00.

At 16:14:12, I wonder what's holding my teammate up. According to our plan, the target should be dead in the street by now, and Whit should have made it to the car already. This is taking too long, and I'm feeling exposed. This is not a country fond of unescorted women. Typically, when women are outside their homes, they have male escorts, often employees of their husband, or they are with their girlfriends. But here I am alone, standing by myself in a parking garage. I'm now getting angry. It is 16:14:20.

And then it happens. I'm leaning on the trunk of our car, when I hear tires screech around the corner, and an old-looking, beat-up sedan comes into view on my right, making its way down the ramp toward me. The vehicle jolts to a stop. No warning. Two men jump out of the back seat, grab me and throw a cloth sack over my head. I feel their guns push against my ribs. In Arabic, they order me to show them my hands, giving me no chance to unlock the weapon wrapped around my left thigh. No one is coming to help me. *Where is Whit?*

The men throw me into the trunk of their car. One of them punches me in the stomach while another holds my neck so I can't move. After all this time carrying out successful missions, which we referred to as "creating change," it's now my turn. I can't see. Some type of cord is secured around my neck. Then there is one last task to perform before I'm locked inside the trunk: I feel the prick of a hypodermic needle in my upper right arm, the contents of which are meant to knock me out but keep me alive. The trunk lid shuts. It's stiflingly hot and hard for me to breathe. I try to fight off the effect of the drug, but it's too strong. As I close my eyes and start to drift out of consciousness, I think about my young sons. How in the hell did I get here?

2

Elizabeth

Kansas City, Kansas
1967

From birth I was part of a system. Labeled as a parentless child, I was shipped from the hospital where I was born to the Prairie Village Country Home for Orphans.

By age three or four, as a ward of the state, I was provided two sets of gray uniforms, one pair of shoes, three meals a day during the week, and two a day on weekends. There was no privacy or space to call my own. The closest to having anything that was truly mine was my bed.

Each 'house' had rows of twin beds lined up in symmetrical rows and covered in white sheets starched so heavily they scratched the skin. I can still smell those over-starched sheets. They smelled as rough as they felt.

We lined up single file by age to enter the 'dining room,'

holding our trays, waiting to receive our one plate of food that looked and tasted gray. As a child, I thought everyone ate like this.

If you thought this was a home, you were wrong; it was not. Here, no one asked, "How are you today?" or "Would you like a hug?" Instead, "Watch out for yourself" and "Don't trust too much in others" were phrases I heard often from the nurses and guards. It was simply a shelter. A place to eat, play, and hope that someday you would be called from the playground to the office where some 'mother' and 'father' would size you up and decide that *you* were the one they wanted to adopt.

We were not treated poorly by the state; it's just that we weren't loved. I was reserved, an observer. Not knowing who my biological parents were or why they decided it was too much for them to raise me as their own created in me a separation from others. I did my assigned chores, ate my three meals a day, and stayed out of the way of the workers.

School was the best part of my day. I wanted more homework than I was given. Before dinner and after getting my chores done, I walked over to the schoolhouse where the teachers had created a library. Inside, rows of books placed on vertical metal racks lined the walls. It was quiet. There usually was no one inside the room. I sat between the rows, head down, absorbed in whatever book I could grab from a lower shelf. I didn't know how to read, but I tried sounding out the letters we'd learned that day in school.

One afternoon a local resident who occasionally volunteered in the library noticed me eyeing some new reading material. "You best let me help you before those books fall on top of you," she said as she pushed the rickety book cart to the side and bent down to see what I was looking at. "What are you reading?"

I answered that I was trying to learn the words that went with the pictures of my favorite book, *Goodnight Moon*. She watched as I carefully pulled its tattered spine from between the titles and held it up. I attempted to pronounce each letter out loud while pointing my index finger over the written word.

"How many letters are here?" she asked, looking at where I'd placed my finger.

"Four," I answered, smiling at her.

"And what is the first letter?"

"G!"

"Come with me," she said, as she led me toward a small table in the corner of the room. We sat on the floor at opposite ends, and I saw a deck of cards in her hand. Placing each flash card in front of me, she asked what letter was on the card. I got all twenty-six cards right! That afternoon changed me.

Her name was Elizabeth. We sat together, her holding one card, then two, then placing three and finally four on the table. She asked me to sound out the letters. She taught me how to read. I was three and half years old.

I have few memories of that time, but I clearly remember her saying "good" out loud and cheering me on. She showed me that I'd sounded out the first word written on the first page of the book. Her eyes gleamed with a sense of excitement and self-satisfaction, like when a parent makes a decisive effort to nurture their child and sees a successful positive outcome.

One day out on the playground, when I was almost four years old, a beautiful, black shiny car with gleaming whitewalls pulled up in front of the office adjacent to where we were playing. A tall man stepped out of the automobile and walked around to the passenger side, extending a hand to an impeccably dressed lady with bright-red hair. She stepped out gracefully and looked our way, her smile warming the cool air. We clung to the chainlink fence, pressing our tiny faces up against the cold rusting metal to catch a glimpse of her face. The tall man escorting her to the office didn't look in our direction.

I watched them enter the office doorway. Whose name would be called? Would today be my day?

3

Loretta:

Welcome to Foster Care

1969

I felt something was special the day the beautiful White couple returned one sunny afternoon, came up to the fence, and asked to take a picture of me. A few days later they were back, and I was allowed to leave the property with them. We went to Sears.

They bought me a beautiful white dress with ruffles and a bow that tied at the waist. The lady brushed my hair, then placed me on a small bench across from a camera. The photographer told me to look at him. The man and lady stood on either side of the camera, trying their best to make me smile as the camera flashed. I was confused. The flash hurt my eyes. But their beautiful eyes made me feel nice inside, an unfamiliar feeling.

I felt this was the day I was going to get a home. I'd been treated with such attention and kindness. But no. This was not my special day. There would be no paper hearts, no candy, no laughter. Feeling sad and alone, I went to sleep without eating dinner.

At night, many children screamed in their sleep. Some called out for make-believe parents, brothers, or sisters—anyone their fertile imaginations had created to help them feel connected to someone. Some slept just a few hours, tossing and turning in their small cots, trying to replace the demons in their brains, hoping today would be different. Darkness comes in many forms.

Months later, after a breakfast of cold, loose scrambled eggs and lumpy cream of wheat, the other children and I were divided into rows, many of us questioning where we were going. Normally we would line up by grade and go to the schoolhouse. The older ones told us this was something different. They said that what you didn't want was your name to be called. If that happened, you would have to step out of line and head to the large office at the front of the building. From there you would be taken away to a temporary home, and you became a meal ticket, whatever that meant.

Our supervising nurse called out several names. Mine was among those called. "Welcome to foster care," she said, as we walked down the hallway.

A huge black woman named Loretta wobbled down the hallway, stopping to breathe several times before she came over to our bench. She said nothing, just stared at us disdainfully, then turned to go into the office, where she spent the next hour signing papers and answering our office manager's questions.

When she was finished, we were instructed to go to our assigned beds, take the contents out of our foot trunks, and pack what would fit into the small duffel bag that lay on each bed. I wondered if it was going to be a trip like I'd had to Sears, but this woman didn't look like she was taking us because she wanted to. She seemed annoyed. She stood, propped up by the doorway, smoking a cigarette. "Hurry up, we don't got all day."

We slid into the back seat of her large, sparkling green Chrysler sedan. Loretta wedged herself between the steering wheel and the driver's seat and told us to be quiet. I was pinned between an older boy of six or seven years old and another young girl who was about three, as well as all our duffel bags. We drove for some time through tree-lined streets with homes on both sides. Loretta kept staring at us through her rearview mirror, scowling the entire drive except for when she blew smoke from her cigarette out her mouth.

We arrived at a small brick house. Loretta took the little girl out of the car and walked her to the front door. She handed the girl's bag off to a tall White woman who was smoking a cigarette just like Loretta. They each put out their cigarettes by tossing them onto the concrete, then stepping on them and grinding them into the cement with their foot. I'd seen the male guards at the orphanage do that before, but never a woman.

After dropping off the small girl, Loretta again hoisted her large body back into the driver's seat and we were on the road again. We drove for several blocks, before she pulled over right in front of a tall, red metal box with a glass door. Inside was a gray and black machine. Loretta got out of the car and opened the glass door. She was too big to close it behind her, so half of her was in the red box and the other half of her facing us in the car. She dropped some coins into the machine, held something to her ear, and spoke into the other end.

The boy said, "We're meal tickets." Not understanding him, I turned to look at Loretta, who was deep in conversation with the black machine. She seemed happy, talking fast and then listening, as if for instructions.

When she returned to the car, we drove straight to the Mason County Social Services Office, where she scooted us out of the back seat quickly. "Time to get paid," she said, and we ran to keep up with her through the glass office doors and down the hall to another room that was filled with solemn kids, chatty adults, and lingering cigarette smoke.

Hours went by. We were cold. The heater kept shutting off. The plastic seats felt like rocks. The boy with me was distant, lost in his own thoughts. Loretta paid no attention to us.

"What's your name?" I asked the boy.

He waited for what seemed like a long time before replying. "Leo," he said. A pause. "I've been here before. They'll ask that woman who brought us here some questions, then she writes something on a paper, and we leave."

"Why?"

"Because when she takes us with her, she gets money."

I didn't understand this. I wanted to go back to what I considered home, back to school after doing my chores. I wanted to sleep in my bed and hear the sounds outside on the playground at night. If it was quiet, you could hear the wind blow through the leaves of the big oak tree and hear its branches swaying. I kept thinking of Elizabeth and my books, eraser, and pencil. The paper she kept for me where I wrote down the letters I was beginning to memorize. I hoped she wasn't mad at me. Would she think I didn't care anymore, or did she know why I didn't show up today for our lesson? Would I see her again?

Across the room where the door opened, I could see a long hallway where two kids were coloring in books. Maybe I could borrow a pencil and maybe a piece of their paper and write my letters today. When I saw Elizabeth, I could give her my lesson. I started to get up from the bench where we were sitting. "Sit down!" Loretta said. "No one told you to get up." I sat down. She was upset, tapping her dark hands on the side of the bench.

After some time had passed, they called her name. She got up and hustled over to the window where a lady was standing on the other side of the glass. They were busy, so I went over to the kids sitting on the floor with the crayons and paper surrounding them.

"Hi! Can I sit with you?"

They both looked up at me without saying a word. I sat down, staring at the paper on the floor. One of the girls was busy drawing flowers in every color she had. The other girl was smaller and was making lines. I wanted to have a piece of that paper. I needed to practice my letters.

The small girl must have understood, because, without saying a word, she passed a piece of paper my way, and I took it, smiling back at her. She let me pick up a red crayon that was next to her left leg. I held it for a minute, trying to remember how Elizabeth had taught me to hold a pencil. I wrote C, C, C, over, and over again. I wrote the letters from my last lesson and was pleased with the way they appeared in red.

Next thing I knew, Loretta was standing over me and

glowering. I could see her from the side of my left eye. "Let's go. Now." We walked through the long hallway, Loretta, the boy, and me, clutching my paper. We walked to another room. "Wait here for me."

Leo said, "What you got there?" pointing to my paper.

"It's my lesson."

"What lesson? You're not in school."

I showed him my red letters on the pale beige paper.

"You trying to learn how to write?"

"I can write."

"You don't want to tell people that. You'll get beat."

"Why?"

At that moment, Loretta reappeared and grabbed both of our hands to walk down the corridor toward the parking lot.

When we arrived at Loretta's apartment, it was past dinner time, and the sky was dark gray. A few young men stood outside the narrow, broken gate that led to the parking lot. Loretta edged through, barely clearing a pole on the driver's side of her car where a side mirror used to be.

We walked through the small complex which smelled like old grease. I looked straight ahead. Leo tried to make eye contact with the boys who were hanging out and tossing a basketball around. They ignored him.

Loretta stopped us in front of a staircase. "Leo, take the bags." She clutched the handrail, huffing as she climbed the five stairs to a small landing. She then turned right and looked up at the next five stairs she would need to conquer. This was getting old for her. The stairs weren't giving in, but her knees and swollen ankles were.

We topped the staircase, and in front of us was a large brown door and doors on the left and right—I don't know how many, but they seemed to go on and on. At number 707 we stopped, and she knocked loudly on it.

Inside children were crying, women yelling at them to be quiet. You could tell this was a place where people were unhappy and children unwanted.

I was far too young then to understand that the reason kids were here was because the adults needed them to live there. An adult had to have a certain number of children to live in public housing. The children could be from multiple sources, different men, the same man, foster kids, or orphans. The tenants couldn't house family members' children, felons, or juvenile delinquents. The kids had to be their own or from the state. Few adults paid attention to the rules. They did only what they needed to do so they could stay living there rent-free.

When Loretta knocked loudly a second time, footsteps came from inside the apartment, and someone walked toward the door and opened it just a crack to reveal a small boy's face. He started to cry.

"Open up!" Loretta said sternly, and when he did, she pushed the child aside. Standing in front of a tattered, black leather couch, she announced, "We're back." No one answered. She kicked the back of the old piece of furniture, and someone started to stir. A grown man was lying on the couch, sound asleep.

"Get up and help me with these kids."

He got up slowly and turned his toward us. He must have been hurt because he hobbled. He lifted our small duffel bags and walked down the dimly lit hallway as she instructed.

He opened the first of two doors on the left. Inside, a small twin mattress and a lamp sat on the floor. A tiny window loomed high above on the wall above the mattress. If I got on my tippy-toes I could probably see some tree branches.

Maybe I could find a chair, put it under the window and try to see something outside. If I stood up straight, maybe I could see between the bars that covered the glass.

He put my suitcase down. "You get your own room."

My stomach was making noises. "Are we going to eat soon?" I asked. "I'm so hungry."

He turned toward me still standing in the doorway and said, "I don't know, but don't ask her. It'll just get her mad."

I sat down on the floor of the small room. I'd never had a room to myself. I felt very grown up but scared at the same time. There was no place to set my few things, so I left them in my bag. I wanted to go to the bathroom, but I didn't know where it was. Outside in the hallway, there was a door at the end and one on the right. I thought I should ask before opening the doors. Loretta was in the kitchen. She could feel me in the room but stared straight ahead.

"Where do I peepee?"

She pointed back to the hallway. "Last door."

The days were long and uneventful, except for the daily yelling between Loretta and the man who lived there. Leo and I figured he was her husband. But no one seemed to pay any attention to us, as if we weren't even there.

I wanted to go outside the gate. Did the volunteer lady miss me? Did she think of me as much as I thought of her?

I sat on the edge of my mattress, looking up at the closed window when Leo burst through the door.

"Let's go to the corner store!" he said.

"Why?"

"To get candy," he said. "I've got ten cents. We can each get something sweet."

I had no idea about money and what chocolate, gum, crackerjacks, or lollipops cost, but I liked the idea of going outside the gate, especially running past the kids who wouldn't let us play in their games.

Loretta had left for the grocery to "get the check." Her husband was asleep, snoring on the couch. "If we don't wake him, we can walk to the store and get back before Loretta does," Leo said.

The husband was fast asleep and smelled like ripe peaches and vinegar. We got close and watched him breathe. When he stopped, like he was holding his breath, he snorted. He twitched and tossed, sounding like a lion or bear, but after a period of silence, like a pig snorting. We started to laugh, but hushed ourselves, afraid we would wake him up. Carefully, we crawled away from the couch to the front door. We got to the triple-locked door just in time. The man moved violently, thrashing side to side, swatting at the musky air around him.

Leo opened the door, tackling each lock like he'd done this before, then stuck his head into the hall to see if Loretta was coming. All clear. We slid out the apartment's front door into the dark, unlit hallway.

"Which way do we go?" I asked him.

"Don't talk. Just follow me," Leo whispered.

But then I remembered the back staircase and its turn to the left, which went down to where the adults parked their cars. I'd known all the exits at the orphanage: every hallway, where each door connected to another hall, which one took you to a staircase, which led to the outside. I could remember which doors unlocked in the middle of the night and the sounds of laughter, nurses breathing deeply.

I took Leo's hand. We hurried down the dark hallway toward the stairs, turned left, then right, and there were the stairs to the outside. One two-handed push on the metal bar attached to the big gray door, and, just like that, we were flooded in sunlight. Both of us had to close our eyes for a few seconds to adjust to the bright-blue sky and warm sunlight surrounding our small bodies. "Hurry," he said as he dropped my hand. "Better get going."

I knew we had to get back before she did. At dinner a few weeks back, I'd taken an extra biscuit. "Who ate the biscuit?" she'd shouted from the kitchen, her back to us as we sat at the small table finishing our food. I said it was me. She told me to get up from the small wooden stool I used as a chair. Standing in front of her, I raised my head slowly, regretting my actions, knowing I had to look her in the eye. She slapped me sharply across the left side of my face, and I tried not to cry. She picked me up and put my face close to the burning metal plate on top of her stove.

"If you take anything from here again, I'll put your face on this hot stove, do you hear me?" I nodded my head up and down as if to say yes, but no words came from my mouth. She dropped me to my feet, and, as she did, the inside of my left knee hit the sizzling black metal burner.

"Answer me or next time you'll be hurting a lot more than you are now."

"Yes, ma'am." I held my knee and tried not to scream from the pain.

But she wasn't here now. Leo grabbed my hand, and we ran to the street. Where was the store? Cars whizzed by us. Lights flashing green, yellow, and red hung by cords across the busy streets. I'd been in a car only a few times, but never on a busy street corner about to cross to the other side. I was about to do something I'd never done before. I wasn't scared. I felt strong. We watched the cars driving by and took one step into the crosswalk and then another. We ran to the other side.

When we made it to the other side of the street where the store was, I heard the rumbling of an old engine that sounded familiar. I turned and froze. Leo tried pulling me into the corner store, but I couldn't move. There she was at the streetlight, staring at us. Our eyes locked, and Leo and I both knew things would be different after this.

"Get in!" Loretta growled. I slinked into the back seat of her car.

"No!" Leo said as he ran into the store.

Now I was afraid. What was Leo doing? He was supposed to be bringing us candy and ice cream.

The traffic light turned to green, and Loretta drove off, turning the corner onto a side street. "You can't be trusted. I tried to help you, but it don't matter. You're all the same." Shaking her head from side to side, she looked at me through the rearview mirror. "I tried to help you, gave you a place to stay, and this is what you do to me. Leave? Don't mind me?"

When we got to her apartment, I hoped Leo was there, doing his chores as if nothing had happened.

"Do his chores first, then yours." That's all she said.

Hours went by. It grew dark outside. And still no Leo.

I was tired, hot, hungry, and scared. I sat in my room waiting for what was to come next. The door flew open. Then the beating started, and it went on and on.

The next morning when I woke up, my duffel was packed. Loretta drove me back to the orphanage.

I never saw Leo again.

4

And Back Again

Prairie Village Country Home for Orphans
1969

The summer dragged on into the same routine. Nothing had changed at the orphanage except for some new faces I didn't recognize. Cars pulled up, and the other children ran to the chainlink fence to see who was coming out of each vehicle. I stayed back.

Being thrown back into the system stung like Loretta's slap across my face. I didn't have the same feeling I once had about visitors coming here. It was no longer the highlight of the day. That summer it became just another part of the afternoon that dragged on with me on the sidelines watching it all go by.

Sometimes, I sat by myself in the yard and watched the other kids play. Other times, I stared out at the street. I remembered the freedom of running to the crosswalk with Leo holding my hand. Everything felt different for those few minutes: the sky was bluer, kids played where they wanted to, music blared from hand radios, buses barreled down the streets trying to get to the next stop on time.

My best time came late at night when the many rows of beds with their starched white sheets caught the moonlight streaming in from the upper-paned windows. I'd gather my sheets together and form a tent with just enough of an opening to allow a bit of moonlight to shine on the pages of whatever book I was reading. If I was lucky, the nurse on duty would take an extra-long break, and I could sneak out of bed with my book under my nightgown, post myself up next to the large-paned window to the right of my twin bed and read by unobscured moonlight. No one bothered me.

When school began in the fall, the volunteer Elizabeth came back to the library. She continued to teach me. Reading and learning how to spell words was the highlight of my day and remained so for the rest of the year. She introduced me to books like *James and the Giant Peach, Where the Wild Things Are,* and *Sal on Blueberry Hill,* all magical. Each one transported me to another place far away from here. My time was spent imagining. Would I one day have a home, a family that I would be a part of? What would my parents be like? Would they love me for only a month or a year? I was no different from the other children there. These thoughts came into and out of our heads, but no one talked about them. I longed to go to public school and have neighborhood friends to play hide and seek and laugh with.

Most of the kids around me looked forward to the next day when the visitors might choose them to come be part of their families. But I knew about the ones who took you just

so they could get money. I couldn't trust adults.
I wasn't yet nine years old.

5

Adoption

1973

Months had gone by since that nice couple had taken me to get my picture taken. When we ate ice cream that afternoon in the park, the woman had asked me if I liked animals. "Would you like to have a puppy, a cat, or a horse?" No one had ever asked me a question like that. Why was she interested in what I liked? Her questions floated around in my head as I fell asleep each night, wondering if I would ever see them again. Probably not. Most couples wanted babies anyway.

One Saturday morning, most of the kids were outside running around, hanging from the monkey bars or fighting over who would have the next turn swinging on the teetering swing set. I was sitting on the lawn reading a Nancy Drew book.

"Come on in and get washed up," said the nurse.

"I'm not sick."

"I know you're not," she said. She led me down the hallway past the office and into the infirmary where she had me take a bath with bubbles in water that smelled like roses. Afterward, she stuck a needle in me to get some blood and then checked my pulse, my ears, eyes, and mouth. I was confused but liked the feeling of being clean from the warm bath. The nurse told me to change into a new uniform and sit in the small room until she returned.

When she came back, she was smiling. "Everything is just fine," she said then walked me down the hallway to the office. I saw them sitting in the waiting room. The woman jumped up and came toward me, smiling and holding out her hands to take mine.

I didn't know that the adoption process with the state had begun months before. The couple had begun the initial paperwork after returning me to the orphanage from our afternoon in the park. The process included a physical examination of both, administered by a state doctor, and interviews with their siblings, parents, and select friends.

"Four long months," she said, as she held my hands. "Every day I looked at your picture praying the adoption would be approved." The head administrator stood across from the man who was bent over her desk signing paper after paper.

I later learned that he—the man who would become my father—was raised in Mount Vernon, New York. She—my new mother—was raised in Midtown Manhattan near the intersection of 51st Street & 3rd Avenue. She taught elementary school before the car accident that left her infertile. He sold clothing for a children's dress manufacturer. Both longed to be parents. Before they came to the home, they tried to adopt a child in New York City; nothing worked out. Applications, endless and invasive interviews, and many false hopes that turned to tears led them to look outside of where they lived.

Both were young: she was twenty-nine, and he thirty-one. Having been married for four years, he wanted to make her happy. She longed for the fulfillment of what she believed would come from being a mother. Societal circles at that time belonged to families, and that meant having children.

He brought her on his business trip to Kansas City, knowing about the Prairie Village Country Home through his customers. They frequently asked for his clothing samples so they could donate them to the home at the end of the year. He thought this could be the place where they might find a child to adopt. He was right.

Two weeks later, I was sitting on an airplane between these two people, heading to California where we would begin life as a family. Most kids would be excited about their first plane ride. I was nervous. I was moving from the Midwest to the West Coast with two adults I had met just once before and who would now be my 'parents.'

My heart pounded as I tried looking out the window, which was partially blocked by her opened *Time* magazine.

"Do you want to switch seats?" she asked gently.

I shook my head up and down as if to say yes. I couldn't form the words. I wanted to say thank you for giving me a home, but the dreaded memories of foster care drifted in and out of my mind.

As we floated high up into the air, I fixed my sights on the billowy white clouds engulfing the plane until it cut through them and rose even higher in the sky. I shut my eyes and fell asleep, hoping that when I woke up, I would be surrounded by love.

6

"Oreo"

*Southern California
1973*

For the very first time I had my own bathroom, towels, soft sheets, and two new pillows. My new mother loved keeping the house in order. She cooked and cleaned and enjoyed cutting roses from her sunny backyard garden that she then arranged in a vase on the dining room table. There was fresh laundry every few days and chocolate chip cookies to devour after dinner. It took no time getting used to living with my new parents. There was laughter, which felt strange to me. Books were abundant, which gave me comfort.

There were not many fifth graders my age at the schools she was researching, but that didn't concern her. She wasn't looking at the children, but at the curriculum to select the most challenging program for me to attend that fall. Until then, I spent carefree days jumping rope in the cul-de-sac and swimming in the large pool at our house. As the summer ended, I grew more excited to start school.

During testing at Collins Street Elementary, the local elementary school, it became evident to my mother that she and her husband had adopted a 'gifted' child. As the principal explained to my parents one evening when he came to visit us before dinner, the Los Angeles Unified School District (LAUSD) was experimenting with an accelerated program for high IQ students. It was being offered at Welby Way Elementary School, twenty minutes from where we lived in the San Fernando Valley. The program was proving to be of merit, and he'd been asked to nominate a student to attend in the fall. My father was ecstatic, but my mother was leery.

"If it doesn't seem right for her, can she come back to your school?" she asked, before signing the paper releasing me from my current class into this new program.

"Of course she can," he said. They shook hands, and I began attending my new school after the winter break.

School became a place to be recognized. It was a place where the teachers celebrated my craving to learn more than what they taught that day. From Italian to Spanish, geometry, spelling, American history, and poetry, all my lessons were exciting and new. I grasped most concepts being taught to the twelve of us students. I found nothing more gratifying than spelling complicated words.

Each night after dinner my mother quizzed me from notecards I'd written. On one side of the card was the word, and on the other, its definition. I was always ready for the spelling bee contests held each Friday morning at school. In June, before school ended for the summer, we had the final spelling bee. Parents were invited. My father was in New York

City working, so my mother came alone. I won the contest.

Afterward, as my classmates and I played outside and ate ice cream to celebrate the last day of school, my mother and the other parents looked disappointed. The program had not been as successful as the district had expected it would be, so, after one year, funding for it was discontinued. I went back to Collins Street Elementary for my sixth grade year.

There are times when you feel a part of your surroundings, and there are times when you know you're not. My neighborhood girlfriends were eleven and twelve years old; I was nine going on ten. I was biracial, adopted by Jewish parents living in a predominantly White, Anglo-Christian middle-class neighborhood. Not looking like the others and observing a different religion at home was uncomfortable at times.

Before, when I was going to school with the neighborhood girls, we were all at the same elementary school. We saw each other at recess, lunch, and on the playground. Half the time they ignored me because I was several years younger, but since they were my neighbors, they allowed me to walk home with them. After class, I walked down the outdoor hallway to the far end where the sixth-grade bungalow classrooms were still in session. I sat at one of the picnic tables outside of their rooms, doing my homework. When the bell rang, Liz, Lisa, and Marion bounded down the metal stairs toward the picnic tables, and we walked home. Not anymore. They were in middle school, blocks away from the elementary school. I walked home by myself that sixth-grade year.

After school each day, the boys in my neighborhood played outside on the cul-de-sac where our house was one of four at the end of the street.

One of the boys hit the softball without paying attention

to where I was walking. Another boy stood at home plate, blocking my way as I walked home. This was Gary, who lived down the street. He was younger and we weren't friends. We rarely spoke to each other in school. To my surprise, he asked if I wanted to join them.

"You would make the teams even at five players each."

"No," I said. I had to get home, knowing that if I stopped to play ball with them, my mother would wonder where I was. Gary remained there, blocking my way.

"Okay. One time. I'll bat." I dropped my things on the sidewalk, my lunch sack resting on its side next to my book bag. I stepped up to the plate. The bat was heavy. The boys surveyed the front yards, looking to see if anyone was outside watching them. Then it happened.

The boy pitching the ball threw it at me. Not what I expected. The softball bounced toward third base after bruising my left forearm. I took a step back, unsure if I should stay put or run. I froze. Then it happened again. Another pitch, but this time near my head. I ducked down and tried not to fall backward. The ball whizzed by the top of my head, causing me to close my eyes. Was he trying to hurt me? I just wanted to help make the teams even as Gary had asked. I opened my eyes. Once more the ball came at me. I closed my grip on the heavy bat and met the ball, driving it past the pitcher and to the right of the second baseman. I froze there on home plate as the kid on third ran home. I just stood there while he pushed me aside to score a run.

"Go home, Oreo," Gary said. "We don't need you anymore. Just leave."

Oreo? What did that mean? His voice was mean and condescending.

At dinner that night, my father asked me how my day

was. I asked him if he knew what it meant when somebody called me an Oreo. By the look on his face, I knew it was something bad. He shot a glance at my mother.

"Who said that to you?" he asked.

"Gary," I replied.

"When did it happen?"

"Today on the way home from school."

"Get up," he said without inflection. Before I knew it, he was out the door and on his way to the street. I followed him across the street up to Gary's front door. He banged on the Kelly green door with me standing close by. Gary answered the door looking confused.

"Where's your father?" my dad asked. Before Gary could answer, his dad Arnie was standing next to him. "I want to know if your son called my daughter an Oreo."

Arnie looked down at Gary, who shrugged his shoulders.

"Answer my question, Arnie," my dad said. More silence.

Then Arnie turned to his son. "Go back to dinner; I'll handle this." Gary looked at me with a look I'll never forget. His eyes were wide, and his face was red. He knew he was in trouble.

"Arnie, I'm a strong man. I could take you out with one punch to the face or maybe the gut, but you better answer me truthfully before I decide what I'll do next."

My father got upset sometimes on the phone, if someone called asking for a donation or there was a sales call, but never with a neighbor.

"I don't know if he said that to her, but I'll find out," Arnie said, trying to convey just the right amount of sympathy to avoid getting punched by my dad.

"Go home," my father said to me. When I turned to leave, I heard him say, "If I ever hear those words said to my daughter again, you won't be standing when I leave." And like that, he left their doorstep.

Once back home, he was silent. I knew something was wrong, but I didn't have the courage to ask my father exactly what those words meant. I didn't want to upset him more than he already was.

That night I lay in bed believing I did not belong in this secluded neighborhood.

7

High School: Many Ways of Learning

San Fernando Valley
1977-1980

In the mid-1970s, most of the population in Southern California's West San Fernando Valley consisted of upper-middle-class White families. Sparkling, crystal-clear pools and ranch-style homes on cul-de-sacs within walking distance of excellent public schools.

And it was a time when many White suburban families started transferring their children to private schools, having been told that small groups of Los Angeles intercity black students from poor neighborhoods would be sharing classrooms, lunch tables, and athletic fields with their children.

I was in high school. A biracial teenager who lived in an upper-middle-class White family in West San Fernando Valley.

School was easy for me when it came to book-learning, but it was difficult socially. The local girls didn't include me in their sleepovers, birthday parties, and after-school get-togethers. At the same time, the black girls who were bused in held a grudge against me because I was lighter skinned than they were, and I lived comfortably only four miles from school.

One afternoon when I was in the eleventh grade, I entered the bathroom during our lunch period and two of the bused-in black girls came up behind me. One grabbed my bookbag, while the other pushed me into the tiled wall. My head hit the wall, and I slumped down, unable to hold myself up. Both started kicking me.

"You think you're all that!" they yelled at me. "Where you came from, girl? You're no better than us."

Just then I felt someone pull me up by my arm. My eyes were still closed for fear of looking at them and having to tell the principal who they were, but Julie, a tall, skinny girl with dyed red hair and earrings in her right ear, was at my side.

"Get away from her," she told my tormentors in a clear direct voice. Then I heard another voice.

"Back up!" it said in an authoritative manner. "I said, back up."

In the doorway stood Darlene Searcy, another student who was bused into the school, but she was different. Her smile lit up a room, along with her laughter. Darlene could throw her head back and laugh so loud you knew it was coming from a place of pure joy. And it was pure joy to be around her. She always smiled at me and said, "Hi there" when we passed each other in the hallway going from class to class. But we weren't friends until that day when she and Julie came to my rescue.

The two bullies turned their anger toward Darlene, but she kicked, scratched, and punched back at them, while Julie blocked the bathroom door until I could get up.

Julie took my arm and rushed me into the hall. "You okay? Does your head hurt?"

"I'm all right. Just can't believe that happened."

"Did you say anything to them?"

"No," I said. "I didn't see them. They came up behind me."

"Cowards."

A minute later Darlene was outside with us. She looked fine, as if no fistfight had occurred. "Don't think they'll give you any more trouble," Darlene said, as she looked me up and down. "Do you know how to fight back?" She shook her head from side to side, knowing the answer to her own question. "Man, you need to learn to fight. I may not be there next time."

"Next time?" I asked, as tears began to drip down my face and torn t-shirt.

"Yeah, there's always a next time. You got to be ready for it." Darlene's eyes were wide. She looked hard at me. "Julie wasn't ready for it, and she got hurt. Really hurt. You got to be ready all the time."

And that's how the three of us became fast friends. Our friendship turned into a sisterhood.

In the mornings, I waited in the parking lot for Darlene's bus to arrive. Then we walked into school together. Julie was always late for class, so we stopped waiting for her. But we all ate lunch together, and, after school, walked to my house where they hung out until four o'clock when my mother drove them back to school.

Back at school, Darlene got on her bus to go home, and Julie walked home. A long walk. Julie never asked my mom to drive her. I think she didn't want us to know where she lived.

In October I asked my mom if Darlene could stay with us during the week. That way she wouldn't have to take the bus every day from Inglewood. Her parents agreed. From then on she stayed at my house until after school on Fridays.

Her sister, Annette, was in the police academy. She was taller than Darlene and thinner. Even with her protective vest on, she looked thin, but she was all muscle. She taught Darlene how to fight, to always be present in her surroundings, and to assess each situation before saying or doing anything.

That summer, Darlene invited me to stay at her house. My dad drove me out to Inglewood, which was about forty miles from where we lived. I remember thinking *How did Darlene do this every day?* It was a long, boring drive.

Their house was small, immaculately clean, with everything in its place. A couch and reclining chair covered in clear plastic were in the small living room. Pictures of Darlene and Annette from their school portraits framed the mantle, along with Annette's police academy graduation picture. The kitchen was half the size of ours. A small four-burner stove with a single oven faced a yellow refrigerator with the freezer on top. Four chairs encircled a round wooden table draped with a yellow plastic tablecloth.

Darlene's mother was kind. She asked me if I'd been in a neighborhood like hers before. I had not, but by the end of the summer it'd become my second home, a place where I was comfortable and enjoyed being a part of a second family.

Their backyard was tiny and made of concrete poured from one side to the other. Some folding chairs and a little table for setting drinks on flanked the back of their house.

You walked through the back of their kitchen to get to the backyard and detached garage. Both entries had an iron protective outer door that locked separately from the wooden door. Once inside, a person felt protected.

Life was very different at Darlene's home than at my own. It was a happy household with lots of genuine laughter. My parents didn't laugh as much or seem to as easily express their joy at home. I was happiest the weekends I spent at Darlene's. At night, I curled up in my sleeping bag on the floor, snug between Annette's and Darlene's twin beds.

Darlene and I spent the days selling lemonade in front of her house or going across the street to her neighbor's home where we played cards or hit a tennis ball against the back of their garage. At Darlene's, the food was delicious. Black-eyed peas, yams, ham, and fried chicken. No fish, liver, or steamed vegetables like in my own home. I enjoyed the food my mother served, but this food had more flavor. Each recipe came from Darlene's great-grandmother, but nothing was written down. Darlene's mother had spent many hours in the kitchen helping her mother and grandmother. She just knew how to prepare each dish by memory and taste.

As we entered our senior year, things began to change. Our friend Julie fell behind a grade. She'd missed too many classes and, as a result, had to repeat her junior year. Darlene had a steady weekend job, so I didn't get to go to her house on weekends like I had before.

And more changed in January 1980 when Darlene's sister, Annette, was shot in the line of duty and died. After that, Darlene's family wanted her close to them. She stopped going to our school. No more mixing between her 'Valley' family and her real one.

Julie saw her right before graduation. She said Darlene

had taken and passed the proficiency test and was going straight into the police academy to carry on the work Annette no longer could. I was going to college in the fall. Our worlds separated, but the time spent with Darlene and her family would remain a warm, happy memory. She taught me how to protect myself and fight back when it was necessary. More importantly, she showed me what real family life was like. I will never forget her.

Spring fever set in. I was starting UCLA that fall. Fortunately, my time was filled with college placement tests which helped me past the pain of missing Darlene. During spring break, many of the cool kids threw parties at their homes. I went to a few. Some of us contracted mononucleosis, probably from sharing a drink among ourselves. It put me in the hospital for several days.

My throat swelled, making it difficult to breathe. I couldn't eat solid food, and I lost the twenty-five pounds of fat that I'd carried on my frame since early childhood. No amount of fresh food, lean protein, steamed vegetables, or fruit had taken it off. Even running in a park-sponsored track club hadn't changed my weight as dramatically as 'mono' did.

My mother was ecstatic, and my father praised my new looks. As a result of my new physique, I started paying attention to what I looked like. I discovered mascara and lip gloss, loving how it altered my appearance.

During this time, my parents encouraged me to apply to the Greek sororities. They worried about my not knowing anyone in a student body of 30,000. In a sorority I would have 'instant friends' and not feel so alone. A new wardrobe and several campus rush parties later, I was a member of Delta Delta Delta and had sixty immediate girlfriends.

8

Moshe

Israel: The Holy Land
1980

Besides graduating from high school and pledging to a sorority, the summer of 1980 was significant for another reason: my youth group took a trip to the Holy Land.

Fourteen of us went, as well as our two youth group advisers. We were excitable teenagers, and most members of the group had never been on an airplane, let alone gone out of the country. I was almost sixteen and would be leaving my family for two full weeks. There were no cell phones or social media then to immediately document and post our every move. We were going to a foreign country and would be completely out of touch with our families. It was going to be a true adventure.

Traveling from LAX via JFK to Ben Gurion Airport

in early July 1980 was an experience. On the flight were foreigners from many Middle Eastern countries including Turks carrying bags of food, religious Jews saying their prayers in the back of the plane, and Muslims praying on small mats in the aisle near the front of the aircraft.

From the moment we landed, armed soldiers were everywhere, lining the tarmac and the public areas of the airport. Guard dogs patrolled the luggage terminal. Members of the Israeli Defense Force, Israel's elite military, were the airport's gatekeepers.

There is a mandatory three-year military service for young men and women in Israel. So after graduating from high school, young students become soldiers with some exceptions made for religious reasons. Young men and women serve their country with pride, and they look forward to the weekend leave given to those in good standing once every six to eight weeks.

Our first night in this unique country became most special to me. After gathering our duffel bags, we boarded a bus heading toward a youth hostel near Jerusalem. Our leaders separated the girls from the boys, and, along with the hostel manager, led each group to its respective rooms.

Naomi and I each grabbed a top bunk. We enjoyed being with each other every week at youth-group meetings. We attended different high schools but spent many weekends together, sleeping over at each other's houses.

"Let's find the showers before we go to sleep," I said to her. It was early in the morning, and we'd been instructed to go to sleep upon arrival as we had only a few hours to sleep before starting our first day of sightseeing. But we were too excited to sleep. Naomi and I both agreed this was the beginning of an adventure. Neither of us had been out of the United States before. We wanted to explore our surroundings; sleep would come later.

We grabbed our soap, shampoo, and shower sandals and crept out into the long hallway, passing the other group members, who seemed fast asleep. Most hostels have separate floors for women and men. Bathrooms form the middle of each floor, with individual toilet stalls and one large group shower that could hold up to six people. We tried not to laugh as we each lathered up, knowing we were breaking the rules.

When we got out of the shower and dried off, Naomi said, "Let's find a place where we can use our blow dryers and not wake the others up." We snuck back to our room where our roommates were fast asleep in their bottom bunks and grabbed our hairdryers. I held a hairbrush and dryer in one hand and my towel in the other, and we crept down to the opposite end of the hall where a pair of double doors blocked our way. We looked at each other and shrugged our shoulders as if to say, *Okay, let's see where this goes.*

I opened one door, and revealed, to our surprise, a group of Israeli soldiers sitting at round tables, playing cards and smoking. They turned toward the noise of the door opening and stared at us in complete shock: two teenagers holding towels around their bodies, holding blow dryers and hairbrushes. The entire room fell quiet. They were probably asking themselves, *Is this real? Am I seeing what I think I'm seeing?* We thought the same. Neither Naomi nor I had slept much during the sixteen-hour trip, and this was a situation neither of us had experienced before.

"Hi," I said, as I stared at the five young men in uniform directly in front of us. They stared back at us. "Do any of you speak English?"

A tall, darkly dressed soldier stood up and addressed us.

"Yes, we all do. How can we help?"

"Do you know where there's an electrical outlet? We want to dry our hair."

The room exploded into laughter. Fueled by our embarrassment, we nervously joined in their laughter. Two of the soldiers approached us and said they would gladly help locate a spot for us to dry our hair.

That was how we met. Moshe was a tall, olive-skinned officer in his fourth year of service, and I was a high school graduate on my first trip out of the country, wearing only a towel and shower sandals and holding a hairbrush.

He and his buddy led us through the smoke-filled room to the other end, through two doors and into a hallway. To our delight, there was an electrical outlet in the middle of the hall. Naomi ran over and plugged in her dryer. She started to dry her straight brown hair with one hand holding the towel above her chest and the other whisking the dryer back and forth, all the while chatting it up with the other soldier.

While I watched the two of them, Moshe left the hall and came back with a t-shirt and a pair of shorts.

"Here, put these on. I think you'll be more comfortable."

"Thank you," I replied, grateful that he'd acknowledged my sense of embarrassment. I would certainly be relieved to be dressed in clothes instead of only a bath towel.

I went around the corner of the hall to slip on the shorts, holding the towel up as I did. He had his back to me, never once turning around. I slipped the large t-shirt over my head. It was more like a nightshirt, and I felt awkward, but safe. We could hear Naomi and the soldier conversing down the hall, neither of us wanting to admit to the other that we also wanted a dialogue of our own.

I started to dry my hair.

Moshe sat on the linoleum floor next to the outlet. "Did you just arrive?'

"Yes. Earlier tonight from JFK to Tel Aviv."

"I want to see New York someday. What's it like to live there?"

"Oh, we don't live there. We live in Los Angeles, but we changed planes in New York to get here."

His eyes grew wide with excitement. "I have an uncle living outside Los Angeles and cousins in San Francisco."

"Have you been there?" I asked.

"Not yet. After I finish my term in the army, I plan to go."

We talked and talked. He stood up and leaned against the wall, observing my attempt at carrying on a conversation while drying my hair.

"Your hair is curly, no?"

"Yes, very."

"Then, why do you try to change it?" It was such a simple question, yet I found it hard to answer him.

"I don't know." I'd been wearing my hair like this since seventh grade. "I guess I never really thought about it."

"You should try to let it dry on its own. This takes too much time."

"Okay. I will." I stopped blowing my semi-dry wavy hair.

He pointed to Naomi and the soldier making out on the far side of the hallway. "You have a friendly friend!" he said in a curious manner.

I blushed and didn't respond, not wanting him to think the same of me.

Then, he said, "I have an idea. Let's go up to the roof and watch the sun rise."

"That sounds great."

We left the other two in the hallway after Moshe told his

buddy where we were going. The other soldier answered that they would join us in a minute.

As we climbed the staircase leading to the roof, Moshe explained why they were there in the hostel for the night. Several officers were assigned to train first-year soldiers who would be educating schoolchildren about points of interest as part of their curriculum. He was one of the supervising officers. When soldiers are providing community service, they can stay in the hostel for free. After the training was completed, he was going to visit his parents in Bat Yam, a suburb outside of Tel Aviv.

We sat on the roof watching the sun rise above the buildings made of ivory and beige Jerusalem stone. The sky was full of color. Purple turned to red and orange before us. It was breathtaking. Neither of us spoke.

The week with my group was full of sightseeing, trying new foods, shopping in the crowded open markets, and learning about this magnificent country. It really had every reason to be thriving given what its citizens had been through. Against all odds, the people are happy, warm, and engaging. They truly wanted us to understand their history and why they loved living here.

We experienced floating in the Dead Sea—the salt keeps a person buoyant. We toured some of the most significant religious locations like Bethlehem, Jerusalem, and the Mount of Olives. We climbed Masada at dawn and watched the sun rise while sitting among ancient relics.

Despite its beauty, however, it didn't compare to the sunrise I watched with Moshe that first morning. As I got on the plane to go back home, I thought about the soldier I'd met, hoping he'd answer the letter I would send to him once I returned home.

9

Blue Blazers

*Los Angeles, California
1980-1982*

Two months after coming back from Israel, I was getting bored and ready to start college. UCLA began in October, much later than most universities. When I applied to attend UCLA, I'd requested to live on campus, even though my home was only twenty miles away. Selection was made by a lottery held during the last week of August. If you were lucky enough to get a room assignment, you could move in the third weekend of September, giving you ten days to enjoy college life before classes began. People were notified by phone. That was etched into my brain.

I was helping my mother prepare dinner. She was nervous, pacing back and forth in our kitchen, the phone just an arm's distance from her.

"What are you doing?" my father asked her.

"Waiting for the phone to ring."

And just like that, it rang. She stopped and stared at the phone, then at me. I couldn't hear what was said, but I could tell she was happy. She hung up the phone, turned to me and said, "You got into Rieber Hall! Now you can start choosing what you want to pack for your dorm."

She and my father hugged, which I thought was strange. They usually didn't show affection toward each other in front of me or my younger brother.

I wasn't as ready for college as I'd thought. Even with the news, my heart sank. I felt as empty as they felt happy. Once again, I was moving, having to create a home all over again. That's all I could think about. That night I went to sleep listening to the sounds of their laughter and the clinking of their wine glasses as they sat in the living room, around the corner from my bedroom door.

The next few weeks I was consumed with sadness, not wanting to eat, or even swim in our pool. I stayed to myself and ended up losing thirteen pounds, which infuriated my father.

"Now she definitely needs new clothes," my mother told him. She was delighted and spent the last week before I moved to campus in New York City seeing friends and shopping for me, even though I wasn't there with her.

The big day came. People scurried back and forth from the overly packed station wagons unloading boxes, shopping bags, and suitcases for their sons and daughters moving into the campus dormitories. You could feel the parents' excitement and the incoming students' anxiety about the unknown.

The rooms in Rieber Dorm were small. In each room, there were two twin beds separated by a tiny nightstand.

At the foot of each bed was a small desk. On either side of the entry was a single bar to hang clothes on and a chest of drawers. Most of my clothes remained in plastic tubs shoved underneath my bed.

I met my roommate, Angela, who loved lips. Her pillows, sheets, and towels were all stamped with lipstick kisses. Her side of the room was marked by pinks and reds, and my side by our school colors of yellow and blue. Living here reminded me of the youth hostels in Jerusalem and Tel Aviv.

My apprehension about moving to UCLA and a new place eventually faded away. School kept me busy. I had taken all my general education courses in high school, giving me an opportunity to explore different majors. By March 1981, the end of my second quarter, I'd decided on English literature with a minor in American history.

Each month I set aside a few hours to write to Moshe. We made a commitment to stay in touch by writing letters to each other. His intention was to complete his fourth year in the Israeli Defence Force (IDF) as an officer and then come to the United States to visit me.

I finished my first year of college without breaking a sweat. High school had prepared me properly. My extra time was spent writing letters to Moshe and trying to enjoy being a teenager with little responsibility except working part time at a neighborhood print shop.

By the spring of 1982, I was finishing my sophomore year of college. Distractions were everywhere. My sorority sisters loved to stay up all night and sleep all day. As grateful as I was to have housing near campus, the environment was not conducive to studying. The girls were snobs. Rude, inconsiderate, spoiled. They were there to find a husband, not to get a degree. All this affected my studies, and my parents decided to move me home after seeing my grades go from A's to C's.

That summer I attended summer school to retake the two courses I'd barely passed so that I could still qualify to become a junior that fall. Once I was a junior, I could apply to go abroad for a quarter of college. That way, I could go to Israel and take classes there, and Moshe and I could spend all our free time together.

Most students who were at the university during the summer were either foreign and trying to acclimate before the fall term, or, like me, students who had barely passed and needed to redo certain courses if they wanted to stay on track. Taking my classes over was the easy part—getting driven to and from school by my father and having to inform him of my progress was a punishment.

As the summer waned, I found myself spending time between classes in Kerckhoff, the student café nestled in the old administrative building between North and South Campuses. Many Iranian students congregated there between or after class. I enjoyed being around people older than me, speaking a language I didn't understand. No one talked to me or paid attention to me as I filtered in and out of their place of socialization.

The Persians kept to themselves. Most had recently fled Iran after the fall of the Shah. They dressed beautifully and enjoyed the camaraderie of their peers. They gravitated toward each other, finding comfort in commonality and relishing the strong community they were creating in West Los Angeles. Outside the café stood small tables nestled under two huge oak trees, and, on the other side of the patio, the beginning of Bruin Walk.

Bruin Walk separated North Campus and South

Campus. It started at the Alumni Center and found its way past Kerckhoff to the Sculpture Gardens tucked into the top of North Campus where the University Research Library stood. Every day along Bruin Walk different school clubs set up booths and tables with literature and signs beckoning students to join their organizations.

Usually, I avoided taking this route to class. There were too many people, and, since I often spent too much time enjoying my late morning coffee, I needed to find the fastest way to class so I wouldn't be tardy.

One day, as I was climbing the steps to get to my French class, a man dressed in a navy blazer passed by me as he walked down. He extended his hand, giving me a small business card with embossed letters saying Federal Bureau of Investigation, and said, "Here, take this."

I looked up and took the card as he continued to walk down the steps, disappearing into the crowd of people coming and going to class. I continued walking to my lecture in Royce Hall. Why would I call the FBI? Once I got to class, I threw the card away.

One month later, as I was walking to my professor's office, a different man—tall with white hair, but also wearing a stylish navy blazer—approached me. He gave me his card and said, "Call me some time," then walked away. I turned to say something to him but decided not to and put the business card in my class notebook. This time I held on to it.

I sat outside my professor's office waiting for my turn to hand in my final paper, the grade for which, if high enough, would enable me to start taking upper-division courses. My mind wandered. *What do they want with me? Should I call? What would I say?*

After turning in my paper, I passed Bruin Walk and

noticed a booth marked Internships Abroad. I took a flyer and kept walking. While I waited for my dad to pick me up, I thought about living in another country. It would be like having an extended vacation from living at home. My parents might go for the idea if I received school credit for the courses I took while working as an intern. Why not get more information?

The flyer directed me to the student center. It would be another twenty minutes before my dad arrived, so I decided to go inside. After signing in and filling out a form asking why I was there, I waited to be called.

"What can I help you with?" the receptionist said.

"I am interested in applying for an internship." I handed her the flyer.

"Do you speak any foreign languages?"

"Some Spanish, Hebrew, and I am taking French this summer." She took notes as I talked.

"Where would you like to go?" she asked,

"I don't care."

She wrote more notes and then handed me an application. "Fill this out and bring it back to me." She got up from her desk. "One last question: Do you have a passport?"

"Yes," I replied, and walked back to my seat. I filled out the one page application that described available options. Was I interested in working on Capitol Hill or for a government agency? I handed it to the student worker at the reception desk. The receptionist sat behind her desk with another student, and I didn't want to bother her. As I was leaving, she looked up from her desk and said to me, "Somebody will call you."

The next day I received a call asking me to return to the student center. My mother took me, convinced I'd made a mistake in registering for two upper-division courses. She thought she was going to have to plead with some associate dean to let me into some random general class so I could keep my school standing. Most courses were already full. I told her she was wrong, but she didn't believe me.

When we got to campus, I could see the disappointment on her face. I tried to ignore it, but it made me feel small, insignificant. I was angry that she immediately thought the worst and had decided not to believe I didn't have the recommendation from my professor.

What changed that summer? I worked hard at summer school and home, offering to help make dinner, clean the house, and wash my clothes and the car—anything to keep busy and stay out of trouble. No alcohol or parties, just studying, working downtown for my father on weekends, and doing any other chore possible at home.

Mother and I entered the student center, and I signed the registration sheet. I left the reason for my being there blank. Moments later my name was called. My mother jumped up, smoothing her tan jacket and skirt. She walked in front of me to the desk. The lady greeted me warmly, which surprised my mother.

"We reviewed your application to study abroad," the woman said. "Have you thought about where you would like to go?"

"No, I haven't really thought about it." *Anywhere but here* was what I was thinking.

She asked my mother, "Do you have any questions about the program?" to which I thought, *Here we go*. The discussion turned into my mother interviewing the lady.

"Why should my daughter enroll in this program instead of taking courses toward her degree? What is the benefit of studying abroad? Will the course work transfer over or will this set her back from graduating early?"

An hour later we walked out of the Westwood Federal Building. I was annoyed but my mother was elated. She found no downside to my studying abroad. "I never received opportunities like this when I was in college, and I graduated with high honors," she said as we walked to the car. I held a small card the lady had given to me. Written on it was a date and time to show up at the federal building in Westwood for testing into the FBI training program.

July was hot. It was the end of the month. My grades came back as all A's. I spent my time going to my parents' tennis club gym, where they had Stairmaster machines, and riding my bike around the neighborhood. I read, swam in our pool, and went to the beach with some of my high school friends, waiting for the arrival of the date and time written on my card: July 25, 1982, 8:30 a.m.

My mother drove me to the federal building that morning. She asked if I had prepared a list of questions for my interview. I had not. She looked disappointed. I figured they'd be asking the questions, not the other way around.

We arrived and entered through the main lobby. A guard asked for our identification. I handed him my college ID as I didn't have a driver's license yet. He told us to take the elevator to the seventh floor. There, another guard led us down a hallway filled with letters framed like pictures lining both walls. We sat on plastic chairs, waiting to be called.

My name was called, and my mother was instructed to wait while another guard led me into a small waiting room. A few moments later, a man entered and asked me to come to his office.

"Hello, my name is Director Mike Smith. Sit down. Let's

talk. Do you know why you're here?"

"I applied for an internship program. Isn't this part of the interview process?"

He smiled and nodded. "We're going to test you this morning. Everyone who applies takes these tests, and, depending on how you do, we'll get back to you."

For the next several hours, I filled out Scantron cards, marking off the answers to questions written in several booklets. Director Smith came back into the room only once, asking if I wanted water or needed to use the restroom.

I completed the test thinking what a bad idea this was. The internship would probably be just as uninteresting as the test.

I handed in the Scantron cards, a hole punched out for each multiple-choice answer, along with the booklets. Next, I filled out numerous forms. When I was finished, I returned to the area where my mom was waiting. As we walked out, she asked me what I had been doing back there for so long.

"Tests," I replied.

"What type of tests?" she asked, as we walked out of the building and passed the US Passport office.

"Reading, writing, looking at symbols and trying to figure out what they mean."

Not what I wanted to do on a Friday in the summer. As we left, the guard in the front lobby said, "Thanks for coming in. Someone will get back to you." I nodded at him in acknowledgment, and my mother and I continued walking to the car.

10

What Kind of Internship is This?

Washington, DC.
1982

The fall semester began, and I felt free. My parents agreed to rent a small apartment for me and a roommate. Ann, a high school friend of mine, had recently transferred to UCLA and needed housing. It worked out for us to share a small one-bedroom, one-bath unit in West Hollywood, about ten miles from campus. A few weeks into the quarter, I received a notification to come back to the student center. I entered the student center and signed in. A man called my name and asked me to his desk.

"Have you considered a career in government?" he asked.

"No. Why?"

"Do you want to study abroad?"

"Yes. That's why I applied to the internship program."

"Are you willing to leave school for one quarter to have some training? In return, we will cover some of your tuition."

I hadn't thought about it, but it did sound good to me. Maybe I could get back to Israel while Moshe was finishing his last year in the army. "What type of training?"

He said that depended on the type of internship I was assigned. "If you choose to take a job with us after the quarterly training, your tuition will be covered, but you have to commit to the job for three years. You would be a student working for us until you graduate and then work full time after that."

Working for us—that was becoming more and more clear to me.

I hadn't thought about what I would do once I graduated from college. I was seventeen, almost eighteen. It seemed far off into the future to think about a full-time job, but the attraction of getting paid while also having my tuition covered was certainly appealing. "I agree to get trained." We shook hands, and I left the center.

Two quarters later, I was notified that, during spring break, I'd be flown to Washington, DC for a one-week orientation. My parents were excited to find out I had received an internship at a local ABC news station. This is what I was told to say. This would be my story: I was an intern working at the Federal Communications Commission (FCC) on Q Street in Washington, DC. My parents had no need to second guess the internship. actually, I would be working with the Federal Bureau of Investigation.

I landed at Dulles Airport outside of DC at a time when

most college students were tanning on some beach and partying the week away. I got off the People Carrier at Dulles Airport and saw a man with a sign that had my name on it. He asked me to follow him and to point out my suitcase as it came off the carousel. He took my bag, and we walked outside to a large black car. I got into the back, and he drove me to Quantico, Virginia.

Once there, we headed toward the FBI training grounds. I thought, *What kind of internship is this?* I knew the information given to my parents from the student center was a cover so they would let me go for the week, but I didn't yet understand what I was doing or for whom.

That became clear once I entered the building and was given two sets of running pants, two shirts and a sweatshirt, one pair of tennis shoes, athletic socks, black dress pants, and a white button-down blouse. Completing the wardrobe was one black belt and one pair of low-heeled black shoes. They also gave me two books, one pen, one pencil, and a notebook.

The week was filled with psychological and physical evaluations. There was firearm training using a Colt .45 and hand/eye coordination exercises. Athletic capabilities like running, jumping, scaling fences and walls, and balancing were all part of the many drills we ran that week. In addition to the physical tests, we had psychological evaluations. All 'interns' spent time with several doctors who asked us about our childhoods, families, schools, and future career goals.

I liked the firearms training best. You had to load the handgun issued to you and fire at a target a hundred feet away, first with the dominant hand then with the weaker hand. Each test was timed. It was difficult, but exciting. I was good at this. My physical tests were decent, but my running and shooting skills were excellent. I'd always enjoyed running and had done well on my high school track team. I wasn't surprised that I tested the highest in the group of young women in running, but I'd never shot a gun before, so this new skill was not only fun but interesting to me. How fast could I load the handgun? How accurate were my shots with my right hand pulling the trigger as opposed to my left? How many times did I hit the target? And where did I hit it? I stayed up at night practicing, trying to master my technique. It became easier to train my right eye to line up the sights, and my non-dominant hand became steadier when holding the gun.

We trained in groups. On many activities the trainers pitted us against each other psychologically and judged our responses. We tried our best to be friendly with each other while knowing we were really competing for whatever positions would be available. But no one discussed it, and no one really knew what we were competing for. Was it a position back home, abroad, or in some government office where we would be attached to some agency? But doing what? Nobody knew. Everyone was curious.

The week ended as it began. We filed into a small room and were told to turn in the clothing and shoes that had been issued to us. Each of us was given an envelope on our way out of the facility on our way to the airport. We could open it when the airplane hit cruising altitude and not before.

The trainers gave no sign that we had either excelled at the tasks or failed them. There were no emotional goodbyes. No indication that we would see these people again or that they would be in touch.

Once on the plane, I held the envelope on my lap over the seat belt. I waited until we took off and cleared the 30,000-foot mark, then carefully undid the seal on the back of the envelope. I was ready to slip the paper out of it when I thought, *What does this say?* I sat back in my seat and closed my eyes. *What's contained in this envelope will change my life. Moving forward, things will never be the same.* I took the paper out and held it on my lap, opened my eyes, and started to read what was going to happen next. The paper said:

> *Congratulations, you have successfully accomplished the first part of a one-year training program provided to give you the skills needed for future assignments. We will contact you with further instructions.*
> *Signed, M. Smith.*

After I returned to Los Angeles, it was time to settle back into the college routine. Before long, however, I received a letter sent from the student center. Once again, I signed the registration list and waited for my name to be called. I sat down, and the man behind the long wooden table asked me for my student identification. He typed something into his computer terminal, then gave me back my ID card.

"You will have an internship in Israel. It will begin in January after you've taken two language tests. The tests will be given to you in late December after the quarter is over. Do you have any questions?"

I was excited to go back to Israel and couldn't think about anything else at that time. "Not now," I said.

"Good," he replied. "We'll be in touch." I got up from the chair and we shook hands. "You have a strong handshake. That's good."

"Thank you," I said, and left the center to go to class.

After class, I called my parents from a payphone on

campus and told them I was going to Israel for my internship beginning in January. They were happy for me but wondered what the connection was between the 'news station' orientation in DC and Israel. I said I didn't know but that I was excited to go back to such a beautiful and historic country. They couldn't have been more pleased and didn't push back on my cavalier answer that did nothing to connect DC to this next adventure. I would see them over the weekend, which would give me time to try to figure out appropriate answers to the questions they would have.

11

At the Kibbutz

Israel
1981-1982

Getting off the plane at Ben Gurion Airport was different this time. There were no friends to share the upcoming experiences with. Memories from my high school graduation trip flooded my head. I had to consciously shake off my thoughts and focus on my surroundings.

Some things felt familiar. Soldiers with military-issued guns protected the tarmac, the plane, and the terminal. Bomb-sniffing dogs circled the baggage claim. Airport workers checked passports and visas. But there wasn't a tour guide or group placard with our names on it. No leadership to guide us onto our prepaid luxury bus transportation. I was on my own this time. I had an address, about fifty dollars in local currency (shekels), and my duffel bag. I was told that everything else would be at the kibbutz.

I felt a sense of independence. My Hebrew was decent, so I was able to navigate the transit system and find the right bus. (Studying it on the plane certainly helped.) I transferred buses at Tel Aviv outside of Bat Yam.

The streets were quiet, not many cars on the road at 2:00 a.m. I was wide awake. The time difference hadn't kicked in yet, and I felt the same excitement I did when Naomi and I had first arrived at the youth hostel on our high school graduation trip.

I arrived at Kibbutz Tzora at 3:10 a.m. The bus pulled off the main road onto a dirt road and stopped at a small bus stop twenty minutes from the heart of Jerusalem. The driver informed me that this was my stop. I thanked him and pulled my duffel bag from the holding rack, stepped off the bus and onto the dirt road.

After the bus pulled away, I decided to sit on the bus stop bench for a moment before walking down the dirt road to the kibbutz. It was dark out and the road was unlit. A dim moon shone on the worn wooden bench.

Time passed with no one coming up or down the road, so I got up and started walking, following the one-way sign written in Hebrew with an arrow pointing forward.

About ten minutes into my walk, I spied lights coming toward me. An open-bed truck slowed down, and the driver stuck his head out the window. "Get in," he said.

He appeared official, but I paused, wondering whether I should get into the back of the truck or into the passenger's seat. He pointed to the open bed, and I tossed in my duffel bag, then pulled myself up. The road was bumpy, and dirt clouds flew up as we traveled down the narrow path. When we approached the front gate, I noticed a sign ahead that said:

Tzora, Built by South Africans in Honor of Religious Freedom.

The sun was far from rising, but it appeared to be the beginning of the workday for this community of farmers. Folks of all ages were walking about. Some were smoking cigarettes, others, drinking coffee. I realized later that this was their morning routine of congregating together outside the community dining room before heading out to the fields for a day of work. The driver stopped past the dining room in front of a small group of buildings resembling two-story duplexes. He motioned toward the middle building.

"Thanks for the ride," I said, and jumped out of the bed of the truck.

Inside the building, an older woman sat behind a desk illuminated by a single light. She was drinking her morning coffee and smoking a cigarette.

"Hello. Welcome," she said. "Coffee?"

"Yes, please."

"How was your trip? Easy?"

"Yes. No problems."

"How is your Hebrew?" she asked at a quickened pace to see if I could understand her.

"All right," I replied.

"Good, it will help you to get to know the people here better if you can speak our language. You will stay in the youth volunteer building. We have volunteers ranging in age from eighteen to twenty-five from many different countries. They come here to work in the fields or with the children. In exchange, we provide their meals, housing, plane ticket, and at the end of the work period they've committed to, a small amount of money to thank them for their labor. You will have two jobs: one in the fields working side by side with them and kibbutz members, and the other in the kitchen washing dishes."

She put out her cigarette, and her businesslike tone became more solemn. "We believe there is a connection between some community members and volunteers passing drugs. Find out what you can and let me know."

She walked me to my room in the volunteer building, adding, "Speak to no one about this. Act as if you are here like any other volunteer. Work hard and keep to yourself."

With that she opened the door to a small room containing bunk beds. The bottom right one was open with a pillow, sheets, and blanket folded on top of a new mattress. Across from the bed sat an open cabinet with three shelves. The bottom one was for shoes, the middle for clothing, and the top for storage. I looked at the other three beds and cabinets, trying to figure out who my roommates were. All were women, some with more belongings than others. All were European from the look of their pictures, but from which countries I had no idea.

"Take some time to put away your things and be in the dining room in thirty minutes," she said. "I will find you in a few weeks, and we will talk."

"*Todah*," I replied, which means "Thank you" in Hebrew.

After making my bed, I showered, changed into some shorts and a t-shirt, and walked over to the community dining room. Inside, picnic tables lined up in five neat rows, and a buffet line had formed on the far right that reminded me of how we used to get our food in the orphanage and in my college dormitory. The kitchen was behind the food line, as it was in my school cafeteria. The dining room was large. Windows looked out to a vegetable garden and, to the far left, the children's quarters.

One aspect of kibbutz living is how the children are raised.

At two years old, kids move from their family's bungalow into a group home with children of about the same age. Kibbutz members manage each group, living with them, nurturing them, preparing their food, and teaching them. On Friday, after school is over, the children go back to their parents' living quarters and return on Sunday morning. Kibbutz children grow up with two families, their biological and communal families, each contributing to the wellbeing of the child: a collective family unit sharing familial and communal responsibilities in a self-sustaining community.

The Israeli government gives the land to the members of the kibbutz. All food is grown on the farm; all clothing is made by mothers and daughters. The governing council purchases machines and farm equipment after the matter is put to a community vote. Almonds and cotton are the commodities sold in bulk and to local markets to pay the bills. Each adult rotates between four types of work: field, kitchen, children's quarters, and facility maintenance.

Community members who'd broken a rule were treated differently. They were given extra work and were not permitted to eat in the communal dining room or take part in group activities, including losing their right to vote. The punishment time ranged from one week to one month, depending on the severity of the offense. After a second violation, the person was required to leave the community. They were given some money in addition to their monthly allowance and a bus ticket, and they were then left to their own devices to make a future for themselves in the outside world.

Kibbutz life was tightly structured. Each afternoon we were given three hours off between jobs. From 4:00 a.m. to 11:00 a.m., we worked in the fields, taking our breakfast there and arriving back to the main area around noon. The sun was at its peak, and no amount of water would keep anyone hydrated enough to do good work past that point.

After showering and changing clothes, most of us got into bed and slept a few hours before waking, eating, and starting our second work assignment. I wasn't used to getting up at 3:00 a.m., and after outdoor physical work and the summer heat, it was easy to fall back asleep. The first week I had a hard time waking and getting to my second job in the kitchen.

The kitchen team was a friendly group of people who welcomed me by preparing a meal upon my arrival. The food was delicious. Lamb, chicken, eggs, homemade bread, saffron rice, plain yogurt, and vegetables grown from their gardens. Although most of the food was homegrown and healthy, no one cared how much or how little you ate. By the end of my second week, my jeans were beginning to feel tight.

After a meal, I was given a sink full of dishes, consisting of fifty to one-hundred plates, pots, pans, and utensils to wash and dry. By the time I finished, there would be the next sink full of dirty kitchen items used to make the evening meal.

After that came the community dishes, which were to be cleaned and put away for the morning. It was a dull routine, but it allowed me to hear everyone's conversations, which were in English, Hebrew, German, and Spanish. It took me a while to get to know who everyone was and what level of respect each person had within the kitchen hierarchy.

After the third week, I started to develop dry patches of skin between my fingers and on my palms. I went to the infirmary and was given an ointment to use every three to four hours by a nurse. "Stay away from the soap," she told me. I was having an allergic reaction to the dish soap. As a result, I had to change jobs.

This meant meeting with the woman I'd met when I'd first

arrived, the one who had given me my assignment: look for possible drug exchanges between volunteers and community members. But what information did I have to share? What conversations had I heard that could be meaningful to her? Almost as if on cue, I got some possible answers when I left the nursing station.

Two of my fellow kitchen workers, Ari and Jared, volunteers from South Africa, stood outside the dining hall. They were talking in hushed tones and glancing around warily.

I kept to the far side of the opposite building so they wouldn't see me. Minutes later they separated, walking in different directions toward the back entrance of the kitchen. I waited for the sound of the back door to shut when I saw the woman from behind the desk exiting the dining hall. I still didn't know her name.

"How are your hands?" She took hold of them above the wrists, turning them palms up then down.

"They itch, but I'm all right."

"Anything you would like to share with me?"

"Not yet," I said.

If I told her about what I just saw, I would be jumping to a conclusion I couldn't support. Get the facts, all the facts that time allows—a lesson learned from my training week at Quantico.

"I need more time, but I believe I'm on to something."

"Good," she said and continued to walk back to her office.

I reported for work at the kitchen and was told to set the tables for dinner. As I grabbed the caddy full of silverware, I noticed a notepad between it and a row of glasses. In English, it read: *You will leave for the city after dinner. Thank you. Don't ask to do the dishes.* I didn't touch the notepad and proceeded to do my work.

After the dinner service was over and the tables were cleaned and prepped for the morning, the driver who'd brought me here that first night appeared in the doorway. "Are you ready?" he asked.

"One minute," I replied. I didn't want the head of the kitchen to think I'd left before she'd dismissed me.

"Not necessary," he said in a firm voice. "She knows you're coming with me."

We left in the same way I'd arrived at the kibbutz: he behind the wheel and me in the open bed of the beat-up truck bumping along the dirt road. When we approached the main highway, the driver pulled over and signaled me to jump out. My hands were hurting. He motioned me to the front cab of the truck and opened the door.

"Give me your hands."

I extended my left hand first, and he peeled back the bandage exposing my raw skin. My hands pulsed from the intense pain.

"The hands call notice to you," he said. "Not now because it's dark, but keep them in your jacket pockets." We drove in silence for the next twenty minutes but were soon on the highway that led to Jerusalem.

This was my first time seeing the city at night. It was lit up beautifully. The Greek Orthodox Temple, with its gleaming gold dome, shined brightly under security flood lights. We passed one of the seven sacred gates leading into the old city where the Arab marketplace resided. The "Shuk," as it's called, is another world.

It winds through the old city, connected by tunnels inside and outside the inner walls to the outside. It's easy to get lost, robbed, or hurt when you look like an American tourist. In other words, you're a 'mark,' or an 'easy target.' We parked the truck across from the King David Gate. The driver told me to remember how we came in. That way if we were separated, I could find my way back to the truck.

We stepped through the gate into the security barrier. Two Israeli policemen stood guard and smoked cigarettes at the entrance to the Shuk, their silhouettes outlined by the floodlights against the stone walls of the city. The driver nodded to acknowledge the police guards and then walked quickly through the entrance. I tried my best to keep up, remembering the lion above the gate's entrance carved into the ancient stone, as if watching over the old city. On my left, an elderly toothless Arab woman was selling cloth, while on my right an old man was bent over and working on blowing a glass bowl. Left then right, then right again. We continued to wind our way through the stalls bordering both sides of the old walkway. Another right, then left. Focusing on how I would make my way back was the exact distraction I needed to forget about the pain in my hands.

My driver pushed through some tourists into a small, dark stall on the right. He waited for me to catch up. "Follow me and stay close." We descended an old stone stairwell and entered a candlelit room.

An old woman sat on the carpeted floor. Her legs were crossed, a box in front of her. She motioned us toward the curtain separating her from the entrance. We stood behind the curtain, not speaking a word. Then came the sound of someone stepping down the same stone stairs.

"*Salem,*" I heard a man say. It was Jared, one of my kitchen workmates I'd seen earlier talking to Ari. He stepped into the room and walked directly to the woman.

The driver and I didn't move. I tried not to breathe.

She held the box up for him to take. He placed a small

bag tied with a cord at her feet. The exchange was quick. Jared turned and walked back up the stairs. We waited until she got up and moved toward the opposite wall from where we hid, then I could breathe again.

She sat down with the bag in front of her and a cup of Turkish coffee at her feet. The smell of the strong brew filled the room. She offered coffee to the driver, but none to me.

The driver opened the small bag. Out spilled several stones onto the handmade carpet. Were they diamonds? I tried to count the pieces as they sparkled in the candlelight. He took one and looked at it through a loop used to assess the quality of a gemstone. Then he set it onto the bag and looked at the next one. He did this with all five stones. When he finished examining them, he returned the stones to the small bag and stuffed the bag inside his jacket pocket. As he got up, he thanked her in Arabic: *"Merci, Salem Alekam."*

The driver moved toward the stairwell, and I followed, after nodding to the woman to say goodnight. He was quick on his feet and was already at the top of the stairs when I noticed the shadow of a man on his left side grab the driver by the arm and move them through the crowd. I tried to follow and realized the abductor was a soldier. This was probably not good. In the few seconds I stood there trying to collect my thoughts, I remembered the driver's instructions. I needed to get back to the truck. My heart was beating fast, sweat forming on my face. The air was humid and full of smoke from candlelit stalls.

I started back the way we'd come. It took a few minutes to navigate the dark marketplace. I rounded a corner, saw floodlights ahead, and, once at the security barrier, the image of the lion. I went through the gate and stepped onto the street.

The truck was still parked where we left it. My hands in my pocket, I walked to an adjacent bus stop and waited for a long time. Finally, a bus came. I got on and asked if would take me to Kibbutz Tzora.

"Ken," said the bus driver, "Yes."

I sat in the cool darkness of the air-conditioned bus watching the old city fade behind me, its lights starting to dim as we approached the highway. My hands hurt, but I had too much else to think about, trying to remember as many details as I could about what I'd witnessed.

The bus driver dropped me off at the dirt road that led toward the entrance of the kibbutz. No truck lights ahead of me this time. I walked it alone, reciting the details of the night over and over.

When I arrived at the entrance, the gate opened. Was the woman—the one who had first greeted me, my connection, here waiting for me? I looked around but saw no one. I entered the compound and headed straight to my bunk.

I tried not to wake my roommates. I left my clothes on, slipped off my sneakers, and got into bed. My heart was still beating fast, and I knew I needed to go see the woman in the office and tell her everything that happened. But what if someone saw me with her? What would they think? It was three hours before it would be time to get up to go to the fields.

I lay in my bunk, restless, wishing it was time to wake up and get ready for work. I would tell my roommates I didn't feel well and stay behind. That way I could go to the office and speak with her while most people were working.

I finally fell asleep, happy with my plan until my bunkmate woke me. It was 3:00 a.m.—time to get up and go work in the fields.

"I don't feel good," I said, as she tried to get me to wake up. "I'm staying in bed."

"You must get up. Three volunteers left yesterday, remember? You told Yoni that you would help take an extra shift until the new volunteers come tonight."

With everything that had happened, I'd forgotten about our having fewer people working that day. Reluctantly, I got up and went to work, uneasy about what I'd seen and when I could share it.

12

Moshe's Family

Bat Yam, Israel
1981-82

While I worked in the fields that morning, I couldn't shake the images from the night before. Should I ask for an explanation, and, if so, who should I contact? Was this a test or had the truck driver really been arrested?

On the back of the open-bed truck leaving the almond fields headed back to the kibbutz, I decided to call Moshe. He would know more about the Shuk and how things worked in this part of the world. He would be able to give me guidance or, at least, listen to what I would share with him. Just how much I would tell him depended on his reaction to my call.

There was a payphone outside the dining hall. I had a few coins and pulled out the piece of paper he'd given me the night we met. It had his family's phone number on it.

I put the coins in the public phone and dialed the number. Nothing happened; the line was silent. Then an operator came on asking for the city. I said, "Bat Yam," and the familiar international dial tone started to sound in my ear. I held the phone, listening, not knowing who would pick up on the other end. It was Moshe's father.

I introduced myself. He said he knew who I was. His son had told him and his wife about me. "Are you back in Israel?" I told him I was and explained that I was volunteering at Kibbutz Tzora. Moshe asked if I would like to spend Friday night Shabbat with him and his family.

"Yes, that would be great!"

"I will come Friday afternoon and pick you up." That was reassuring. I wanted a change of scenery and realized there would be no bus service beginning tomorrow, Friday at 5:00 p.m., until sundown Saturday, out of respect for the weekly Sabbath, or day of rest.

We arranged to meet at the kibbutz after I finished setting the tables for Shabbat dinner. He said he would call ahead and give the office his reason for coming, as well as his car's make, model, and license plate number. Security measures were being taken seriously at the kibbutz, as recently there had been several nearby incidents where Palestinians had tried to bomb kibbutz members who were out farming or taking care of their children.

When the time came, I was excited to hear he'd arrived, and our kitchen boss was excited that I had a visitor. I saw a small white Toyota Corolla nearing the end of its front-gate security inspection. The air was still, and the night was quiet, and most workers were finishing up their afternoon shift before showering and getting ready for the beginning of the Shabbat, where they would eat with their families, relax, and enjoy being together at the end of the work week.

I came out of the dining hall as the car pulled up. Moshe's father sat behind the steering wheel, and a tall, thin girl sat next to him. I thought this must be Moshe's younger sister, as she appeared to be high school age. Moshe had mentioned her, but I couldn't remember her name. She stepped out of the car before her father and greeted me with a warm smile.

"Hi. I'm Moshe's sister, Miri. My English is better, so my dad thought I should come with him."

"Hello, Miri. Thank you for picking me up. Hello, Mr. Salem. I really appreciate it," I said, while trying to return as friendly and warm a smile as Miri's.

They were both tall and slender with dark eyes that lit up when they greeted me. I felt comfortable and happy. It would be so nice to be in someone's home, especially Moshe's, and to get to know his mother. I was looking forward to her cooking, which he had raved about, and discussing the day's events with his family at their dining table after enjoying the delicious meal she would make.

When Moshe spoke of his family the night we'd met, it was as if he was tasting his mother's food again and trying to feel he was back with the family that he missed. He was the only son and the smartest of the three children, and his parents treated his army homecomings as family holidays when food and conversation were bountiful.

After signing the appropriate log so the kibbutz director knew who was going to pick me up and where I was going, we were off to Bat Yam, city by the sea, located on Israel's Mediterranean coast, south of Tel Aviv. The town was made up of a small Hasidic enclave, but mostly of Jews who had relocated from Turkey in the 1960s and the former Soviet Union in the early '80s.

The narrow streets were lined with tall concrete buildings that looked like offices but were apartments. The windows and balconies looked onto the streets, and people strung their laundry from lines to dry in the warm sun. We were fortunate to find a parking space just outside the apartment's narrow doorway.

"You bring us luck," Miri said. "Parking is hard to find around here." The streets were crammed with cars of all sizes, lining the right side of the street, almost touching end to end.

Their building had no elevator, so we walked up five flights of stairs to their front door. I wondered how long they had lived here and what the home would look like. I hadn't been inside anyone's personal residence in Israel, so I had no idea what to expect. "We Americans have more than most people," my father had told me growing up. His words came back to me as the door opened to a small room, half the size of my bedroom back home.

Along the far wall sat a small couch, an easy chair, a coffee table, and a small television. A beautiful Persian rug that filled the entire room lay on top of an old white-tile floor. I could hear noise from the kitchen. Pots were simmering, and the room was filled with the smell of chicken baking, potatoes and vegetables cooking on the stove, and some type of soup that was bubbling on the side. The smell of turmeric, saffron, and peppers made my stomach dance in anticipation of the type of meal Moshe had described.

"Your son said you are the best cook in town."

His mother turned from the stove, wooden spoon in one hand and dish towel in the other. Miri translated: "I am not, but if my son thinks so, then so be it."

She shooed us out of the kitchen and into the living room where Mr. Salem was in his chair, feet propped up on the coffee table, reading the evening paper.

Miri then showed me to the room that would be mine for the weekend. It was next to hers and had been Moshe's childhood room. The bedroom was modest. A twin bed hugged the right wall, with a small desk and chair across from the headboard, that was separated by a window that looked out to another apartment building. A small, paved walkway separated the two midrise units.

We were five stories high. I thought the building had eight or nine floors, but I wasn't sure. Moshe told me his parents decided on this apartment because it had a third bedroom. They had sacrificed being higher up, where they would have had a view, for him to have his own room.

I placed my small travel bag on the floor at the foot of the bed, feeling his presence around me. I was safe, and about to sleep in his childhood bed that night. I felt special, and yet I wondered if any other girl he'd met from another town or country had been invited to stay with his family. *Maybe this is just what kind, hospitable Israelis do.*

Just as I was thinking whether to ask Miri this, she poked her head through the door and said, "You know something?" I looked at her and shrugged. "You are the first girl to stay in my brother's room. I think my mother is having a difficult time ... that my brother is not here. She is very shy. Please do not think she does not like you, for her to have you here without my brother is difficult." Her voice lowered to a whisper as if she was speaking to herself. "If he was here, you would not be a stranger, so she will just have to know you tonight and tomorrow will be better." We sat on Moshe's twin bed, her swinging her feet back and forth as if she were swinging from a tree.

"Would you like to see something?" I asked. I unpacked

my sack and pulled out two wrapped parcels. One was wrapped in pink tissue and the other in purple. I had one more for her older sister, not knowing if she'd be here or not. It would have been difficult to bring gifts for only two of three women in the Salem household.

I asked Miri to pick out a color and hoped she would pick pink, since I had picked out that gift for her. "Pink, please." As she opened it, her eyes grew wide with pleasure. It was a handmade headband with little appliqued flowers sewn on it. A woman on the kibbutz made them by hand. Miri's hair was dark brown, thick, glossy, and very long. She walked to the bathroom mirror on the other side of the doorway and affixed it, pulling her hair back off her face.

"I love it. Thank you. *Todah*."

"*Todah Raba*. You're welcome."

"You know Hebrew," Miri said.

"Not much, but I'm trying to learn."

"I will teach you! You will be able to speak a few important sentences by the end of Shabbat."

Her mother's words rang over her own. We were told to wash our hands and come to the table for dinner. While walking from the restroom to the table across from the open kitchen/balcony, I noted the number of pots and pans used to make our meal. Every Friday is special in this country. People forget work and their problems, as well as their political fears. The time between sundown Friday and sundown Saturday is to be spent in prayer and with family.

I sat next to Miri, across from the two empty seats reserved for the eldest daughter and her husband, who lived just down the street. The parents sat on either end of the table. I wanted to give Moshe's mother her gift, but it was clear she was not in the mood for it—she was upset that her daughter and son-in-law were running late—so I decided to give it to her later. "We will start dinner anyway," she said in Hebrew, and I knew what she meant as she closed her eyes, stood in front of the two candlesticks, and lowered a white headscarf over her face.

She lit the candles, surprising and amazing me that she did it with her eyes closed. It was hard for me to judge a person's age, especially when that person is a mom, but I supposed if she had been observing the Shabbat since birth, at her age she could do the whole ritual with her eyes closed. The prayer was familiar to me, as my mother had sung it on many Friday nights when I was in middle and high school. The Hebrew words were the same and the melody similar, but with a little different accent. It felt good to be here.

As she finished the prayer welcoming in the Sabbath, the door opened. There stood Moshe's older sister, pregnant and glowing, with her husband next to her.

"Come sit," said her mother, and they sat down directly across from me. We were introduced in English, and then the meal began: chicken soup with large pieces of celery, carrots, onion, and chicken meat that could have served as the entire meal. The color was golden, and it tasted rich and smooth.

Then came the lamb, roasted turnips, lentil beans, and saffron rice. Moshe's parents were from Egypt, so these traditional foods were part of their Friday meal. Each dish was delicious and hearty, and the flavors danced in your mouth. We washed down the dinner with a dark beer, like ale. I loved this drink and vowed that it would become part of my weekly Sabbath meal in recognition of the week being turned off for twenty-four hours. When we finished, everyone congratulated Mrs. Salem on the feast we'd just devoured and thanked her for her hard work. The meal had taken hours to prepare, and she was grateful for the recognition.

I asked if I could be excused, as I wanted to get the small gifts I'd brought for her and her older daughter. She seemed to understand, and, when I returned to the room, they were in full conversation, speaking Arabic so quickly I couldn't understand any of them.

"Do you know this language?" Miri asked me, as her sister opened her gift.

"I knew you were speaking Arabic, but I couldn't understand what you were saying."

She replied, "You will have to come back for me to teach you. It will take more time than Hebrew," her voice almost a wink.

The ladies liked their presents, and I was happy to see them try on the Shabbat scarf and small earrings, all made at the kibbutz where I was living.

The conversation at dinner was filled with questions: by Miri to me in English and then her translating my responses to her parents in Arabic. What did I like best about Israel? How long would I be here? What was college like? Where did I live in the United States? What was my family like, and had they been here before? I wondered how many questions came from her parents and how many were all her own. I was polite, but I tried to make my answers brief and turn the conversation back to my being the one to ask the questions.

"Have you been outside of the country, and what did you like most?" I asked Miri. Then I asked the couple seated across from me: "How did you two meet and how long have you been married? Is this your first child? How many do you want to have?"

With Moshe's parents, I decided to not pry. I was in their home, eating their food, and sleeping in their only son's bed;

it was best to be polite and try to help as much as possible.

I feel most comfortable working. I will do any chore. Any dish or pot that needs to be cleaned, dried, and put away is a no-brainer for me. After dinner, I cleared the table, helped clean the kitchen, and took part in preparing the table for the morning meal that was to be enjoyed before Moshe's father went to the temple. After all this was done and Moshe's mother had said goodnight, I sat with Mr. Salem and Miri in the living room.

He was tired, and his eyes closed as he pretended to listen to us talk about his son. I told Miri how we met, leaving out the part about my being dressed in a towel. She liked going to youth hostels so that was all she needed to know. That, and the fact that we stayed up all night talking, laughing, and watching the sun rise that morning before saying, "So long for now." Moshe and I had agreed not to say goodbye.

While I got ready to sleep, I looked around Moshe's bedroom. The pictures of his grandparents, parents, sisters, and friends, graduation from high school, and his first officer training surrounded me. He was here in the room, his presence all around me. As I fell asleep, I thought how lucky he was to have a family that loved him so much that they were kind to me, a stranger, and never made me feel unwanted even though he wasn't here.

I woke to the sound of the front door opening. It was dark outside, early morning. I thought it was too early for his father to walk to temple, but what did I know? I wasn't very religious and hadn't been to a synagogue here. Then I heard the familiar sound of a rifle being placed along the wall, after the cartridge had been dislodged and the chamber checked. I sat up in Moshe's bed and looked around. He was stood in the doorway, beaming, with his hand over his mouth, signaling me to not say a word. He would go to his parents first and let them know he was home; then, I hoped, he would come back to his room where I'd been soundly sleeping.

Once his parents knew he was back, Moshe's mother came out of their bedroom to greet him, then straight to the kitchen to prepare him something to eat. He returned to his bed, knelt, and gave me a hug. It felt good, strong. I was excited to see him, more than I thought I would be.

"Go back to sleep," he said. "I will see you in the morning when everyone is awake."

"But where will you sleep?"

"I'm fine," he replied. "See you in the morning." And he shut the door.

I lay in bed, wanting to stay awake and resume our conversation from where it had last ended, but this is what he'd asked of me. "Go back to sleep," he said. It was his home, his family, so I did what he asked, my heart warm and pounding.

He sat with his mother in the early hours of Saturday morning, and she asked him how long he could stay and how long I would be staying with them.

He told her that we'd be leaving that evening after sundown. During that precious time he spent with his mother, she seemed worried. He tried to assure her that I was a nice college student here as a volunteer working in the almond field and kitchen so that I could have an "experience abroad." Mothers know their sons better than they know themselves at a certain age, possibly because they've lived through their early twenties and told their parents the same reassuring words as he was doing now, but she knew better.

They enjoyed the strong Turkish coffee she'd made with such care so as not to burn it, and she tried to enjoy her time with her son, the young officer who had come home for eighteen hours and who kept trying to convince her all was good. He was happy to be home even if it was for less than a day.

Early in the afternoon, Moshe suggested we take a walk along the water. Bat Yam is a beach town. The main square borders the ocean, with cafés, shops, and children playing in and around the waves. It's a peaceful, happy town full of families, not tourists. The ocean breeze cooled my face as we walked barefoot along the water's edge.

"So what is your plan?"

I looked at him inquisitively, thinking it was a strange thing to ask me.

"My plan? What do you mean?" I asked.

He stopped walking. Looking directly into my eyes, not flinching, he inquired where I was going after my volunteer time at the kibbutz came to an end.

"I'm not sure." We stood facing each other, neither wanting to say too much, especially outside with people passing by on bicycle and foot. He was sizing me up. Would I talk to him directly, honestly, and if so, was I going to share why I was here, what I saw, and that I was waiting for directions from my superiors?

Finally, he said, "Not here." He took my hand, and we walked the remainder of the concrete promenade separating the café patrons from the beach.

When we returned to his home, he told me to follow his lead, to not look surprised, and to leave as graciously as I had arrived. I nodded assent. We walked up the five flights of stairs, listening to the sounds of clanging dishes and pots, and savoring the smell of supper and Turkish coffee.

His father was sitting in his favorite chair and looked

up from his evening paper as we entered through the front door. His mother was in the kitchen, putting the finishing touches on their evening meal. Moshe spoke Hebrew to her. She looked both disappointed and understanding at the same time. He then turned to me and said, "Gather your things. Mother will make us some food that we can eat on the way. We will leave in ten minutes, before the evening rush of people fill the buses."

I left the kitchen, excited to leave, even though I would've liked to have had one more meal with Moshe's family. I missed being around family; plus, her food was delicious. As I collected my few things and put them in my travel bag, I heard Moshe speaking Arabic to his father at a fast clip. It was hard to recognize individual words until I heard his father say, *"Ya la.* Let's go."

I felt bad not saying goodbye to Moshe's sister. He reassured me his mother would let her know, and he would tell her himself when he returned. I assumed that he was going to take me with him, but I didn't know where.

His father went into the bathroom to splash his face with cold water and came back to the kitchen looking refreshed and awake. He grabbed the car keys from the side entry table and walked out the door. I thanked his mother, and she gave me a faint, polite hug. We left their home, his father leading us down the stairs to the car on the street, parked there from the night before.

He drove us to the bus station. In Israel, soldiers ride the buses for free. All public transportation stops from Friday at sundown to Saturday evening when the Sabbath ends. We said goodbye to his father, me smiling and shaking his hand and Moshe hugging him. His father didn't want to let his son go, but Moshe gave him a kiss on the cheek, picked up our bags, and turned to enter the bus station.

I bought my ticket with Moshe's help. He told the clerk, "One way to East Jerusalem." I handed her the money and felt slightly uncomfortable because of the way she looked at me. He was dressed in his army fatigues, soldier's boots, and officer's cap. I was in a pair of Levi's, a white V-neck shirt, and a Members Only jacket. My old, navy blue Keds needed a good cleaning.

We sat and waited for our bus number to be announced. We didn't talk. Maybe the clerk thought we weren't traveling together and that he was doing what IDF soldiers do: help others. Or perhaps she thought we were heading to his base and that I worked there or for him. Either way, her look didn't make me feel secure. Had I only made up in my head a love story between us? Where were we going, and why did we leave his home right after Shabbat ended?

When our stop was called, he took our bags and placed them outside the bus, to the left of the glass entry door. "Get on, and I'll be there shortly." Now I really felt unsure about the present situation. Why wasn't he boarding the bus with me? Was my bag safe, and would it make it onto the luggage bin underneath the sitting area of the bus? I watched from the window seat, trying to make out where he was going, until he turned a corner and was out of sight.

My body temperature started to rise. I was sweating, nervous to be alone. I scanned the busy crowd standing next to the bay where the bus was parked. I just wanted to see him and feel what I had the night we met. Just as the driver started to speak on the loudspeaker announcing our destination and time of arrival, I could see his officer's red beret moving toward us through the crowd. He had no weapon. So that's what he was doing.

To ride on public transportation, Israeli soldiers must turn in their rifles, log them with the duty officer at that station, count and verify how much ammunition they were carrying, and get a ticket to pick up their weapon at the destination.

Moshe boarded the bus, looking for me, and made his way down the narrow aisle close to where I was sitting. He sat down ahead of me, two rows to my right, looked back and grinned; I must have grinned back because he started to laugh and then turned to the woman next to him, who seemed to have been talking to him from the moment he had sat down.

I nestled into my seat as the bus backed up and left the station toward Jerusalem.

13

Israeli Defense Force Army Base

Jericho, West Bank
1981

After a two-hour bus ride, we arrived at the eastern end of the ancient city. I must have fallen asleep. It was nighttime, and the streets were quiet.

The area was full of mosques, synagogues, and the first Eastern Orthodox temple. All these different religions and cultures resided together peacefully. The olive trees that lined the street swayed in the night breeze. The streetlights were dim. We left the station and walked to the corner, where I saw lights on in many apartments.

We continued down the street, each of us carrying our

own bag. Moshe had retrieved his rifle and counted the bullets before checking out of the station. I could hear the metal buckle of his shoulder holster marking time with the sound of his boots on the pavement.

Down one street, and then another. It had been twelve minutes since we'd left the station. My Timex watch glowed in the dark. The volunteer librarian back at the orphanage taught me to tell time and gave me this watch—her own—before I left with my new adopted parents. The Timex had dangled from my wrist until I grew into it.

Moshe and I approached the iron gate that separated us from the small patio planters that lined the entry and the landing at the top of an outdoor staircase.

"Is this your place?" I asked as we climbed the stairs to the second-floor apartment.

"It was my grandmother's home for many years. I stay here when I get time off and don't want to go home. My parents wanted to keep it after she died, so it's my family's home away from home."

He unlocked and opened the door. The antiques, pictures, and furniture had to be his grandmother's. The room was bathed in soft white light that almost looked pink, the color bouncing off the many floral pictures and patterns on the furniture. He took his boots off at the doorway, shut the door, and put down his rifle, resting it on the edge of the dining room table.

"Come outside." He motioned me toward the beveled glass doors that led to a balcony filled with flowering plants. It was warm outside and clear. The sky was black except for a few stars that pierced through the darkness. A small wrought iron table and two matching chairs sat on the balcony.

We sat in silence, looking at the street below and the stars.

As I searched for the right words, he said without turning toward me, "I know you are not just a kibbutz volunteer."

"No. That's true," I replied without emotion. But what to say next? Do I offer any information, or do I just listen to what he thinks he knows about me?

"How long are you here?"

"I'm not sure. I'm waiting to hear from home, but right now no one knows where I am because I'm here with you."

"Then, we're all alone," he said, as he got up and went inside to the kitchen.

After a few minutes, he came back outside with two beers and the food his mother had prepared for us. "Eat," he said, as he laid out foods different than I'd had the night before: eggplant, pita, leben, and cooked vegetables. I was hungry. He drank his beer and went back to get another. He ate, but not much.

We sat there for a while on the sweet-smelling floral balcony, then he got up, back toward the door, and stood in front of me, put his hands on either side of my waist, and raised me out of the chair. The street was dark. Everyone seemed asleep or away from home.

In the quiet of that evening, he kissed me slowly, tenderly, and without a care that there could be someone watching. We went inside the apartment through the kitchen; I could see the shower and small bedroom. He took my hand and led me into the bathroom. Before he turned away from me to start the water, I could see he was aroused, and I felt goose bumps on my arms and legs. While the water heated up, he slowly undressed me, putting each piece of clothing on the counter next to the sink. Then he undressed himself, removing each layer of clothing until he was down to his briefs, and, while looking straight into my eyes, he took them off.

Both of us stood there wanting to see each other's bodies, but not wanting to be the first to break our gaze. Still looking at me, eyes open, he kissed me again and led me into the shower. Under the hot water in that small space, he kissed each part of me. My head was spinning, my heart was racing. I was feeling faint but excited at the same time. We stayed in that shower, soaping each other's bodies, every part, while kissing deeply and passionately. And then he turned me around and pushed himself against my back, behind my legs and behind. I could feel his hardness against my skin. He then turned off the water, grabbed a fresh towel, and dried me, starting with my feet and moving all the way up to my hair.

We held our towels over our private parts and grabbed a beer before going back outside. He laughed quietly. "This reminds me of when I met you in a towel." We both laughed, recalling that fateful night in the youth hostel. He said in the morning he would take me somewhere safe until he came back. I didn't question him. He was an officer in the Israeli Army. He could be trusted.

That night, each with our towels around us, me in his arms, he sang "Besame Mucho" in Spanish, until I was fast asleep.

In the morning, the sun was shining, and we woke to the sounds of birds chirping. No buses, no honking horns from cars on the main boulevards. Moshe asked me what time I needed to get back to the kibbutz.

"No idea," I replied. "I need to get to a payphone."

"Payphone, why? Use the phone here, it works." We stood on opposite sides of the bed and paused while tucking the sheets in and smoothing the comforter. He said, "I want you to talk to me. You can, and I will listen."

This was my worst fear. What should I say? If I told him

what I saw in the Shuk, would he think I was crazy, or would he jump to conclusions about why I was here? Trusting people is one of the hardest things for me to do. I felt uneasy. My early years were spent in a collective environment that breeds competition for attention, warmth, and personal touch. No emotion was acknowledged. As a result, there was a blank space resembling a black hole inside of me. I wanted to trust, to feel each emotion, but any feelings were foreign, empty, and uncomfortable.

Moshe reached for me, lowering me to the freshly made bed. He held me tightly. "You are like no one I have ever met. I am going to help you." We kissed softly. "I want you to feel safe."

After a traditional breakfast of coffee, leben, tomatoes, and cucumbers, Moshe decided he would go back to Kibbutz Tzora and gather my belongings. This meant I didn't have to call the kibbutz office. He would find out how long I could be gone for without jepardizing my volunteer position. From there we would go to his army base in Jericho. I sat down at the tiny kitchen table, making a list of my things to pack. I was unsure how long I would be gone and what I should leave at the kibbutz. He asked me to relax and stay in the apartment until he returned.

In the three hours I was left alone, I found stationary, envelopes, and stamps in an old rolltop secretary. I wrote two letters, the first one to my parents asking for Marlboros, Levi's, and a new jacket. These would be useful for trade if, or when, I needed to do so. I also asked for a new pair of Keds tennis shoes, but most important, a visit. I missed my mom and knew how badly she wanted to see Israel. Maybe this could be her chance.

My mother. A gifted musician on both oboe and clarinet

as a young woman, she missed her chance to attend and graduate from Julliard. Maybe 'missed' isn't the right word; rather, was distracted, at the time, by what she thought might have been a better calling.

She had grown up in New York City, one of three children. Their parents, Russian immigrants, had created a comfortable life, owning a summer camp in the Berkshire Mountains that children from wealthy families attended while their parents vacationed without them.

In the summer of 1955, while young campers were in the Berkshires, my mother visited her older sister, Edi, in Los Angeles. Edi, who, at one time, aspired to be a ballerina, fell in love and married a handsome, brilliant Duke University Medical School graduate. He loved horses and the couple lived in an equestrian community northwest of the city in the San Fernando Valley while he completed his residency at Cedar Sinai Hospital.

All this was quite attractive to Edi's seven-year-younger sister: a lovely suburban home, planning for children, and a perfect married life. So my mother enrolled in classes at Los Angeles City College, deciding to shift gears, get a teaching certificate, and leave behind the rigors of practicing her musical instruments five to six hours a day. Instead, she would enjoy touring California with her sister, spend time at the beach, learn to cook and take care of a house.

This was the plan until their mother appeared. Straight from Manhattan, she had come to take her youngest child back home. Even at ages twenty and twenty-seven, my mother and her sister were the disciplined children of strong parents; when their parents gave an order, it was obeyed. Once back in New York, Mother enrolled in Hunter College, waiting for an audition date at Julliard and the life her parents wanted for her.

But she'd changed: more independent, less mindful than before. And, one night in Scarsdale, New York, she met a recent graduate of Syracuse University who worked for his family's successful business. His father had died when he was only ten years old, and raised by a highly protective and indulgent mother, he was privileged, self-absorbed, loud, and raucous. Instead of graduating from Julliard, she married him and got the teacher's certificate after all.

This was the mother I was writing while waiting for Moshe's return to the apartment. This was the mother I missed and who I hoped would get her wish, take the chance to come visit me in Israel.

After reading over the letter, I folded it, put it in one of the envelopes, sealed it, then went outside onto the patio.

The fragrance of flowers surrounded me. It was heady, full of the scent of geraniums, gardenias, and honeysuckle. I felt like I was back home in Southern California, remembering games of hide and seek in our backyard, stooping down low in the honeysuckle bushes, and trying to stay out of sight while sucking on the sweet flowers that were full of juice.

Now to figure out what to say in the second letter. I needed to find out how long I would be here and what I had to do before I returned home or before I encouraged my mother to come to Israel. Who should I send it to? To my kibbutz contact? To Mr. Smith of the FBI in West Los Angeles?

I wrote a short note to Mike Smith to tell him that I was fine, but that I needed direction and a timeline. No mention of the Jerusalem Shuk, seeing Moshe, or visiting his family.

The door opened as I finished the letter, and Moshe walked in with two bags. One was my duffel, stuffed full of my belongings, and the other with fruits, vegetables, and baked goods.

"Here are your things, except for your bedding and several items at the group laundry facility. I have signed permission for you to be with me."

"For how long?"

"A few weeks." My heartbeat started to calm, and my breathing relaxed. A few weeks would give me time to hear back from my letters and have some direction.

"Thank you."

He looked back at me as he unpacked the bag of food. *"Toda, Raba."* You are welcome.

We ate, laughed, and walked the neighborhood. At sunset, he announced we were leaving and that I would need to collect the few things on the bathroom counter that were mine.

"You may want to shower here before we go." Not certain what the showers would be like at his base, I took his advice and savored the water as it poured down my face and body.

We left as quietly as we'd arrived. Throughout the two-hour bus ride, we kept to ourselves. The night air was still and hot.

On our approach to Jericho, Moshe signaled toward the door, and we left the bus. Palm trees lined both sides of the unpaved road, and an old dilapidated Arab market sat off to one side. It was good to be there at night and not in the 100-degree heat during the day. We sat on the bench, looking at the night sky as the bus pulled away, leaving us behind in a cloud of dust to wait for our ride to the army base.

Before I could see the vehicle, we heard it coming down the dirt road. Loud and boisterous, the truck rounded the corner, and soldiers' voices pierced the silent night. "My friends," Moshe said.

He stood up and gathered our two bags. This was our ride. The three military personnel looked at me with blank expressions. Moshe lifted me into the open jeep and gave some order to the soldiers in Hebrew that I didn't understand. They wore black berets, signifying a lesser rank than his.

We traveled down the dark, bumpy road with me holding onto the railing with both hands. Moshe sat across from me. Two soldiers sat in front, one driving and the other navigating, while a third sat with his back to me, knees up and positioned with his rifle pointed out the back of the open vehicle.

At the base, surrounded by a barbed-wire fence, floodlights drenched the sky, and guards stood on either side of the entrance. It was the army base: IDF Jericho.

Moshe had told me that we were going from his grandmother's apartment to an army base. Now I was full of anxiety. Was I going to be held here, and in what way? A jail cell, or treated like a party favor, passed around the troops? My mind raced, and I'm sure I looked scared.

On entering the base, I heard many different voices. Rows of tents stood side by side on the left side of the main road. To the right was a large black expanse. Probably a training field, but at night with no lights on it was hard to make out what I was seeing. We stopped in front of the main building, a bungalow that had a metal roof and siding. My thoughts started to ease. I saw no barracks that appeared to be guarded or blocked off. This was, as Moshe had told me, a military base, not a jail.

Moshe and one of the soldiers who had ridden to Jericho with us escorted me through the metal building to a washroom on its back side. After I cleaned up, they took me to a neighboring tent. Inside was a small cot, pillow, and white sheets, pressed and starched. A green fatigue-colored blanket lay folded at the foot of the bed. One locker sat underneath the cot. A small cloth mat separated the tarped ground cover from the cot.

"Here is where you'll sleep. I'll be back to wake you in the morning. You are safe. Yuri will stand guard outside your tent, and I'm close by." Moshe kissed my forehead and walked through the tent flap.

I lay down on the cot, my mind racing through the past forty-eight hours. I still felt uneasy, but not afraid. The night was cooler than in Jerusalem. I could smell the tobacco from the cigarette Yuri must have been smoking. There was no noise. No floodlights, just silence and darkness. The air was fresh and still. It was the time of night when most of humankind was fast asleep, and you realize that you're in the small category of those who are not. I lay there thinking about the morning and what would come, but somehow I fell asleep.

I woke to the sounds of rifles blasting in the air. I jumped out of bed, disoriented and shaking. Where was I? What was I hearing so close to me? Then I remembered that I was in Jericho at Moshe's army base. I looked outside the tent, and there was Yuri standing across from me, leaning on his issued AR-40.

"*Boker tov.* Good morning," he said.

"*Boker tov,*" I replied, happy that he'd addressed me in English. "Where is the range?"

"Come," he said, warmly and motioned for me to follow. Perhaps he thought I was there to observe, to write about or report on their unit. I was grateful that he didn't question me nor look disturbed that I was inquiring about the gunshots. As the two soldiers spoke, the master sergeant kept an eye on me. He must have thought the same as Yuri: that I was here to observe. He motioned for me to come closer.

Yuri introduced us and we shook hands. He asked me in English where my notebook was. I told him I had no notebook, that I wanted no physical evidence that I was here, just my memory. He liked that, and proceeded to show me their drill area.

Twelve soldiers were there, suited in camouflage, wearing additional artillery, and aiming at various targets. Some moved; others stayed stationary. I walked with the MA behind the firing line, watching each soldier observe his surroundings, take aim, and fire. Precise shooting from 100 to 150 feet away. The targets were different from what I had been 'trained' on. Moving back and forth, some side to side. It was exciting to watch the shooter reposition himself. I was fascinated by how each could adjust his stance and scope so quickly. Every shot was dead on, perfectly positioned.

"How do they train so that this becomes second nature?"

"So you would like to learn?"

"Oh, yes, please." I'd forgotten Moshe's request from the night before: "Stay in the tent until I come get you." All I wanted was to learn how to move like these soldiers did. I wasn't thinking about anything else.

We walked to another part of the base where there were many low concrete buildings lined up, side by side. We entered the third building and I sat, waiting for instructions. A small, young woman came out from the back. At first, I was surprised to see another girl, but I remembered that in Israel, starting at age eighteen, both males and females serve a mandatory three years in the army. After that, they can remain soldiers or leave to work or attend college. She asked me in perfect English if I would like to see the training rooms.

"Yes," I replied. I followed her behind the desk where she

gave me earmuffs and a pair of goggles.

The master sergeant said, "I hope you like it," and off he went through the front door.

We exited through the door where the young woman had entered and into a room with three chairs. One of them had a big, gray box with wires, nobs, and monitors on it. She sat down and asked me to put on the earmuffs.

"We will test your hearing." She held up both index fingers. "You will hear a noise and point to the finger in the direction you heard it from, left or right."

She hooked up my earphones to the gray box. Before I knew it, I could hear faint beeps coming from either side. I pointed to the right or to the left, accordingly. Then the noises became loud far-piercing sounds of bombs, blasts, and gunshots, then faint, almost like whispering children trying not to get in trouble. This went on for ten to fifteen minutes. I was alert and felt the adrenaline flowing inside me when it was over.

"Very good."

I was excited to hear that, my competitive side always present. Still much the child in the orphanage, needing to count for something, to matter.

The hearing test completed, my tester and I moved to another building. It had a large screen and a man sitting behind a projector. "Stand here," she said, referring to the front of the screen, left of the man.

In this test objects flashed across the screen, coming from all directions. I was to reach for the symbol, person, tool, or color as quickly and precisely as I could. This test was fun. I jumped, leaped, lurched so that nothing would escape me. At the end, the female soldier once again looked at me approvingly.

"Are you hungry?" she asked.

"Oh yes." Which was a complete understatement. I'd been hungry since the day before, but I hadn't thought about food the entire morning. All I wanted was to be pushed and tested and win approval.

We arrived at the mess hall to the sounds of voracious young men and women. All were head down, concentrating on their plates and how much food they could consume before they had to return to work. I gazed at the food that spread out in front of me. Hard-boiled eggs, cucumbers, chicken wings and thighs, yogurt, berries, tomatoes, pita bread, hot foods like shakshuka (over-easy eggs on top of cooked tomatoes and peppers), falafel, and cooked lentils, saffron rice, and spicy eggplant.

I felt as though I was in a buffet line in Las Vegas where you begin with the cold foods and end three plates deep with dessert. But not here. I didn't know that the food remained the same, three times a day. What changed was the hot beverage. Tea for morning and night; Turkish coffee during the afternoon meal.

Moshe spotted me sauntering down the food aisle. He tapped me on the shoulder, which immediately woke me from my food-induced trance.

"Go slow," he said, chuckling.

With my plate overflowing, I smiled and followed him to an empty spot, sat down and dug in. He and his fellow officers watched me with fascination. How could she eat so much and remain petite? Where did it go? For the longest time, I was a chubby child. My 'baby fat' was still there during high school until spring break in my senior year when I lost weight due to mononucleosis.

That was a temporary weight loss. It wasn't until college

that my weight truly changed. During my first year in the dormitory, nothing but the salad bar and M&Ms appealed to me. My body slimmed down, remaining that way through college, muscles from track and field emerging. I could see a difference in how people looked at me, both in school and out and about when I walked around Westwood with my sorority sisters. I could feel myself being looked at in a positive way, and it felt good.

As I ate, Moshe asked me about the morning. Where had I gone, why had I not waited for him as he'd told me to do the night before? I apologized between bites, a barely audible, "I'm sorry." The others at the table mostly talked among themselves. Moshe was the only one who spoke with me.

When the others got up to leave the table, they each addressed him and he them. Then it was the two of us alone at the table.

"So you want to learn how to shoot like us?"

"Oh, yes," I replied, more excited than ever.

"We will see," he said. "First, I want you to come and see the group I'm commanding and then we can talk." I dutifully agreed, and we got up and left the air-conditioned mess hall.

Outside was hot. Desert hot. Dry heat, 110-112 degrees. Not the weather for eating as much as I had. The body can't metabolize food at this temperature. Water is all one needs, and I learned quickly what "go slow" really meant. If you don't pace your food intake, most of it will not stay with you.

As the morning turned into afternoon, my stomach churned, and, before long, I was throwing up all the wonderful breakfast I had devoured earlier. My body paced itself for me. I spent the rest of the afternoon in my tent, in and out of sleep, when I wasn't running to the latrine. Moshe came to my tent several times, bringing water mixed with lemon juice. He sat next to the cot, on the ground, rubbed my shoulders, and told me I'd be all right. "Just rest."

When I woke, all was still. It was dark outside. No lights showed through the thick canvas tent. I stood up, feeling somewhat light-headed, but not sick. When I moved, the ground stayed below me, no longer jumping up at me like it had before. I noticed Yuri wasn't there. After washing my face and brushing my teeth, I changed clothes and decided to look around the base. No one was there to say, "Don't leave your tent." So I did.

I moved toward a noise that turned out to be laughter. Around the corner after the long row of tents, soldiers sat around a firepit. Another four soldiers played cards at a table in the far corner of the open area, lit up by one lantern. Several looked up from the fire and clapped at my approach. My face turned red with embarrassment. "She's back!" I was.

They motioned for me to sit down, and I sat by the fire, gladly welcoming their company, and not thinking of protocol. Each one of them scrutinized me. After a long silence, the soldier who invited me to sit with them asked, "Got any Marlboros?" With that simple question, I became their best friend.

I ran back to my tent and returned with a pack. The look on the men's faces amazed me. Like water is to a lost desert soul, these magical white tobacco sticks were the key to survival for many a soldier. Each held out a dirty hand, taking one at a time from the pack. As they lit one cigarette and passed the flame around to one another, I realized I had the greatest bargaining chip I could have and would use it judiciously thereafter. This lesson stayed with me throughout my career. Find the carrot, for every person has a different desire. Once found, use it wisely to entice.

During my time at the army base, I learned how to shoot at both close and long range. Long-distance scope shooting was my favorite. I loved lining up the cross hairs on the target and holding my breath for seconds before squeezing the trigger while exhaling. And I learned new exotic dishes from the Arab chefs who ran the kitchen, each enticed by a Marlboro in exchange for a family recipe.

The soldiers relaxed at night. We played blackjack, poker, and spades, all for money or Marlboros. I was invited each time there was a betting game. Not for my card skills, but for what I brought to the pot.

A month in, my time was coming close to an end. Word came from the kibbutz that I was to return there before leaving for the States. My last night on the base was memorable.

Each soldier I had befriended came to say, "So long, Shalom," which means "Be well" in Hebrew. Even Yuri stopped by. He told me, "We never say goodbye. We say, 'Until we see each other again.'" Another lesson I learned at that time was soldiers do not think in terms of finality. "Goodbye" was replaced with "So long" in my vocabulary.

Back on the kibbutz, I continued to work in the fields and the dining hall. Nothing had changed except that Jared, the volunteer I saw that night in the Shuk with the diamonds, was no longer around. I wondered why I was taken there that night. Was it part of my training?

During my second week back, I received a letter from my mother. She was coming to Israel! We would have a week together touring the country, and then she would accompany me back to California. I would need permission to end my volunteering and for her to come to the kibbutz, so I now had a reason to go to the office and speak with the woman at the desk.

"Elena will be back in a few weeks," said the young man who was sitting at her desk. I knew I'd be gone by then, so how would I get to tell her what I saw? After he signed the paper granting me permission to end volunteering the day my mother was to arrive at the kibbutz, I asked him if I could leave Elena a note thanking her for helping me get settled when I first arrived and to say, "So long."

He was happily surprised. "That is very kind of you. I'm sure she will appreciate a note." He gave me paper and an envelope. I left the office and went to my bunk. It was quiet. Most of the volunteers were still at their second jobs.

I took my time and wrote down everything I could remember from the night in the Shuk. I wondered what had happened to the driver and the diamonds, and whether Jared had been arrested. Word around the kibbutz was he was part of a group smuggling diamonds from South Africa. Would I need to testify about what I saw that night?

Putting those thoughts out of my head, I began to focus on getting ready to end my stay at Tzora and to prepare for my mother's coming to Israel.

She arrived in Tel Aviv seven days later. My father had hired a driver for the week so she could get to the kibbutz, then tour the cities safely. I saw her grinning as the old Mercedes taxi made its way through the gate. Her arrival was cause for celebration.

My companion kibbutzniks joined me in welcoming my mom with the excitement reserved for a foreign diplomat coming to their country, and, in return, she was gracious, acknowledging each of them. We ate, laughed, and toured the entire campus, including the fields where each morning I worked picking the almonds or cotton that provided the kibbutz's main revenue. She was amazed at how many people it took to make a kibbutz run. To her, I was a student, learning in another country. No reason at all to know or even suspect an FBI connection. I was not yet an official 'hire,' but I was in training.

As Mother and I were leaving to tour Jerusalem, Haifa, and Moshe's home city of Bat Yam, a young man from the kibbutz office gave me a letter from Moshe. He said he hoped I would receive it, not knowing when I was leaving the kibbutz or Israel. For the last two weeks his unit had been stationed in the Sinai Desert. Now they were back on base in Jericho, giving him the chance to write and send a letter.

Before we'd left each other, I'd given Moshe the Jewish star charm that my parents had given me when I graduated middle school. Small, yet strong, the beautiful gold symbol lay encased inside a gold disk that resembled a flower. He was touched and vowed he would think of me every day, protecting the pendant by securing it to his gold chain worn under his uniform.

He told me that one night he reached for the charm in the tent, as he did every night, to touch it before he slept, but it was gone. In a panic, he sifted through the sand beneath his tarp. It was nowhere to be found.

When the sun rose and soldiers rolled up their blankets and unpitched their tents, Moshe continued to search the area where his tent had been before they left the area. He wrote:

> *As we were leaving camp, I saw a glimmer of gold in the sand in front of me. I ran toward it. There it was, sitting on top of the Sinai with the sun beating down on it! I will never lose it again.*

I read his letter to my mother while we drove down the

dirt road leaving the kibbutz.

"I wondered why you weren't wearing your necklace," she said.

I was relieved that she wasn't upset that I'd given it away.

"I would love to meet him," she said as we continued to Jerusalem.

14

Josh

Los Angeles, California/Bogota, Colombia
1983

Coming back to California and to UCLA from Israel was an adjustment, another major life transition. I was almost eighteen years old and entering my junior year.

Kibbutz life had been good for me. The physical work and healthy foods had kept me in shape. College, on the other hand, was centered around socializing, drinking, and occasionally going to class; decisions were made based on what felt good, not what was good for you.

Hanging out with my sorority sisters occupied my time outside of class. They were primarily interested in dating as many students as they could, in search of finding someone their parents would consider 'marriage material.' I had one beau in college. I say "beau" because my true love was Moshe, who was still committed to the IDF and not to me.

One Thursday evening, my fellow sorority sisters encouraged me to come with them to the Zeta Beta Tau (ZBT) fraternity house. Thursday nights were reserved for fraternity parties. It was funny that my parents felt my being home with them on weekends saved me from attending mindless parties, when on campus everyone knew the party nights were Wednesday and Thursday.

At the ZBT house, I met a nice young man. Josh was quiet, not a social animal. No one would have given him a second look except for the fact he was blond-haired and blue-eyed in a predominately Jewish fraternity. He was standing next to the bar when we walked inside.

That night the party was really jumping, Josh motioned me to the dance floor. We danced in the fraternity house Tiki lounge for hours, then about midnight we made our way down Gayley Avenue to the hottest club in Westwood.

The Red Onion was *the* place to be. Everybody wanted to get in, but few did. By day, it was a Mexican restaurant, and a nightclub dance party at night. Most of us were underage, so admission was tough to begin with. The 21+ crowd would stand for hours in line hoping to get in. The velvet rope opened for only a very few, so most had to resign themselves to the fact that they were wasting their Thursday night standing in a line without getting to dance to Donna Summer's "I Feel Love" under the huge glimmering disco ball.

Five of us—Josh, his frat brother Bob, two of my sorority sisters, and I—approached the line of people waiting to get inside. I took my place at the end of the line, but Bob laughed. "We're not getting in line."

Josh was up ahead waving for us to follow him inside. All eyes were on us as we passed the line of hopefuls. I felt uneasy. No one said anything, but it felt like we were doing something wrong.

Inside, it was dark and hot. There had to be several hundred people, most of whom were on the dance floor. Before I knew it, I was separated from my two friends. A man's hand grasped my wrist. It was Bob's. He looked like a football player: tall, broad, and 250 pounds, and he played second-string defense on the football team. His red hair gleamed under the hot spotlights as he pulled me through the crowd, angling from side to side, cutting our way through to the edge of the dance floor where Josh waited. Bob let go of my wrist and stood beside him.

"You all right?" Josh asked.

"I'm fine, but I can't find my friends."

Josh turned to Bob, and he moved in the direction of the bar where I hoped he would find them.

The dance floor was packed with sweaty bodies trying to move to the music. It was loud. This was my first time in a club, and I loved feeling the music, the pounding beat.

"Brick House" by The Commodores began to play, and the crowd on the dance floor grew even more. They started pushing each other to make room.

"Dancing at the frat house was better, don't you think?" Josh asked.

"Way better!" And with that we left.

When we got outside, we found Bob and my two friends standing on the sidewalk, tipsy and sweating, as if they, too, had been dancing between drinks. Bob held each girl by the wrist and guided them back to the frat house.

When we arrived outside the house, Bob sat my friends down on the cool, grassy front lawn and asked me to stay with them. He followed Josh inside and returned a few minutes later. "Can you stay for a bit? Josh asked me to ask you. First, I will get these two ladies home, then come back for you."

I felt reluctant to oblige, but the night was electric, and I was wide awake and not ready to go back to the house and sleep. Students older than I sprawled across the front lawn, falling, throwing up, or passed out on the freshly cut frat house lawn. By today's standards, the early 1980s was an innocent time. Drugs weren't laced with stuff, although drinks were consistently 'mixed' with clear liquors like Everclear, intensifying the alcohol percentage to deadly limits. Sorority girls knew better than to accept a drink at a frat party. We did our drinking before going across the campus from sorority row on Hilgard Avenue to fraternity row on Gayley Avenue.

I waited, as Bob had requested. Others rambled off; some lay on the lawn, either lacking the desire to get up and walk home or already asleep, face-planted in the freshly-mown grass. I sat alone on a vacant corner of the lawn.

Bob came back not too long after leaving with my friends. He extended his large hand toward me, pulling me up to my feet, and then led me into the massive frat house. I cautiously walked up the staircase toward the front door, trying not to step on sorority sisters and frat boys who'd had far too much to drink.

Inside, music we'd danced to earlier was still booming, although most everyone had left except for the guys who lived there. We entered the main foyer and walked up a flight of stairs that led to a long hallway. Not certain why I was here, I asked Bob, "Where are we going?"

"To meet someone," he said, affably.

Someone?

We approached a door near the end of the hall. He swung it open proudly and said, "I live here."

Okay, I thought. *Why should I care?* I didn't know this guy and couldn't care less where he lived, but I tried to look impressed. He shut the door.

The door to the left of his room was wider and looked new. He knocked on the freshly painted door, then stood back on his heels, waiting for a response. No sound came from the other side. We stood there for what seemed like a few minutes.

"What time is it?" I asked.

"No clue," he said. "Probably close to 4:00 a.m."

He knocked again. This time the door opened, and a slight young man invited us in, saying, "He'll be out in a second." Then he disappeared.

Bob had said we were going to meet "someone." Who were we waiting on?

Bob and I stood in the middle of the largest dorm room I'd ever seen. It must've been three rooms combined. Dark wood paneling walled the living room, and windows spanned an entire wall, looking out toward the back yard. A dark-blue couch, leather wing chairs, and a glass coffee table sat in a group. Behind the long couch were hundreds of books. I scanned the top shelf and saw Ayn Rand's *Atlas Shrugged*, several John Grisham bestsellers, and a biography of Henry Kissinger. *Interesting mix,* I thought.

Bob sat down on one of the leather chairs, and I noticed a turntable surrounded by record albums in the far corner of the room. Whose room was this and why was I here?

The door across the room slid open and out stepped Josh. Nondescript and slightly built, he walked over to me with an air of confidence and authority and extended his hand. "Hello," he said, smiling his perfect, gleaming, white-toothed smile. I noticed he'd changed out of his sweat-soaked dance clothes.

"Hello," I said and shook his hand.

"We didn't talk much earlier, and I want to get to know you," he said matter-of-factly. "When I'm interested in someone or something, I make it my job to learn all I can about that person or thing."

He motioned me to sit down and sat opposite me in the other leather chair. By this point Bob was curled up on the ottoman, sound asleep. Josh and I both laughed when Bob snored—though not loud enough to wake him.

"He's my best friend, but not my closest friend. That would be my brother, Aaron."

"The one who opened the door?"

"Yes. That was Aaron."

I'd seen him before but couldn't place where. Maybe from earlier that evening, or from class, but he looked familiar. Josh didn't.

"Why haven't I seen you before?" I asked. "Our sorority and your fraternity do lots of activities together."

"I keep to myself. I don't go out much." He looked directly at me, almost through me. We sat in silence; he seemed to be measuring who I was. "Your first time at the Red Onion?"

"It was," I replied.

"What did you think? Would you have stood in line more than an hour to get in?"

"I loved the music. If I didn't have an early class the next morning, I would stand in line to get in." My answer brought a smile to his face.

"You care about school. I can tell you study more than you party. Do you party?" he asked.

"I like to dance," was my reply, not knowing if it really answered his question.

"When will you graduate?"

"Two more years. What about you?"

"This year."

"What are you majoring in?" I asked.

"Business economics."

"What will you do after you graduate?"

"Grow my business."

"You have a business?"

"Yes."

"Doing what?"

"I'm a provider of goods."

Not understanding what he meant, I probably looked confused, which amused him. His laughter woke up Bob, who looked startled, wondering if he'd really fallen asleep.

"Perfect timing," Josh said. He stood and extended his hand to help me up from the couch. "Bob will walk you home. I am glad we met, Sally." And with that he said goodnight and left through the same pocket door from which he'd appeared.

Bob stood up, looking wide awake. "Ready?"

"Okay," I said, and we left the apartment inside the fraternity house, careful not to wake anyone we passed on our way outside.

Ten minutes later, I was in my own bed. Bob had walked me through campus to Hilgard, directly to my front door. As I closed it behind me, I waved and thanked him.

I lay in bed with my mind replaying the night's events. How many times had Josh been to the Red Onion before that night? At the frat house, how many other girls had he danced with before he approached me? I was curious why he wanted to meet me, but I hadn't asked him why, which was strange. Usually, I was the first to ask questions. I could still hear the disco music in my mind. Donna Summer's "Hot

Stuff" serenaded me to sleep.

In the morning, I woke up on time as usual. After four hours' sleep, I showered, dressed for class and walked out the door with enough time to get some hot tea and a muffin before my 9:00 a.m. English literature lecture began.

I wasn't interested in Chaucer that morning. Nothing could stop me from thinking about last night's introduction. Who was this guy, Josh, and where had he seen me? Why did he want to meet me after everyone had left and the party was over? Why not just talk to me during the party or at the club? Why wait until close to 4:00 a.m. and then have me escorted by his best friend to his room? I'd ask my roommate, Allyson, if she knew him. She knew most of the guys in that house. After class was over for the day, I decided to go to the sorority house and talk with her, if she was there.

As a rule, Allyson didn't wake up early. She was averse to mornings and didn't take a class earlier than 11:00 a.m. She was tall—five foot, ten inches—and long-legged, with milky white porcelain skin and dark hair. She looked like a cross between Snow White and Twiggy. She grew up in Beverly Hills and was quite familiar with Westwood, the UCLA campus, and the entire west side of Los Angeles. This was her home away from home. Her mother lived in a high-rise condo two miles away.

We made a great pair. I was an early bird, and Allyson was a night owl. Most of the time it was like living alone. I went to sleep without the sounds of someone on the phone with her beau or having to dodge the functions, and I respected hers.

We met during the sorority rush at the beginning of the school year. My fellow Tri-Delts thought she was too loud, not funny, and too pushy. She did have one thing going for her though: she was a singer, a born entertainer, and with her talent, we would be assured a place in the final songfest championship.

She once sang at a rush tea, showing her interviewer that she truly was a soprano in the university's Madrigal Choir, an honor that only sixteen students would receive during their four-year term. Once you auditioned and were accepted in your freshman year, you were committed until graduation. The teacups and petit fours dishes became silent when she stood commanding the room with her solo rendition of "Ave Maria." Not one sister could deny her talent or the sweet craving of competing, knowing she had a real chance to win it all. That day sealed her fate to become a Tri-Delt and my roommate, her sophomore, and my junior year.

I walked from class to find and talk to Allyson. I heard her sweet singing behind me. Before I knew it, she was by my side.

"Do you like it? We learned a new verse today and next week they're auditioning for the two solo parts."

"Are you going for a solo?"

"Of course, silly. Why wouldn't I?" That was Allyson, self-assured, talented, and beautiful. Also, loud, borderline obnoxious, and self-absorbed.

"I have a question," I said. "Did you go to the ZBT party last night? I didn't see you there."

"No. I had pledge duty after choir practice and was too tired to go once I was done cleaning the kitchen and mopping the dining-room floors." She looked me in the eye, holding my shoulders firmly with both hands, and said, "They made me mop the floor twice. Can you believe that? Twice. I was exhausted."

She wasn't lying. Born into money, she didn't know what a chore was until she became a pledge. Her parents had divorced when she was four years old. She was raised by a nanny, who also cooked for her mother and grandmother when she was young.

Once Allyson calmed down over having to redo her mopping, I asked if she knew who Josh was.

"Josh Gigmon? Really? Why are you asking? Did you meet him? Did you talk to him? What did he say to you?"

I didn't know where to begin. "Yes, I guess that's his last name. I'm not exactly sure."

"Did he have blond hair, pale with huge blue eyes, and the most gorgeous smile you've ever seen?" She was practically rabid.

"It was late. I'm not sure about the eyes."

"Did you meet at the frat house?"

"Hmmm, um," I replied, trying to get her to keep walking without multiple stops and questions.

"It has to be him," she said. "But wait." Once again, she stopped me. "What did he say to you … and why you?"

I knew her question meant no harm, and she was seriously trying to understand why *me*. I had no answer; I just shrugged and continued walking.

"He doesn't socialize; he barely exists. Mostly he runs the frat house and has others do his work, classwork included. Last month one of the senior economic students was suspended from school. He was caught taping the professor's lecture. When the professor asked him why he was stealing his 'intellectual property,' the student said he had a debt to settle, and this was the consideration he was asked to tender. The funny part was that the professor never asked for the tape, so it was known that the transcribed notes could only have been given to one person. Josh."

After explaining this, she'd forgotten her original question of why me? I was relieved and just wanted to get back in time for dinner before going to work.

When we'd made our way through North Campus, down to the midpoint, Kerckhoff, between South and North buildings, she waved me off. "Gotta go. See you later."

Wednesday and Thursday nights were the busiest on campus. I was grateful when Friday came as most students wouldn't be caught dead on campus unless they were on academic probation or had to work. The North Campus eatery, where I worked part time, was quiet. A few faculty members sat at a table near the sculpture garden, one or two students picked their way through the salad bar, and I used the cash register as a pillow, head down as I tried to fight off sleep.

"Just make it to 10:00 p.m.," I said to myself. "You can do it." My head bobbed up and down as I tried to stave off sleep.

"Wake up, Sleeping Beauty." I looked up, and, to my surprise, it was him. Josh stood right in front of me holding a Styrofoam cup full of hot chocolate.

"Hello! You surprised me."

"Glad it was me and not some angry student resentful that they're on campus Friday at 9:30 p.m.?" he asked. Then, "Want some company?"

"Sure," I replied, happy to see him again, but even happier to just have anyone to talk to until closing. He reached into his wallet for his student card, but I quickly rang up his drink on my number.

"No card needed." I smiled but was met with a look of disappointment.

"When a man offers to pay, a lady says, 'Thank you.' Ladies don't pay for men, especially not me."

"I was just ..."

"I know what you were doing. You were being gracious and kind, and I appreciate it, but when it comes to paying for something, that's my job." He paused. "Understood?"

"Yes. Understood." I felt ashamed, as if I'd hurt him and myself by my hospitality. It was a relief when another customer came up with a burger, salad, and drink. "That will be eight dollars," I said. He gave me a twenty dollar bill, and I gave him twelve dollars back.

As the student walked away, Josh asked if I was all right. "I'm fine, just tired."

"Last night was late. Tonight, you should go right to sleep after work."

That was exactly what I planned to do.

Before I knew it, it was 10:00 p.m. The lights in the eatery dimmed automatically, signaling the time to lock up the register and usher the remaining patrons out of the dining room so the janitors could come in. Every night I worked I was allowed one free meal. But I didn't need it because I ate at the sorority house before starting my shift. So I asked the janitor what he would like and used my meal to feed him.

I had the happiest crew cleaning after I was finished and the cleanest dining room. Once my manager asked me why it was so clean after each of my shifts. I responded, "Milton and Ronny are the best janitors. I'm just lucky they work the same nights I do."

Josh watched as Ronny gave me his order and I disappeared into the kitchen, returning with a full plate of food. On that night, Josh was the last to leave. He said he'd wait to walk me home. I gathered my receipts and cashbox, walked to the back office, and collected my sweater and purse. When I walked out the back door, he was standing there.

He invited me into the sculpture garden that was next

door to the eatery. I'd worked here for two years and hadn't once entered this area of campus. It was magical. Bronze and silver statues peered down at us while we sat on a stone bench surrounded by mature trees and freshly cut grass.

"Take it in," he instructed. He closed his eyes and took in a deep, long breath. "We live in a beautiful place. People are too busy with insignificant things and don't appreciate the beauty that's all around us every day." Was he speaking to me or himself? It was hard to tell.

Months went by, and we became closer. Josh was a renaissance man. A free thinker exemplifying no worries or care in his work. He was strong with others, sensitive with me. He held himself above the pettiness we students regularly felt. He was above it all. Perhaps this was why his fraternity brothers held him in high esteem.

One night in October, we were in his living room listening to jazz. I was taking a music appreciation class, and he was adamant about my knowing the difference between John Coltrane and Thelonious Monk. I liked Al Jarreau and Jonathan Butler. That was jazz to me, so he decided to become my tutor and educate me in the ways of trebles and clefs.

"I need to ask you something," he said.

"Okay. What?"

"I've never asked anyone this before, and I'm struggling for the right words." Sometimes, he closed his eyes as if to have a private conversation with himself. "Please know how much I respect you." He started off with those exact words.

Here it comes.

I thought he would tell me how he was moving on, and as much he'd enjoyed our time together, he was over it. Instead, he said, "I want to protect you and make you smile every day. I love you."

Now I was the one to close my eyes, trying to absorb the words so many of my peers wanted to hear from this guy. I wanted to feel some overwhelming sentiment, but felt nothing. Yes, I wanted to enjoy our time together, and I did, but love? My ideas about love were unformed. I instantly thought of Moshe and searched for what to say at this awkward moment.

"Thank you for your honesty. I want you to know how much I enjoy our time together. My feelings are formulating, but I want to let you know that I want to protect you, too, make you laugh and leave every encounter together with a mutual smile." He stood next to me and his phonograph and held me tightly, kissing my neck as the sound of Coltrane played in the background.

The next day when I walked out of class, he was standing there again, grinning broadly. We walked across the courtyard separating Royce Hall from the Liberal Arts Library, and I could see he was excited to tell me something.

"Have you ever been to Colombia?" he asked.

"The country? No, never."

"Not many people have," he said. "Would you like to go this weekend? I want you to come with me. Will you, please?"

I should have asked some questions, gotten more information. But I was young, smitten, and thrilled by the attention.

"I want to. Let me see if I can trade shifts and work Sunday instead of Friday. Will that work?"

"It should be fine, but you may want to ask for Monday in case we run late. I wouldn't want you to miss work if you're committed to being there."

It was Tuesday, so I had to get my request in quickly. After my last class of the day, I went over to North Campus and wrote my supervisor a note requesting the weekend off; to make up for this absence, I offered to do double shifts the following weekend. During lunch shift the following day, I got a note back approving my request.

When I saw Josh that night, he was ecstatic. "This will be the best time. I promise you that!"

On Friday my house mother knocked on my room door and announced: "You have two visitors."

"Thank you. I'll be downstairs in a minute."

At all sorority houses, visitors were announced to verify whether they were welcome or not. No visitors were allowed upstairs: living and dining room only. I grabbed my bag and raced down the back staircase, which led to a sitting room. From there I could peer into the main entry and check to see if it was Josh. Our house mother had said two visitors. I was unsure who the other person would be.

I looked into the mirror that reflected down toward the front door and saw not only Josh, but also Aaron. Pleasantly surprised, I walked into the entry where both men entertained our housemother.

She was laughing and smiling, all the while smoothing her pleated skirt and tucking her straight blond hair behind her pearl earrings. Josh and his brother seemed to have a strong effect on everyone. She was very nice to them both and asked no questions of me in front of them. That was a first. We said our goodbyes, and Aaron opened the front door for me.

At the car, I got in back with Josh, while Aaron got behind the wheel. I sat back watching campus dissolve in the background. Josh and I held hands and excitedly discussed the plane ride ahead. We were going to Santa Monica Airport, which is a private facility. He said his friend had a plane that would take us to Colombia that night and back on Sunday.

It was going to be a quick trip, but an escape from the school routine and Westwood life. I wondered if they'd brought their passports and how we'd deal with customs in a private airport, but when I was around Josh those details didn't matter. Doors just seemed to open for him, and details were of no concern.

Fifteen minutes later, we arrived at the private airport's security gate. Aaron pushed the panel and the gate opened. We rode slowly down the drive. Planes were parked on either side: Cessnas, Embraers, and sleek planes that looked like they'd just come off the assembly line. We rounded the hangar on our right, and directly in front of us was an old military transport plane; its ID numbers had been painted over, but it still had the markings of a transport. This was our plane? I was surprised but not concerned. It wasn't what I expected, but Josh and Aaron didn't seem out of sorts.

"Have you been on this plane before?" I asked.

"I have, but Josh hasn't," Aaron replied. It would be an adventure, beginning with my guardian housemother waving me off in the company of two young men, to the flight and then to the foreign country we were about to visit.

We boarded the plane and were told to find a place near the middle, up against the wall. There were no seats, just a rope that went from front to back that attached to a mesh cargo hold. Toward the back of the plane stood a thick-shouldered man holding a can of Coors beer, a rifle slung across his left shoulder.

"Don't sit next to those boxes. They tend to slide during the flight."

I found a small space far away from the cargo but kept it in my line of sight just in case some of it should dislodge and come flying toward me. It was strange being on this transport. I had no idea why we were traveling like this, but, at the same time, I didn't feel comfortable asking questions. I was Josh's guest. Along for the ride. He was a gentleman.

He gave me his nylon Members Only jacket to sit on so my jeans wouldn't get too dirty, and sat across from me on the side with the cargo. Aaron sat on my right where he could talk to the pilot, who was in front of and diagonal to him. The beer-drinking crew member sat on top of a long metal trunk in the back of the plane. While we waited to take off, I caught a glimpse of the sun setting; it would soon be night.

Cargo planes are tricky. If you enjoy rollercoasters, they're a close second. Dips and turns are all exaggerated. The mesh comes in handy. You can steady yourself against the thrust of the metal cage you're in by holding on to it. There aren't any windows. If you tend to get nauseous during car rides and the like and need to look outside to calm your nerves and your stomach, you're doomed. This wasn't a cruise ship where you could get on deck and steady yourself by focusing on the horizon.

Not long after takeoff, Josh turned an entire shade whiter than what was normal for him. He tucked his head between his legs and proceeded to throw up on his pants and shoes. Aaron was of no help. He was fixated on the pilot's controls and trying to listen to the commands the co-pilot was giving into a speaker on the dash. I tried to steady myself but was thrown to the ground as the plane climbed to reach altitude. Josh was left to sit in his own mess until the big guy from the back came with some wet paper towels and helped him to his feet.

In the darkness in the back of the aircraft, Josh cleaned himself up, changed clothes, and attempted to settle back into the flight. We climbed into the sky. I closed my eyes and wondered where and when we would land. I tried to sleep, never leaving my little space until the big guy handed each of us a cold beer. "It'll help settle your stomach. If you're real lucky, it will help you sleep." It did both, and I slept the entire flight.

The jolt and fierce bounce of the plane landing woke me. I wiped the sleep from my eyes but could barely make out the view of the blue sky through the pilot's windshield.

"We're here," the co-pilot said. He reached around his seat to grab a metal box strapped to the back of his chair. The crew member began his routine of securing the outer staircase and unlatching the door. We made our way to a standing position.

I had to go to the bathroom and wanted to sprint down the stairs, but I waited patiently until instructed otherwise. "Ladies first," said the crew member.

I approached the open door and realized we'd landed in a field. There was no one around. Trees swayed in the breeze. They lined the large patch of dirt where our plane sat. Behind them stood dense, dark jungle.

I turned back to ask where I could find a bathroom, then realized it was a stupid question. "Bathroom?" I asked, trying not to make it sound as asinine as I knew it was. The man's response was merely pointing toward the trees.

A warm and wonderful breeze blew on my face and through my hair. I walked straight toward the open field and away from the plane's engines that were idling down to their stop position. The grass grew taller, and I unzipped my Levi's and pulled them away from me, trying to keep them clear of the flow. I could hear their voices behind me, but I couldn't make out what was being discussed.

Walking back toward the plane, I saw the co-pilot and crewman on either side of the airplane with guns pointed away from themselves and from the engines. What were they doing with guns and who, when, and where was our ride out of this field to the city? Aaron and Josh stood in the doorway and on the metal staircase having a conversation with the pilot. Surely, he was radioing someone to pick us up. Maybe we'd run out of gas and had to stop before we reached the airport. I didn't believe we were supposed to be here.

"We should be picked up soon," Josh said, and the pilot nodded in agreement.

"It's beautiful scenery," I said.

"Yup, it is. Wait until you see the city and eat the food. It's incredible!"

Food. I was ready to eat.

The men took turns going into the field, trying not to get too far from the plane. We welcomed the sound of a jeep and the dust it kicked up behind its exhaust as it approached. Our crew member handed Josh and me our bags, and we walked toward the open jeep.

Aaron came a few minutes later. He spoke Spanish and gave the driver some instructions and then thanked him for the ride. Josh was quiet, not saying a word. I wondered if he felt better or if this bumpy road was going to make him sick again.

We left the dirt road, and the fields turned to brush. The jeep climbed over the divide and onto the pavement. Soon we saw stucco houses with no windows or doors.

The male villagers were dressed in t-shirts and shorts; the women wore dresses with their hair tied back or on top of their heads, secured by colorful scarves. We picked up speed, passing billboards of beautiful women striking poses and holding cigarettes. We were tired and hungry.

The sight of Bogotá city made me forget those feelings.

Music came from the open-air apartments and stores that lined the street. Bicycles mixed with cars. People walked freely from store to store; old men sat on outdoor chairs smoking cigars and drinking coffee—the sights, smells, and sounds of a foreign town. I loved watching it unfold in front of me.

Aaron, Josh, and I arrived in front of a large two-story building that looked like a huge home. Pink and purple flowers in clay pots lined the stairs leading up to a large wooden door. It was beautiful, old, built with purpose, and surrounded by workers full of pride.

Our room had a balcony lined with potted plants and flowers that overlooked the back garden. Tables and chairs sat underneath a bougainvillea that arched, making a natural canopy. The long wooden table in our room had a bench on one side, and chairs at the head of the table.

We showered, then I sat on the bench admiring the garden below, listening to other guests and the sounds of chinaware and glasses clinking as waiters went back and forth from the kitchen. Josh stepped onto the balcony, looking much better than before.

"Aaron and I need to go out for a while. The employees here will be bringing your dinner. It's a nice night. You should eat out here."

Not wanting to look disappointed, I said his suggestion sounded good and asked if he wanted me to wait until they got back so we could eat together. He didn't know when they would return exactly and didn't want me to wait any longer. Josh placed a candle that sat at the side of the bed on top of the outdoor table with some matches so I could eat by candlelight.

The sun set, and I ate and ate. Slow-cooked pork, grilled chicken on skewers, mangoes, both green and red salsa, and homemade tortillas with Oaxaca cheese, which was creamy and sweet. Afterward, I thanked the attendant as she cleared the many plates that were left empty on the table. She appeared delighted and offered to light the candles, then came back with a small cup of strong coffee. It reminded me of the Turkish blend I loved, but this coffee was darker, sweeter, with no 'mud' at the bottom of the cup. It was simply delicious.

Although I wondered why I was left alone so soon after arriving and where Josh and his brother had gone, I was enjoying the moment, but then the door abruptly opened.

Aaron blew past me, saying, "We need to go," then he went into the bathroom and gathered his things.

I looked at Josh.

"Did you enjoy your dinner?" he said, his calmness a contrast to Aaron's apparent hurry.

"I did. Thank you."

"Get your things. We need to leave. They're waiting downstairs for us."

I didn't know if we were going somewhere else or back to the plane, so before I walked out the door I went to the bathroom.

"Let's go!" Aaron said, raising his voice in agitation, trying to get me to move faster.

Why the rush? We'd just arrived a few hours earlier. Again, I didn't ask.

We rode in silence to the plane, which was waiting for us as if it had never left that spot in the open field. As we took off, I noticed a movement in the trees bordering the jungle and wondered if it was an animal or person making the tall weeds ripple beneath us. The plane was loud, making it impossible to speak. I focused on the sound of the engine instead of trying to ignore it and after a few hours, I fell asleep.

Thud. We landed with a loud jolt, bumped down the runway and came to a stop.

A harsh light shone into the cockpit from outside the aircraft.

"US agents," someone shouted. "Come out of the cockpit and let us on now!"

Was what I'd just heard real?

Before I could process what had been said, a megaphone repeated the same words. "The plane is surrounded. Come out of the cockpit and let us on!"

Were we back in California?

The crewman hastily opened the metal boxes and removed bags marked "sugar and sugar cane." The federal agents weren't pleased that the plane's staircase hadn't been lowered, though the pilot and co-pilot were busy opening the door. I was confused. What was the big guy doing with sugar bags, and why were federal agents outside our plane?

The door opened, and a white, glaring light covered the hull. I could barely see my own hands. Josh and Aaron were invisible to me. Heavy steps stomped up the stairs. An agent entered the plane and barked orders from the flight deck, telling the pilot and co-pilot to gather the flight logs.

More US authorities boarded. Machine guns pointed at the four of us replaced the glaring lights. *Stay calm. Don't react. Focus on them. Look each of them in the eye.* I didn't think anything was wrong, so I stayed with my knees tucked under my chin, both hands wrapped around my legs.

Josh and Aaron told the crewman to get away from the cargo. With the guns pointed at them, the brothers looked like frightened deer blinded by headlights just as the car is about to make contact. We froze in place, watching the agents shout orders at the crewman and pilots, Josh started to shake like a scared little boy crying for his mother. Aaron wasn't much better. Both looked like their worlds were changing, and not for the better.

The Drug Enforcement Agency (DEA) group boarded and rifled through each metal box stacked in the back cargo hull. "You have violated penal code ..."

After a moment of this, I stood up, thinking they must be kidding if they thought I'd done something wrong.

"Sit down," one of the agents said. Then he said my name. How did he know it? And then, there he was.

At six foot, two inches Director Mike Smith looked stronger standing up than he had sitting behind a desk. "Let's go," he said without a trace of anger in his voice. Stern, direct, matter-of-fact.

He stepped aside to let me pass the two agents on either side of Josh and Aaron, who were not the same all-American, confident, perfect-looking college guys that they'd appeared to be earlier. They looked broken and weak. I moved past them, and Director Smith followed me down the staircase where a gray Bonneville waited, idling on the tarmac.

"Sit here," someone in the car said. I got into the back passenger seat next to a young man I didn't recognize. Director Smith opened the passenger door and sat down. We were silent for the first few minutes as we rode in the large, unmarked government vehicle. When we exited Santa Monica Airport and onto Cloverfield Avenue, which would lead us to the 405 N freeway entrance, Smith turned to look at me.

"Do you know what they were doing?"

I shook my head side to side and said, "No."

Silence for the rest of the ride to Westwood.

We exited at Wilshire Boulevard, then went east and drove

to the gated parking lot and into the underground parking beneath the building. The concrete was being power washed and numbers painted on the columns to indicate each level of the parking structure. We parked adjacent to a bank of elevators marked "Bureau Entrance." An armed guard stood next to the elevators. He acknowledged the director and used his key to unlock the elevator.

The doors opened. We entered behind Smith, and the guard closed the door. Again, still, silence. I stared at the crease running vertically down the back of Smith's navy blazer. He was so tall. Why didn't I remember that? The doors opened onto the office floor.

Walking past the pastel-colored walls of the small waiting room where my mother and I had sat almost one year ago, I found it hard to think of that time now. Images of Josh, Aaron, the frightened crewman, the delicious dinner, and the housekeeper lighting the candle so I could enjoy my after-dinner coffee outside on the balcony filled my head.

I followed Smith into the coffee room. He poured two cups of strong, black coffee and then turned toward his office. The driver and young man remained in the small kitchen.

"Sit down," he instructed as he walked around to his chair. He placed a cup of the steaming hot coffee in front of me.

"Thank you," I said softly.

He studied me, and I looked down at the floor. I'd disappointed him. It was hard to raise my head when he began to speak, but not meeting his eyes would be worse than enduring whatever he was about to say.

"Did you know I read your college application essay?" he said. "I read the entire essay." Then he didn't speak for what seemed like a painfully long time. "You're smart. Not just book smart, but street smart, which for someone your age, and female, is very unusual. You've had to figure things out from a young age. No classic family structure where you could learn from parents or siblings. No, not until later. But your foundation was formed from and by yourself." He paused. "Unusual?" he asked.

Here it comes. He would tell me how disappointed he was in me, that I'd had a great opportunity to join the Bureau and serve my country, but I blew it.

He continued. "I realized as soon as I got the field report that you knew nothing. You probably didn't know what these two brothers were up to, and I have to say there was something different about your demeanor that I don't see very often, even from agents that I've worked with for a long time."

Wait. What was happening here? I'd been uneasy since the plane landed in the South American field, but now I thought my hearing or capacity to understand the English language was seriously impaired. Was he praising me? If so, why?

"You display a lack of emotion given this stressful situation." We locked eyes, and the silence hung between us. "You will be a true fit for the organization."

I was still confused, wanting to ask him what had just occurred. Where were Josh and Aaron? What was their 'business' in Bogotá?

"As we move forward, your training will become your job outside of class. No more cashiering, no more sorority social events. The volunteering is important, though, and you will need to continue showing the others around you that everything is the same as before. That is, except for Josh. Make it appear as if you and Josh broke up. Don't answer questions about him or his brother. They are gone from your world now. They don't exist. Understood?"

I shook my head signifying, yes, but he continued staring at me. "Yes, sir," I said in as strong a voice as I could.

"Did you know Josh was a drug dealer?" He must have seen the shock on my face.

"No, sir."

He stood up and looked at me from across his massive wooden desk. "He is *the* dealer on campus."

I got up, shaking inside but calm on the outside. "May I go?"

"Soon. Go get cleaned up, and we'll get you back to your dorm, or whatever you call where all you girls live."

"Thank you, director." I smiled as best I could and left his office, walking down the long linoleum hallway, trying not to get sick as Josh had done on the airplane.

15

Official and Undercover

Washington, DC.
1983-1984

In November 1983, right before Thanksgiving, Moshe came to Los Angeles. We'd stayed in touch by writing long letters to each other over the two years we were apart. My parents had heard everything about him, and they'd told his mother and father that we'd take care of him.

He arrived with one duffel bag, wearing his best pair of Levi's and a flannel button-down shirt—looking like an extra in a B Western movie. He was a fish out of water in Los Angeles. Besides his native Hebrew, Moshe spoke English, Italian, French, Spanish, and Arabic fluently, but he had opted to stay in the Israeli military beyond the mandatory three years, and never went to college. I couldn't understand why he was so different from how I remembered him, which made our reunion uncomfortable. I was immature, and, instead of easing his anxiety, I added to it by pushing him away. My lack of feeling for him was not his fault—it was mine.

After the holiday weekend, I happily went back to college, putting distance between us. My parents kept their promise. They housed, fed, and clothed him. My father bought him his first car. Moshe lived with my parents for four months.

My mother adored him. She enjoyed their conversations about politics, art, music, and life in Israel versus the United States. My father loved him. He was the kind of son he never had: independent, smart, articulate, and, most of all, determined. Moshe had goals. Coming to the United States was a gift that he would take full advantage of. Never mind that we were no longer an item, he was going to be financially successful.

He began working for a moving company, where he learned to perfect his English and Spanish. He also befriended the owner of the company, who taught him how to run a business.

After a few months of living in their home, Moshe told my parents that he was going to visit a distant relative in San Francisco. He stayed there for a month. Once back, he gathered his belongings, told my parents how much he appreciated their hospitality and that he loved them, then he moved in with some of his workmates from the moving company.

On Mondays and Tuesdays, he started working in downtown Los Angeles, learning the diamond trade. His Northern California relative had connections in the Southern California diamond district and connected him to influential people in the industry. Moshe was astute, a quick learner. After several months, he saved enough money to open a small jewelry booth on Hill Street in the diamond district, selling gold jewelry to the public. Moshe still came to see my parents once a month, usually for dinner.

One evening, in early June, I was home studying for my final exams when a knock came at the front door. My mother was busy in the kitchen preparing a delicious meal, which I'd thought was because I was home for a few days before final exams began. I opened the front door, and there was Moshe. Tall, olive-skinned with well-built arms due to his moving job, he looked like a Greek god. I was in shock, unaware that he was regularly communicating with my parents.

My father rushed to the door, welcoming Moshe inside. They hugged and went into my dad's study. I wasn't invited to be part of their conversation, so I waited until they got settled, then stood at the front of the hallway where I could hear their conversation without their seeing me.

Moshe said it was difficult deciding whether to come over for dinner that night. He was mad at me and wanted to tell me how much I'd hurt him, but also that he still loved me and wanted to get back together. My father suggested he share his feelings with me.

During dinner Moshe talked about his work and how he liked living in North Hollywood. The four of us sat at my parents' dining room table, Moshe and I trying to not look each other in the eye. I didn't want to acknowledge his pain and my lack of concern for it. By the end of the meal, he'd had enough. "I want to speak with you, in private."

We left the dining-room table and went into the backyard. He had much to say, but he wasn't angry, only hurt. That was the first time I understood how my actions could cause someone pain. As a child I would say, "I'm sorry," but not really mean it. Foster care taught me that whether I was genuinely sorry or not, I would still be punished for my actions. But that night I felt the pain I caused him. He was the first to open my heart. I truly hurt over what I'd done.

We sat under an old oak tree directly outside my bedroom window. I took his hand and held it to my heart. "Can you feel how fast my heart is beating?"

He nodded, yes.

"I am truly sorry. I think this is the first time I've meant these words. Will you forgive me?" I asked reluctantly.

As he moved his hand away, he caught sight of the chain around my neck. "You still wear the chain?" He sounded surprised. "I still have your pendant."

We made up that evening with a promise to each other. We would start over, seeing each other on weekends and determine if we could have a relationship again.

My official hire date with the FBI was November 10, 1983, two weeks shy of my eighteenth birthday. The paperwork showed my age to be nineteen to avoid calling attention to my underage status.

In June of 1984, I graduated from UCLA. My parents drove all of us to UCLA that June morning: my grandfather, brother, mom, dad, and me. My dad didn't want a repeat of my high school graduation when I showed up minutes before the ceremony started. It was a busy day.

Thirty thousand students walked in their caps and gowns across the stage set up on Drake Stadium's field. Each individual school and subject matter had its moment, but, unlike high school, the graduate's name wasn't read aloud.

It was close to 100 degrees. There were too many people and not enough shade. People passed out. No guest should sit in the hot Southern California sun for that long. By the time the commencement was over, my family was miserable. We decided not to eat out but to go back home. That suited me just fine. I jumped in the pool and enjoyed my free afternoon at the house.

Moshe and I had decided to give one another some space over the summer. He could expand his jewelry business, and I could pursue a career after college.

Our relationship could wait.

The next day I was off to Washington, DC. My cover was to be part of an internship program the UC Regents had established in collaboration with various government agencies. My English literature background gave me a solid writing foundation. I could compose memos, take dictation from department heads, and edit better than most full-time staffers.

On paper, UCLA had me placed in the Enforcement Division of the United States Securities and Exchange Commission. I was training part time at Quantico and working undercover at the commission verifying allegations of employee misconduct.

Part of my field training was learning to blend in. "Do not bring attention to yourself," our instructor drilled into us daily during training.

After three weeks, it was time to test what we'd learned. I'd waitressed in college and was comfortable with the fast pace of family dining, so my first assignment was to learn how to tend bar.

Houlihan's was a hot drinking spot. Popular with undergraduates for their cheap, potent drinks and with local government workers who wanted to decompress after work before going home to the family. It took up three floors of an old building in Georgetown, the most popular area in the District of Columbia.

Houlihan's was located at the corner of Georgetown and

Wisconsin Avenues. Trendy taverns and chic boutiques lined Wisconsin Avenue. It was the place to be seen. The restaurant's bright, stained-glass windows filtered the afternoon sunlight across a massive wooden bar and mirrored backstop.

It took a sliding ladder to reach the top shelf where many liquor bottles were positioned by category, one row lining up behind another, three deep. Even on quiet afternoons, it was easy for the main bar to go through ten bottles of Tanqueray or Absolut during 'happy hour.' The menu boasted a variety of mixed drinks, and I learned how to make the East Coast patrons' favorite cocktails: Whiskey sours, Manhattans, and vodka or gin martinis. The most popular drink among the younger crowd was the Long Island Iced Tea. Consisting of five different liquors, it packed a punch. Despite its name, this drink contained no tea; rather, it was made of triple sec, light rum, gin, vodka, tequila, a shot of orange liquor on top of the sour mix and finished with a dash of Coca-Cola. This gave Houlihan's Long Island its uniqueness—limited to two per customer, unless the tip was generous or the patron local.

I loved my time learning how to be a bartender. This area was dynamic, full of college preppies, wealthy visitors to our nation's capital, and loads of happy hour-seeking government employees. Turn the corner and the entire area was different.

Up Georgetown Avenue was the prestigious Four Seasons Hotel. I walked from the Foggy Bottom DC Metro Station past its beautiful, red-brick facade every day. *Someday I'll be able to stay in this hotel,* I thought. *I'll be able to reflect on when I first began working in this town.* I fantasized sitting in the big red-leather chairs at a white-tablecloth-topped dining table, drink in hand, watching others walk from the station to their destinations. I walked briskly so I wouldn't be late for my Houlihan's job, daydreaming all the way.

After work, walking from Houlihan's to the apartment I shared with five other trainees, I heard music booming across the street and saw a crowd of black men dressed sharply in their 'evening' suits surrounding a storefront. I'd walked by this bookstore named The Library almost every night after my bar training shift, thinking it was a bookstore. But it was a club. One of the few black clubs in Georgetown. Exclusive, not calling attention to itself.

"Hey, hello there," a very nicely dressed man in his forties said to me. "Stop. Where are you going?"

I just kept walking, determined not to look back or continue any conversation. "Come back in your party dress!" he called to me as I quickly stepped up my gait to put distance between us. "Don't forget your dancing shoes!" he called, laughing afterward.

As the next day of training was coming to an end, I asked one of the older Houlihan's bartenders if he knew of the nightclub.

"Oh, yeah. I know it," he answered, "Did you get invited in?"

"No," I replied. "I was just curious."

He told me admittance to the club was by invitation only, and it was only open Thursday through Saturday nights, strictly for a crowd he wasn't a part of. My usual bartending training nights were Sunday through Wednesday. No wonder I hadn't noticed the crowd or heard the music before.

He went on to explain that many 'information' exchanges occurred inside that club along with many undescribed indiscretions. Secrets were exchanged between DC policemen, government agents, and private investigators for payoffs in drugs, sex, or cash. "At The Library, besides a stiff drink, getting information is what it's known for," said my bartender mentor.

At Quantico the next day, after training class, I asked my instructor if I could speak with him privately. Although the weather was getting hotter, the humidity wasn't too bad, so we took a walk outside.

I explained what I was told about The Library and my 'invitation' from the man in the doorway.

"Why are you telling me this?" my instructor asked.

"I thought I'd go after work and check it out."

"Who invited you?"

"I don't know the man's name, but he was signaling the bodyguard to let me in, so I think he's in charge."

"Let me ask a few people before you go there, all right?"

"Sure, I just thought—"

He cut me off right there. "I know what you're thinking, but I don't think you're ready to go check out places alone."

We walked back to the main building in silence. The next morning after class he handed me an envelope. I waited until I got on the Metro heading back to DC, then opened it. Inside was small piece of paper reading, "Permission granted. You will have backup."

That night before I left work at Houlihan's, my manager asked if I would trade shifts with another bartender trainee the next night. This meant I would work a Thursday night, the same night the club was open. I agreed, thinking this must be the signal for me to go to the club after my shift at Houlihan's.

After a busy evening, I waited until the crowd thinned out. It was very late. When most everyone had left, I slipped into the restaurant's public restroom to change into clothing I'd borrowed from one of my roommates.

I didn't want to use the employee restroom for fear

someone who worked there would see me dressed like this. My new outfit consisted of jet-black fishnet stockings, black patent-leather pumps, and a tight purple dress made of shining material that felt and looked like satin. I had to adjust my breasts to fit into the pushup bra I borrowed, which was two sizes larger than the regular sports bras I normally wore. When I was younger, I'd been somewhat 'endowed' in the chest area, but after not being able to digest most of the food served in the cafeteria those first two years of college, my chest had shrunk. The bra and dress were sized for D cup breasts. My 'B+' size wasn't providing the silhouette that I was longing for. Viewing my body from the side in the brassy mirror, I got an idea.

Grabbing some toilet paper from the nearby stall, I wadded it up and placed it under my left breast. Now the left side of the dress was wrinkle-free. My chest was upright and pitched forward. Repeating this fix under my right breast seemed to do the trick. I viewed myself in the bathroom mirror from side to side, then from the front. I was pleased with my look. The dress fit like a glove.

To complete my new look, I needed to change my hair and wear some makeup. Normally my hair curled around my face in a short, soft afro-like style. I decided to slick it back using my roommate's hair gel. After lining my eyes in black and applying a fierce burgundy color to my lips, I looked nothing like the girl who'd walked in earlier that afternoon to begin her shift behind the bar.

My first instinct was to walk out the back door as we normally did after work, but that would signal to anyone who saw me that I worked there. I needed to test whether I could be seen like this and not be recognized. Could I walk past my workstation without anyone noticing it was me? If yes, then I'd know I did a good job disguising my looks. If I was recognized, maybe my idea to go to The Library wasn't as great as I'd once thought.

The lights were dim inside the restaurant's main bar area. It was 1:00 a.m. A few regulars stood around the bar, but most people were gone. Several Georgetown students were hanging out, waiting for their late-night order of burger and fries. The wait staff was at a minimum.

Holding my bag full of makeup and my Houlihan's uniform, I walked past the right side of the bar where I'd clocked out thirty minutes before. "Wow," said a voice from the far side of the bar. I kept walking. No one behind the long wood and brass structure said a word to me. As I made my way past the empty tables, the assistant manager, Tony, who knew me well, said, "Goodnight. May I get you a cab?"

"No, thank you," I replied without looking directly at him. I pushed the glass roundabout and exited onto the sidewalk. Outside in front of the restaurant sat the same car and agent, Stan, that I'd met that morning at Quantico. I walked past my backup's car and was astonished that Stan didn't recognize me. I turned back to the car, thinking that this might work.

It was my first assignment in DC. I was to gather as much information as I could against an official to help justify opening an investigation. My instructor had told me, "Powerful people in DC think the rules don't apply to them. When the elite apply the rules, they create for others and not for themselves. DC's ivory tower seems to get loftier." I was determined to help gather whatever information I could.

I tapped my long cigarette holder against the driver's window, rousing my partner. Stan shook off sleep. He'd been sitting in the unmarked car since 11:00 p.m., waiting for me to finish work.

"Wake up, sleepy!"

He rolled the window down just enough to eye me once over through the partially rolled-down window. "Is that you?" he asked, still half asleep. It was 1:00 a.m. Although the street was dimly lit, he could see my face.

"Who did you think it was? Your mother?"

He looked puzzled, not comprehending my sarcasm. "Hope my mother would never look like that," he replied, with a slight laugh. So maybe he did get my humor.

I handed him my bag and started walking up the street toward the club. Stopping a few feet away, I turned back toward the car and said, "Maybe she did."

He yelled back at me. "Not funny."

Giving him a slight wave, I said, "See you outside, and don't be late."

He yelled back, "Don't talk about my mother!"

The walk took longer in four-inch heels than it did in my regular shoes. I wasn't used to wearing high heels and was careful not to tear them up on the cracked concrete sidewalks. Walking the paved streets would've been easier if it wasn't for having to wear these heels and watching out for drunk drivers careening around the corners and hitting anything in their way.

The line outside the club was twenty people deep. Dark purple and ruby red ropes blocked the entrance. The line went around the front door toward the side street that faced a White Castle hamburger shop. I surveyed the line looking for anyone I'd seen while studying the entrance of the club for the past two months, no one looked familiar except one of the two bouncers blocking the anxious, want-to-be patrons from entering.

"Packy," or "Pac-Man," had worked the line before becoming lead bouncer. He knew everyone who frequented the place and many more of the outliers who the insiders needed to keep their stellar reputations intact. That was all the Washington elite wanted the public outside the Beltway to know about them. Their true character was for a select few to see and not to divulge.

If anyone asked me who I was, I was a young dancer looking for the right club to work at. I was looking for guidance and a recommendation from the insiders so I could get a coveted spot at a reputable club. The Thursday-Saturday lineup was a dancer's main time to make money: such spots didn't open frequently. Most 'dancing' clubs were basically strip joints where one-dollar bills flew throughout the drunken hours of midnight to 4:00 a.m. That wasn't the type of club where I was headed.

I was aiming for the most exclusive clubs, the ones where powerful Washington officials partied the night away and displayed their debauchery, where their secrets were safe inside the padded, rose-colored, silk-lined walls or the black-painted sex dungeons for the provocative, who licked their leather whips before striking the flesh of their bounded prey. This was the information I sought, known only by a select few.

Packy eyed the line as I walked past the front door. "Pull the rope," he commanded and muscled his way through the men who were awaiting entrance. He extended his huge hand toward me. I grabbed his index finger and pulled myself toward him. A few of the men looked me up and down, but didn't put up an argument about letting me in before them. Several women didn't share their view and snapped at me. I nodded to them as I walked through the door. *Those high school girls won't get me tonight,* I thought. Gone were the days of being jumped in the bathroom stall, getting beat up and having my head submerged in the toilet, glasses and all. I smiled even wider, thinking those girls helped me get here. I went from not belonging to being a few feet away from a crowd of untouchables.

Once inside the velvet ropes, through the mass of people, I was faced with several decisions. Should I stay on the top level, mingling with the well-dressed crowd or try to work my way downstairs to the cigar bar and the exclusive party rooms lined with waitstaff doubling as bodyguards? It was my first night in, and I needed to go slow and not attract any undue attention. I was to memorize the entrance and surrounding exits and nurse one drink for several hours, which, I had learned, was itself a victory not known to many in my profession. My mind had to remain clear, my reactions sharp. Alcohol would slow my step and cloud my brain.

This night offered a treasure trove of information that had escaped our group up until then. Director Smith had told me a few months before that he'd not been able to find the right person to penetrate this world. We'd spoken by phone one morning while I was at Quantico. He'd tracked me down and pulled me out of behavioral science class to speak with him. So this was what Mr. Smith was talking about. It was all coming together: why he gave me this assignment.

I knew very little except that, first, I had to learn Georgetown's Wisconsin Avenue's trendy scene, bartending, and now The Library. My gut told me there was more to come, but, for now, this was my first assignment. I closed my eyes, allowing them to adjust to the dim, soft rose-colored lighting of the first floor and vowed to myself that I wouldn't fail.

I recalled the map of the floor given to me two months ago. I knew where the bar was, the drawing rooms, and the exits. Now I needed to verify the accuracy of the map. That was the plan for tonight. Nothing more. I focused on where I was in relation to the side exit near the bar's right side.

A man approached my left side, slightly touching my arm. "Hello. I haven't seen you here before; first time?"

"Hi," I said. "What a beautiful place."

It was simply regal. Gold tones mixed with brown high-back bar stools and winged-back armchairs. A mix of old world and black high-class, over-the-top touches, like the bar backlit to show off the multitude of cognac choices. I wasn't going to be deterred. My attention was on sight-mapping my territory and not on making small talk.

"A drink?" he said softly, whispering in my ear. The music of Rick James pounded in the background. I nodded, indicating yes, and he marched off in the direction of the bar like a soldier who had just received an order from command.

It was time to roam, before he got back. I walked through the large room in the opposite direction of the bar, trying to confirm each entrance I saw. Maps are God's gift to intelligence gathering. The drawings of the layout that I'd memorized now surrounded me. I tried to keep my excitement in check. The map was unfolding before my eyes.

I felt connected to each wall, ceiling, floor, and doorjamb. My mind was trying to race through the diagram. I had to slow myself down and note one door, one entrance, and one exit at a time. After walking through the bar and adjacent living-room area, I noticed a staircase leading down at the end of the hall where I was standing. I found that interesting. This had been a townhouse, which usually meant that staircases led up since the houses were built side by side on narrow lots with multiple stories. This was probably a basement staircase that many of the older homes had. Provisions could be stored underground next to or below the kitchen. Dumbwaiters were used to deliver the various goods up to the kitchen for preparation.

I was making my way to the top stairs when an arm reached out and touched my shoulder, pushing me forward. My drink, mostly ice at this point, slipped from my hand, breaking into tiny shards on the dark wood floor. I bent down to clean it up.

I began to pick up the largest pieces of glass, careful not to cut myself, then I sensed someone standing in front of me. "Leave it," he said. "You'll hurt yourself. I don't want that here at my place."

I looked up and realized I was face to face with Ronald "Renard" Brown. Known as "The Player," he was part of an exclusive elite circle of influential black men rumored to help certain high-level government officials.

Handsome, fortyish, and tall, his dark skin glowed from the candlelight reflecting off the red-velvet walls that surrounded us. He was the quintessential East Coast, well-dressed black man. Exuding charisma, his smile lit up the room. He commanded the crowd and romanced the women with his deep, dark, sexy looks. He reached his hand down toward me, and our eyes locked. His skin was warm, his hand strong and firm. He displayed confidence in spades. His hand grasped mine and pulled me up, the broken glass between us.

"Hello," I said.

He smiled and led me past the bar, holding my hand as we made our way through the crowd. He pushed a door open. Then a second door. We walked through the kitchen galley and around the corner away from the hustling, loud activity of the busy kitchen. "Sit here, I'll be right back."

I didn't say a word but sat on the comfortable black-leather desk chair, smoothing my dress and adjusting my black pumps that now showed water spots on the toes. He came back with a bar towel and bent down to wipe off my shoes. I could smell the dark, musky scent of his cologne and I caught myself with thoughts of him wrapping his arms around me as we pulled each other in and out of one another. My head spun. Never had I had such lusty thoughts where I could envision each move with my eyes open. *Stop,* I told myself.

"Now they look better than before," he said, then walked around the corner and out of sight.

I surveyed where I was, some type of office. Papers were neatly arranged in manila folders with dates written on the tabs, backward as if not to be obvious. A telephone sat on the right side of the desk, a typewriter in the middle, and more files on either side. These had names marked on the labels like "Nank," "Broman," "Richey," "Ti," and "Lords." I quickly made a mental note of where this desk was and how many files I saw.

Still no Renard.

I opened one file that was placed to the right of the typewriter. Inside, "Lords" was written at the top of the four pages. Each page looked like an accounting ledger full of transactions. Dates, amounts, no descriptions, but a running tab of tens of thousands of dollars. I closed the file, looked both ways, and saw a door to my left. It was time to leave, but I couldn't go out a different way than where I'd come in. This place was bound to have 'eyes' of some sort on all exits. It was a club known for discreet information exchanges.

I decided to navigate my way back through the kitchen that was still quite busy. A digital clock on the wall displayed the numbers 0320.

"Where's the bathroom?" I asked a waiter, as I held the

swinging door open for him. He balanced a tray of hamburgers and sandwiches in one hand and pointed to a hall with his left index finger.

"This way, ma'am." I followed and found the ladies' room. Once inside, I adjusted my padded bra, fixed my hair, and touched my lips, trying to spread what was left of my lipstick evenly. I came out of the restroom to see Renard in action-greeting-mode with a group of well-dressed men and their lady companions. He saw me as I walked to the exit.

"Hope to see you again," he said.

I smiled and kept walking. Better not to say anything and get stuck having to make unnecessary conversation. My smile would suffice for now. Once outside, I noticed there was no longer a line of people trying to get inside. It was past 'last call,' so all the partygoers were already inside the club for the rest of the night.

I turned the corner, and there was my partner's car, the engine quietly idling across the street. It was a good night. My first real assignment in DC. I got into the car, and we drove off. There were no words between us, except for Stan's saying, "Right on time."

16

First Arrest: J. Fedders

Washington, DC.
1984-1985

Paintings of William Barraud's hunting scenes lined the left wall of a conference room on the ninth floor of the DC bureau's office. On the right, Polaroid snapshots were thumbtacked to a large cork bulletin board: images of a bruised neck, a bloodied left ear, another of a black eye, more shots of a woman's bruised legs, arms, back, and abdomen.

A woman stared back from the photos: hollow, empty, as if she was looking far past the camera. She'd been beaten repeatedly over a sixteen-year marriage. "He beat me around the abdomen when I was pregnant with our first son."

They had five children, all boys. He was six foot, ten inches, a former Marquette University basketball player, and one of the top law enforcement officers of the Reagan administration. Earlier that year, her relatives had taken the wife-beating allegations to the White House, but there was no investigation, no justice for Charlotte.

We sat around the huge, highly polished conference table with our morning cups of coffee and notepads. Assignments were distributed, routine at the beginning of a new case.

What was unusual was that this meeting was behind closed doors. There were seven of us. We were waiting for Deputy FBI Chief Dale Watson to enter the room. The deputy bureau chief is the second-most senior FBI official and assists the director by leading prominent investigations. All agents report to the director, who reports to the deputy chief.

The mood in the room was conversational, but the pictures posted in front of us stared back as if to say, "How can you be sitting there drinking your coffee, chatting, and not helping me? Someone, help me!"

The door opened and all participants at the table stopped mid-sentence and straightened up in their respective chairs. The deputy walked to the head of the oblong table. He set down a manila folder. We waited for him to talk.

"This will be a difficult investigation for you. Anytime we investigate a prominent government official, we must ask ourselves, have we uncovered every certifiable fact? Has any question been left unanswered? What evidence do we have that won't be admissible in court? Have we substantiated the truth with a minimum three sources? Are those sources credible?

"One question each of you must ask yourself now and be true to yourself in your answer is: will I treat this suspect differently because he was appointed by the president of the United States? If you say yes—and it's a natural response—then you must leave this room now. Do not discuss what you saw or heard in here with anyone."

Most of the men looked uncomfortable, surprisingly so. Yet, no one got up. No one moved.

The deputy walked to the bulletin board and surveyed the pictures. He took his time, giving each of us an extra moment to think through his questions now stirring in our minds.

Many of these agents were longtime bureau employees with long lists of arrests. There were no amateurs except for me, and another recent college graduate named Martin. He was short, pale, and quiet. I'd seen him during my time at Quantico. He looked around the table, twitching nervously. This entire scene was troubling to him. His world was looking for inconsistencies, imperfections, and inaccuracies in numbers that, by their very nature, should be logical and precise. His world was a desk stacked with ledgers.

But he and I were novices to the bureau. Just why we were here in the conference room with veterans was unclear, but exciting.

The alleged suspect was Commissioner John M. Fedders. At age forty-three, Fedders was a rising star in the world of United States law enforcement. Heading the US Securities and Exchange Commission, he personified the perceived decorum of DC: powerful, hardworking, and thorough. Fedders had a reputation as a vigilant prosecutor, disclosing fraud and insider trading with a level of detail so meticulous that even Martin was impressed.

The room was still as copies of the initial analysis were distributed. Facts and physical descriptions of the alleged wife beater were clearly presented within the documents. I asked myself: how many beatings had his wife allegedly incurred? When did they start? Where had she been hit? The document, called an "analysis brief," listed multiple hospital reports, including two rape-kit forensic reports written by certified examiners. The information was extensive. What was not here was *why* he was physically abusive to his wife. Where did he go before and after work? Was this a pattern? Were there other women? What relationships had he had with women at work, with his neighbors, and did he belong to a church or any clubs?

As part of the discussion, each veteran agent took turns stating why he or she should lead this preliminary investigation. Each bragged about arrest records like a professional sports team would celebrate its wins. There was a bravado among these veterans, as if they had seen it all and the clear reason they were sitting here about to devote all their time and experience to this case was because it was for the Securities and Exchange Commission (SEC) Commissioner John Fedders. Anyone else wouldn't warrant their years of experience.

It was my turn. I looked around the room, knowing I was the youngest member at the table, one of three women. I began to state my name, but the deputy director interrupted me. "We have a young cadet still in training. She is working The Library right now and will be able to go underground better than the rest of us."

A silence hung over the group.

"That works," said the older agent sitting next to me.

Now I knew my role, as did the rest of the team. I learned that morning that the deputy director's decision stands. It may be debated by the senior agents, but, at the end of the day, the deputy director decides who is on the team.

I was now going to have two worlds cross over into one. My information gathering at The Library would be used when or if needed by the Fedders task force. I wondered if Renard knew people who knew Fedders. Would anything I find out make a difference?

That night, someone else took my shift at Houlihan's, so I was able to take my time applying my makeup, fixing my hair and dressing for The Library.

Once again, I looked into the mirror sideways, to view my silhouette. The black fishnet stockings, black-leather miniskirt, and purple blouse fit like a glove. While adjusting the skirt, I saw my waist was getting smaller. I was losing the weight I'd gained over my last year in college. The clothes were fitting better, and my fellow agent who'd lent them to me was starting to regret her decision. She would like to be in my place, and that made me uncomfortable. But we both knew I was younger than she was and had a different look. Midwest-girl-next-door was not going to gain entrance into The Library.

As it turned out, Fedders' choice in women was Asian, perhaps because they were physically smaller than most Caucasian women and he could feel superior when striking them. I understood how he could prefer someone smaller: she would be weaker. But smaller doesn't mean dumber. Smaller doesn't mean insignificant.

It would be really satisfying to bring a man who thinks he's above others to justice. Now was the opportunity to answer the demons in my head telling me that I didn't matter, that I was insignificant. I heard Loretta in my head saying, *No one gonna adopt you, child.*

I can recall what she said as she took my bound hands and whipped them with her boyfriend's leather belt. I was a foster kid, the equal of a paycheck. Nothing more. If she could see me now, she'd think I was a prostitute, earning money with my body by trying to find genuine parental love that had eluded me since childhood. I laughed out loud as I peered closely into the mirror, lining my eyes in deep black eyeliner. *Watch me now.*

I was dropped off in the same place as the night before. After this visit, I was to wait three nights between visits to avoid looking like a groupie.

The line outside The Library stretched around the corner. Some of the women gave me dirty looks before and after their men eyed me. It was strange standing in line by myself; I felt like it called unnecessary attention to me. Most people my age go out in groups or with a significant other. I was alone.

Then someone touched my shoulder, causing me to reel around. Renard stood behind me on the outside of the line. "Come with me, my dear." I took his extended hand, and he walked me to the front of the ropes. The bodyguard created an opening for us to enter the club.

Someone who'd been ahead of me in line yelled out, "Hey, man, what gives? We're in line here." Renard turned toward the voice and glared. "Sorry, my man. Didn't realize it was you."

Once inside, it took a moment for my eyes to adjust to the light. The rooms were buzzing. "Brick House" by The Commodores was blaring and the drinks were piled high on the side of the bar, waiting for servers to deliver them to the proper table. We stood on the side of the bar where Renard could view the whole room. He was taller than most people and could get the lay of the land by positioning his body with his back to the bar, his left side to the line of drinks still waiting to be picked up by his servers.

He could see that, at some tables, folks were starting to get agitated as they looked around for their server. "I'll be back." He exited through the side door on his left.

Moments later five additional servers stood in line next to the awaiting drinks. One bartender placed the orders on silver trays with precise execution. Within a few minutes, thirty-odd drinks that had been on the side of the bar were now gone.

I could barely see Renard through the crush of the crowd. Glimpses of his mahogany-brown velvet blazer with flecks of gold caught my eye as he walked from table to table.

"He's the best host around," said a deep voice next to me. "He handpicks everyone who works here. They're loyal to him and won't leave unless he personally tells them to. People beg to work here. Do you know why?"

The small, dark-skinned man speaking to me wore a black leather jacket, buttoned-down blue shirt, and black-and-blue tie. I couldn't tell the color of his pants or shoes, as he was leaning up against the bar, blocking the view of his body from the chest down.

"Why?" I said.

"Because this is the place to be. Everyone that's a player comes through here."

"Player?" I asked.

"Player. A man's man. A person you want to know … be tied to. That's why."

I asked, "Are you a player?"

"Me? No." He laughed. "I'm that man's best friend." He pointed to Renard, who was making his way over to us.

Best friend, I thought. *Why would he say that?* Before I could ask, he volunteered the information.

"Anything a player needs, I provide. That's my job."

Interesting. This is what I needed to know.

"What's your name?" I asked.

"Ace. And yours?"

Before I could reply, Renard was back at my side. "Hey, Ace. Busy night?"

"Yes, it is." And with that answer, Ace was off. Just like that. Gone.

I tried to play it off, but I was frustrated that the person I wanted to get to know had just been pushed out by the person I needed to know.

Renard said, "I want us to be better acquainted. Ask me any questions you have, not Ace."

So there it was. A warning to stay away from that guy, but why? Renard excused himself to attend to an upset patron causing a scene.

I moved across the room toward the bathroom. When I walked through the dark-paneled door separating the restrooms from the hallway, Ace was standing outside the men's room.

"Here's my card. I hope we can continue our conversation another time at another place. I would like that."

"Me, too."

After using the restroom, repositioning my padded bra, and retouching my lipstick, I left as I came, exiting through the front and eyeing the opposite end of the hallway where I'd been my first time here.

This night was important. I had established a contact or at least someone who knew things I needed and wanted to know. My instincts about Renard seemed to be correct. He was interested in me. He ran the place. He wanted me to stay away from Ace.

"Good night's work," said my current partner when I debriefed him about my time inside The Library. He was onboard with the way things were progressing until I mentioned my being in line by myself and needing him to come with me the next time.

I needed a date to show Renard that I wasn't available. I

needed a man who was a 'player' and who would be respected by this crowd. My partner, Agent Mike Charles, was the perfect guy for the job.

It didn't take long for the deputy director to approve my lead agent's request to have Agent Charles double as my date. This would show Renard that I was taken, spoken for, not as easy to have as he might've been thinking.

Agent Charles was a street cop turned agent after his partner was gunned down during a domestic dispute. His wife begged him to leave the force, which he did, but only to take on a job in another law enforcement agency. Finding justice for others was in his bones.

This case, like so many before, was why he did what he did so well. There was something about men who beat women and took their pathetic anger out on others that made Agent Charles passionate about his job. Seeing your partner of thirteen years gunned down by a sobbing man who stood over the beaten lifeless body of his wife, her children cowering in the doorway so scared that one had peed in his pajamas, leaving a pool of urine on the linoleum floor—all this shook him to the core.

Agent Charles had stood with the children and tried to block them from the sight, while his partner tried reasoning with the suspect. Words had no effect. The suspect pulled a gun from his shorts and fired directly into the heart of the officer. With no body armor to protect him, Agent Charles's partner died immediately.

It took months for him to get the faces of those two little boys out of his head. He even went so far as to try to adopt them when their mother overdosed on crack.

Justice came in the form of one life sentence and one sentence for manslaughter. The suspect would never leave prison. No parole was granted. The boys would grow up in a loving home with a doting aunt, and Agent Charles and his wife played active roles in their lives.

Agents admired Mike because of his control. He could reach the point of beating a suspect down to submission but have the discipline to not kill him. His own demons created his anger. The difference was he could repress then channel his rage, releasing it on the job when needed against men who hurt women, children, or his fellow officers.

Agent Charles and I were finally allowed past the red crushed-velvet ropes and into the large lounge where the bar was located. On this night, he would meet Ace and start the process of building trust with the informant. If Renard showed up, Mike C. would act the part of my protective boyfriend.

My 'date' and I grabbed a table in the corner of the room, and he went to the bar to get our drinks. As soon as he left, I spied Ace on the other side of the room. He waved to me, and I waved back. Mike watched from his spot at the bar and slowly made his way toward Ace. After exchanging pleasantries, he invited Ace to our table, and the friendship began.

Agent Mike Charles and I became regulars at the club. For the next three months, we'd hang out with Ace, and, sometimes, with Renard three to four times a week. All the information Ace gave during that time proved to be accurate. He gave us names of clubs frequented by 'players' and their favorite street corners where money was exchanged for women. Not just sexual encounters, but bondage sessions, foot-fetish gatherings, and places where patrons paid to hit, kick, and maim women.

Ace described such a club to us. "The Alcove" presented itself as a strip bar; however, tucked away from the dancers and the crowd throwing single dollar bills at them were seven dark, small rooms. If the rooms could talk, they would tell stories that would make a person's skin crawl. It was here where the elite of DC came to indulge their perversions.

After a night with Ace, Agent Charles and I wrote down everything he'd told us. Sometimes we worked straight through to the morning briefing, as was the case on this morning.

"You both must have some intel from last night," the deputy director said. "I want you to start the briefing this morning with any new information you two have."

We described The Alcove based on Ace's description. Next, I asked to work there. "Agent Mike can ask Ace for Renard to recommend me. Then perhaps we have a shot at getting inside."

Agent Charles looked at me like I was crazy. "You want to go work at The Alcove?"

"How else will we know if Fedders or other high ups go there? How will we really know what goes on inside if one of us isn't there to see and hear it?"

The thirty task force members sitting around the conference table said nothing. Then the deputy director broke the silence. "I'm good with it. If you want to go inside, then do it," he said before getting up and leaving the room.

Getting a job as a cocktail waitress at The Alcove was easy once Renard mentioned me to his buddy who knew the owner. The hard part was getting the women who worked there to become my friends. They went to work, collected their cash, and went home to their children. Most were single mothers. They didn't talk much to each other, keeping what they experienced, saw, or heard to themselves. The money was too good and the line of others wanting to replace them too long to jeopardize their job. Silence was their bond to each other and to the owner.

I began determining who came to The Alcove and on what night, but I wanted to get more information firsthand. One evening I decided to go downstairs with a tray of drinks for patrons in the strip club. If anyone stopped me, I'd say that one of the patrons had asked me to bring the drinks down to him.

As I descended the steep staircase with the tray, I heard the muffled sounds of a woman crying. Once downstairs, I noticed a light on in a room to my right and saw a young Asian woman holding a wet hand towel to her left eye. In the reflection of the mirror, her puffy, bruised face was clearly visible.

Now I was getting somewhere. I set the tray of drinks down and knocked on the door. From the other side, I heard someone panting, breathing hard. I knocked again. The door opened ever so slightly, and a man snapped at me.

"What do you want?"

"I have your drink, sir."

"I didn't order anything to drink. I'm busy."

Before he shut the door, I saw the long black whip he was holding in his left hand away from the opening. My mind was racing. I knew I had to go upstairs, but I wanted to know more about what was happening behind each of these closed doors.

My next shift was a few nights later. I tried to find the same small woman that I'd seen earlier that week. My questions went unanswered. Where was she? Why didn't I see any bruised or battered people here? Where did they go if they weren't upstairs with the public?"

I went around the back of the club, volunteering to take out the trash, which was part of the job at the end of our shift. No one wanted that chore. As the new person, I was given that task and accepted it graciously. It allowed me time to look around the back alley for other entrances into the building. There had to be one.

I noticed how clean the alley was. No trash, no people, no cars. But from the end of the alley, I heard a man yelling, and then I saw it. He was hitting this small person, striking her to the ground.

Rushing over, I yelled, "Hey, what are you doing?"

The small figure looked up at me and said, "I'm doing what I'm paid to do."

At that point, the man kicked her in the side as she cowered on the cold stone ground. "Get out of here before I start on you," he said to me. "I'd like to do you two at the same time."

I wanted to memorize her face. Just then the man raised his fat hand as if to strike me but stopped and, instead, kicked her again. I took off, leaving her and the trash bags outside.

Once inside, I tried to collect myself before going to get paid for the night. If the owner knew something was upsetting me, he might ask too many questions, which would not be good.

I straightened my hair after washing my hands and got in line to be paid. The money was good. Strippers had to give 10 percent of their take to us, plus we got our own tips that we didn't have to share. I had more single dollar bills on my person than I'd ever imagined I would.

I didn't keep the money. It wasn't mine; it belonged to the government as part of the investigation.

Each morning, I took the dollar bills to the bureau office, placed them in envelopes marked with the dates I received them at the club. I typed up what had occurred the night before. Once done, I placed my report in a manila folder, along with the money envelope clipped inside. Then I delivered it to the deputy's secretary, placing it directly in her hand.

Materials that could become evidence in a trial are handled with extreme care. As many attorneys know, if law enforcement breaks the 'chain of custody' when working with evidence, that material can be thrown out during trial. During training at Quantico, we learned what to do and what not to do when handling evidence. "Do not take chances with leaving materials on your desk or out of your sight until they are processed by an authorized agent."

It was time to catch a break in the case. Three months had passed, and we still hadn't seen Fedders at any of the locations that Ace had informed us were the player clubs, where a policy of "don't ask, don't tell" was enforced. Our timeline was shrinking.

Fedders' wife was growing weary of being married to a wife beater. She was strong, but how long would it take until she could sleep through the night not having to worry that she would be rousted out of bed, told to prepare a meal or draw a bath, and, while obeying his demands, get thanked by being his personal punching bag? Would his sons start to put two and two together? When would she not be able to hide the bruises and her tears?

This day was a new day with a new plan. I was to assist Kevin, who had been placed by the FBI at the beginning of the investigation to collect information on the employees working directly with Fedders. Since Fedders was the chief law enforcement officer for the Securities and Exchange Commission, befriending some of the attorneys who worked in his Enforcement Division could reveal where their boss went after work and with whom.

I knew nothing about stocks, data logging, or insider

trading, but I was about to get an education. None of it interested me, and the days were long as I tried my best to be pleasant while learning detailed information I couldn't care less about.

It was during my second week working with Kevin that I got the break we were looking for. I'd left my desk for a while to use the bathroom. Inside, two young secretaries stood in front of a tall mirror opposite the sinks adjusting their skirts and hair.

"He's so tall that sometimes when he bends down to lick my toes, even in my highest heels, I come up to his armpits."

"That's crazy! He licks your toes?"

"That's not all he licks."

I could not believe she was talking so openly in the presence of a stranger.

I shut the stall door to use the toilet, and she went on, "I take this long black whip, and he likes to lick it while he's behind me, then wrap it around my ankles and pull my heels up so they hit, then scrape his balls."

"This sounds like a horror movie."

"If you don't let him do what he wants, it would be. I've seen pictures of what he's done to girls younger and older than me, and it's bad. He showed them to me, warning me to be good or else."

I exited the stall to wash my hands, when one of them said, "You're the new assistant right?"

"Yes, I'm working with Kevin."

"Hi. We sit around the corner from you."

I smiled, trying to hear every word over the water. I could see their faces in the mirror in front of me. Then, with a friendly wave, they left. My heart was racing. Could this be the information that would help tie Fedders to the allegations? Who were the other women she saw pictures of and where were those pictures now? Where did they meet for their encounters? When was the first and last time they met?

I gathered my thoughts, knowing I had to get back to my desk and write down everything I had heard. I needed to find where these two women sat. I knew it was on the same floor I was on—"around the corner" from Kevin—but hundreds of people worked on this floor.

I rounded the corner, ready to write down what I'd just heard, but Kevin was standing there waiting for me.

"You're three minutes late," he said in a frustrated tone.

"I'm sorry, but this is important."

He stopped himself from responding to my comment. Maybe it was something in my face that told him this was serious. He watched as I sat down and took out my pad and pen. I wrote down every piece of information that I'd heard, marked the sheet with my name and the date and time of the conversation. Kevin read it all. I clearly indicated the floor, restroom, and time of the dialogue. Location was important. If it was 'him,' and the women speaking worked directly for him, then Fedders would also be violating employment laws.

Kevin said, "I need to go look for someone."

I asked if he needed my help.

"Yes. Come with me. Let's look for a meeting room. Follow me."

We left our desks, which were in the unsecured part of the second floor. Some spaces had small windows looking down on the roof below, while others had floor-to-ceiling windows where one could watch the street traffic around the square and the comings and goings of Foggy Bottom's Metro stop.

The attorneys working for the SEC sat in a row based on their seniority. This was an enforcement agency. The longer attorneys worked here, the more cases they were given, and, coupled with the number of cases they won, this was what gave them their seniority.

The number of years spent in government service also helped in securing a stellar office view. These elements were also part of the decision process for what some thought was the most coveted perk of the job: one's own secretary, rather than someone who was shared with three or four other attorneys.

We began our search for a meeting room by walking along the long corridor separating staff from attorneys. I couldn't help but realize how sexist this environment was. Every person sitting in an interior spot was female. On my left, in the rooms with the view, were men of all ages and a few women, each of whom looked to be in their late fifties and tired.

Where was the young woman I saw in the restroom with dark hair pulled back in a perfect ponytail, wearing a pretty, soft-pink cardigan and cream-colored blouse? I kept scanning each desk while Kevin tried looking for an open meeting room.

We turned the second corner, and there she was, sitting in front of an IBM Selectric typewriter, focused on the legal brief she was typing. The nameplate in front of her typewriter, placed front and center on her L-shaped wooden desk, said "Danielle Aspery."

We kept walking. As we rounded the third corner, I stopped and told Kevin I needed to go back to the desk now. "Okay," he said, conveying that he understood I'd found the person I was looking for. Now I knew her name and could add it to my notes. Once back at my desk, I detailed my walk around the office floor with Kevin, adding to the report Danielle's name, along with where she sat.

When we left the office that day, I tried looking for Danielle's pink sweater among the throngs of 8-5:30 p.m. workers pouring into the street, vying for position on the first bus or Metro car out of the city toward home. I rode the bus occasionally, but most of the time I walked. It took thirty-eight minutes during the late summer months to go from Georgetown to Washington Square.

Walking the crowded streets of DC as the summer turned to fall was peaceful and beautiful. The evening air was starting to cool, and the sun, although still out and shining, was low in the sky at 5:30 p.m. Trees lined most streets in DC, with each beginning to show off its fall-colored leaves—colors ranging from a deep, dark green to burnt gold or rusty red.

This was my favorite time of year. Football games dominated the weekends. Most tourists stayed away from DC during the fall, making it the best time to steal an afternoon away at one of the Smithsonian museums, admiring the presidential china and the gowns worn by our first ladies.

My favorite lunch-time getaway spot was the National Portrait Gallery. I'd buy a coffee and sit outside the side entrance on a stone bench, watching people come and go. If I had time, I went in and sat with the Raphaels, Gauguins, and Van Goghs. The painted faces stared through me. I dreamed they knew what I was doing, who I was, and even the parts of me still undefined.

While I investigated the faces painted at the height of the Renaissance, I felt their sadness. They were the chosen: the intelligent, beautiful muses of the greatest painters of their time. Could they have been objectified, beaten, broken down as some women are today? Did they hold the same secrets as our accuser? Those thoughts made me jump up and rush out, feeling guilty for taking time away from what I needed to do. My job was my world. I was completely 'all in' and didn't want anyone to question why I'd been selected for this team.

The night after identifying Danielle was a game changer. Ace was holding down the bar when Mike and I got inside The Library. We needed to know whether Fedders had frequented an area near the capitol where some clubs prided themselves on their perversions.

My partner was good at coaxing out the smallest of facts from Ace. I say "facts" because the information exchanged between the two of them was always truthful. Mike never crossed the line. He gave just as much data as he needed to gain trust, then demanded it back, generally receiving more than he'd given.

It was that type of night. Ace gave Mike names, addresses, and passwords needed to get into two clubs at the district. This is how I got a job at one of those clubs. When we left The Library, I felt I was seeing it for the last time. Our work here was done. What came next was spotting Fedders at one of the establishments Ace had described to my partner.

We shared Tanqueray and tonic with Ace in the lounge, and something pulled at me, as if I was saying goodbye to a good friend. We'd experienced much laughter and genuinely good times here. It sounds crazy—good times and genuine conversation with an informant. We were not being truthful; he was. He didn't know our true identities and why we were there seeking him out. He befriended us. It was that simple. We were the dishonest ones. Our friendship arose not from a sense of camaraderie, but necessity. I felt a knot in my stomach. If this new information turned out to be true and was corroborated that night, Ace would be arrested along with the others. He would simply be collateral damage from this five-month investigation.

The location, date, and time, and the descriptions that Ace confirmed for us left us with nothing more to discuss. We needed to document our conversation before the gin kicked in. Off we went, waving our farewells as we walked hand-in-hand to the door.

"See you Thursday, Charlie?"

"Yeah, sure, Ace."

That was the last time we saw him.

DC is a mysterious place. People come and go. Power changes hands. New faces appear. Despite all the public privilege and high-profile insiders, there is a real power group that stays under the radar. Out of sight. Like the dinners that had taken place in the White House kitchen far away from public view, our club owner and keeper of many of the secrets of Washington's elite had paved the way for their night of sexual satisfaction.

With the times spent at The Library behind us, Agent Mike and I focused on the club where Ace had told us we could find Fedders. At 1:00 a.m., we awaited a signal from a waitress we'd paid to turn a light on in the upstairs bathroom when she saw our suspect.

At 1:04 a.m., the light went on. I walked quickly to the back-alley door that she'd left slightly ajar. Once in, I made my way through the hallway toward the last door on the left. I could hear the same faint whimpering sounds I'd heard before at The Alcove—where I'd seen that shy, beaten girl months before holding a hand towel over her swollen eye.

Staying clear of the door, I walked into the breakroom. As I waited, I held my gun next to my stomach, thinking it would be difficult to draw and shoot before getting the shot. Why we had decided that I would wear a black, skin-tight leather skirt and slouchy sweater and stick my .45 caliber weapon between my stomach and waistband was beyond me.

I looked through the dimly lit hallway and heard the door open.

"Stay here," said a loud, deep voice to whomever was in that room. He emerged as a tall silhouette, all 6'10" of his frame outlined by the dim hallway light, but I saw his face as he walked toward the staircase that led to the public area of the club. He walked slowly, like a fighter who'd just gone nine rounds. He climbed the stairs without looking back.

Perfect, I thought. From behind the door, I could get a shot off, but that wasn't the plan. My job was to identify the SEC Enforcement Chief, then turn the light off. Mike would see my signal, drive to the front, and take the target's picture as he left the club. I needed to stay out of sight and wait until I heard Mike's car idling in the alley, waiting to pick me up. I had just seen John Fedders. Now we had the information needed to bring him in.

But someone else was downstairs, and that wasn't in the plan. Fedders's victim was still in the room. There were no sounds. I couldn't tell who she was or what condition she was in. All I knew was Fedders's wife had agreed to testify against him; we had confirmed his whereabouts, his fetishes, and the receipts that were collected at the various clubs, and we had also gotten testimony from two girls whom he regularly beat for money. Both were illegals and would become US citizens in exchange for that testimony. The door creaked open, and a slight figure clinging to her torn blouse hobbled into the light. It was Danielle.

Her right heel was broken, the front and sleeve of her blouse were torn, and her hair was no longer in a tight ponytail, but was disheveled and wet with sweat. She tried stepping forward and fell, making a loud thud on the wooden floor.

Every part of me wanted to go and help her, but I couldn't. I had to stay out of sight. How could I get Mike's attention that someone here needed our help? I closed the door, trying not to call attention to anyone, and I turned on the light. If I knew Mike like I thought I did, he'd understand that someone else was down here needing help.

Danielle's face was bathed in the murky light of an old, yellowish bulb swinging from a wire in the middle of the hallway. Puffy, bleeding. I closed my eyes, trying not to breathe. I wanted to remember her face so I could testify if necessary.

Then I heard my partner's voice, along with two or three other men.

"FBI. We have you," one of them said. "It's okay. We're taking you to the hospital." With that, he picked Danielle up and carried her away.

The hall was clear. No one in sight. A single lightbulb swung from the ceiling, guiding me to the alley door. I crept down the hall, praying no door would open, that no one would know I was there. When I pulled the outside door open, Mike grabbed my wrist and spun me around. Surprised to see him out of the car, but extremely relieved, I said, "I was hoping it was going to be you." We jumped inside the car and sped off to headquarters.

That night sealed Fedders's fate. We had identified the man while keeping me out of sight. More importantly, we got him in the same location as one of his employees.

The next morning task members all met at 5:00 a.m. at headquarters. The arrest would be taking place that day. Danielle was safe. She would not be going back to work. If she testified, the government would move her to a different agency so she would not be subjected to her coworkers asking her what had happened. But we knew the story. The report taken at the hospital had been read to us during the morning briefing. Kevin looked like a ghost. I thought he was going to vomit as the deputy directors recited details of what Fedders did to Danielle.

At 11:00 a.m., I got up I from my desk at the SEC. Kevin stayed in his chair as if nothing was different. I went to the elevator bank and could hear the old cables as they lifted my teammates to the fourth floor. I took the stairs.

When my team members exited the elevator, I opened the access door and met them in the hall. Fedders's redwood-paneled office had windows facing Washington Square and the Smithsonian skyline. It was majestic. We walked five agents strong down the hall past the senior attorneys and their secretaries. As we approached Fedders's office, his assistant was already on her feet proclaiming he was not to be disturbed. My senior agent blew past her and opened the door.

There he was, sitting at his magnificent marble-topped desk and talking on the phone. While his rights were being read, he looked out the windows at the full trees and gray sky. That would be the last day he held any real power. As a result of spousal abuse, coupled with rape, abuse of power, and committing sexual assault on an employee, John M. Fedders was convicted and sentenced to thirteen years in jail. He served seven.

17

Daniel

Los Angeles, California
1985

If you were in the FBI between 1984 and 1999, you lived and worked in a different city from where your loved ones did. But when the Fedders case ended, most of the senior agents went back to their normal lives. For many of them, this meant leaving DC. Many older agents, usually those managing a department or heading a desk at their local bureau office, were able to live and work in the same community, raise their children, and be a part of their community.

When you're young, it's commonplace to leave home, sow your oats, find yourself, and succeed far away from the day-to-day family squabbles and demands. Those of us who were still just starting out with the FBI expected to be assigned far away from home.

My family, however, wanted to see me, and questioned how an 'internship' could take so much time out of each day that weeks went by without my even calling. For my mother whose full-time job had been raising her two adopted children—yes, I still haven't talked about my brother—the idea of no communication for extended periods of time was difficult to explain, rarely justified, and mostly uncomfortable. I tried to keep up my end of the communication deal.

Whenever I called, my parents had questions like, "Are you having fun? Do you have enough money? Are you staying within your budget? When will you know if you'll finish your internship and be hired?"

Lying was hard. I felt isolated from them and they from the real me. What I did each day and what I shared with them were two very different stories.

One year turned into two, and I couldn't ignore more questions about full-time work. If I did admit I was working, when would I say I was hired? Every agency within the US government had directories. A citizen could request those logs and look up a relative if they researched and found out how to get that information. Maybe, I thought, they would go to those lengths to figure out what I was doing. If so, then what would I counter with? Another lie that I had been transferred to another position and department. I decided not to say much and stay clear of family holidays until it became necessary to come home.

The holiday season in 1985 in Los Angeles was magical and special. Although I was out of college and felt grown up, sitting in the back of my father's car as we rode through the streets and peering through the car windows at the beautifully lit-up houses while playing "Silent Night" and "Here Comes

Santa Claus" on the radio made me feel like a kid again. No worries, no watching my back, no cares in the world.

Christmas Day meant going to the movies and enjoying family friends and company in the late afternoon. We usually ordered Chinese food for Christmas night dinner, a tradition many of my parents' friends shared. I didn't have to discuss my work or make up any stories: my parents were preoccupied with their friends, who cared little about what other people's children were doing. If you went to college, graduated, and were either married if you were a woman or had a profession if you were a man, they left you alone. Dating someone of interest? Then, you were in the clear.

Since I wasn't dating at the time, I made strategic use of my calendar. Pop into an old family friend's house with my folks, and, about twenty minutes later, another friend would arrive to take me to a party with people our own age.

My parents encouraged me to socialize—in other words, try to meet a nice guy. During that week back home, several college friends had parties I attended. Most of these had a high girl-to-guy ratio. We gals had a great time catching up, but then it was time to move on to a scene where there would be ample opportunity for meeting guys. There's something about the time between Christmas and New Year's Day. People are warmer and friendlier, and, if you're single, it's easier to meet someone of the opposite sex to your liking.

Toward the end of my time at home, Sharon, a college friend, threw a party in her re-married mother's home. The home was newly remodeled and sparkled with chrome, glass, and black lacquer. Not my style, but very clean and modern.

There were plenty of young guys there. Mostly law school buddies and fellow UCLA graduates, along with a few doctors and nurses. Sharon worked at a local hospital where her father had been chief of medicine for the last seven years. As I made my way outside to the bar, I noticed a group of older guys, probably in their thirties, hanging out on an old outdoor couch, enjoying the crowd.

Sharon was outside, too. She looked beautiful, a sparkly silver dress clinging to her tiny hundred-pound figure, her long hair curled, and her makeup flawless. She looked as she should, the soon-to-be housewife of a UCLA law school grad, living in the valley, awaiting children that would consume her life, much as we had the lives of our own mothers. We hugged, and she told me there was someone there she wanted me to meet. He was older, thirty-three, and he was the architect who had redone her mother and stepfather's home, taking the traditional California ranch-style family abode from kid-friendly to nightclub chic.

I looked around the outside, with its floor-to-ceiling glass walls and brightly lit rooms, each of which could be seen at night from my poolside vantage point, and I realized this was nothing like the house I used to visit several weekends a month. If Sharon's mom had chosen this guy to redesign her home, he had to be cool.

Sharon led me through the group surrounding the bar toward a sofa at the far end of the pool. He sat with an older couple, who were the designer and contractor he worked with. Sharon introduced us, and he asked if I'd like to sit down for a while. His name was Daniel.

We talked throughout the night about the remodel, Sharon's parents, Sharon, her boyfriend, and the party. Then, as it usually goes, either each of you is interested in finding out about the other or it's time to say your goodbyes and move on. I stayed. He asked how long I had known Sharon, when I graduated, where I grew up. Then he shared his background.

After playing football most of his junior high and high school years, he was rated among the top fifty California players the summer before his senior year. He accepted a full scholarship to play quarterback at UCLA, already knowing that he wanted to be an architect after his football days were over.

During the second-to-last game of the regular season, he was tackled from behind and broke his throwing arm. His college football career was over before it had begun. But instead of worrying about his future, he ran. Every day he ran faster and longer, to the point where the track coach thought some universities might look at him for track and field. He was the third of four children, so money was tight, and there would be no college if there was no scholarship. His coach made a few calls, and he was given an opportunity to attend Cal Poly, San Luis Obispo, one of the premier architectural colleges in the country, on a track scholarship. After one year of general studies, he could test into the architectural program.

It was disappointing to him that his college-educated parents neither pushed for nor supported higher education for their children. He was the first of the four siblings to attend college, and only because of the full scholarship that he earned through his track and field skills and the high grades he received in all his classes.

He was so talented in the 440 that his coach arranged for him to compete at the Olympic trials. He finished as an honorary runner-up, mere seconds away from claiming one of the two coveted spots on the team. Before completing the third year of a five-year architectural program, he qualified, with one of his teammates, to compete in the Maccabi Games, Israel's version of the Olympics.

As history recounts, the Jewish people were not welcome

in Nazi Germany's Olympian venue, nor were they treated fairly in the years after World War II. The slaughter of the team during the 1972 games in Munich further convinced the Israeli government to create their own version of the games whereby athletes could come and try their hand at competing for a medal without fear of retribution. Daniel and his teammate did well, bringing home a silver in the 440 and a bronze in the 440 relay.

But at the same time his university was praising him, Daniel and his family were becoming more estranged. He and his mother, in particular.

She was from Kerry, Ireland, a devout Catholic raised on a small farm in Des Moines, Iowa. Her parents were corn farmers. She was the youngest of five children and was very independent thinking. Growing up, she became a highly touted swimmer for her high school team and won a swimming scholarship to attend the University of Iowa. While there she met another competitive swimmer from Chicago, Illinois.

Her parents never spoke to her again; she had disgraced them by marrying a non-Catholic. Worse, she had married a Jew.

As the years passed, she became withdrawn and turned to alcohol. Once her children had grown up, she decided her work was done and packed her bags the night before Daniel's high school graduation. After the ceremony, while the rest of his family celebrated his going to San Luis Obispo, she left a note on a chair next to the front door and walked out. By the time of his competing in the Maccabi Games in Tel Aviv, Daniels's communication was sparse with his father and nonexistent with his mother.

In the interval, Daniel stayed in Los Angeles where he

started his own business remodeling and designing custom homes. I went back to work in DC. No one, including my family and Daniel, knew what I was really doing.

18

The Wedding

Los Angeles, California
June, 1987

It was good to be back in Los Angeles for a while. Daniel and I had time to spend together. We both enjoyed being outside, jogging with his two dogs, and making picnic lunches that we ate at the park near the house he rented.

I got to know his dad and stepmother and encouraged him to reconnect with his mother. It took time, but it happened. Daniel, his mother, and I spent Christmas Eve together; she taught me to make her special holiday rum balls. I was very happy. Daniel and I decided that, in six months, we would get married.

My mother was ecstatic. She was going to plan the party of her life.

We looked at several beautiful hotels in Los Angeles: Hotel

Bel-Air, the Graystone Mansion, and, finally, the Beverly Hills Hotel. Nothing compared to it. Mother and I knew this was the place for my wedding. It felt magical walking down between the pink and green banana-leaf-wallpapered walls, through the Polo Lounge, named after the polo fields on which the hotel was built, and to the ballroom where we met with the hotel's event planners.

I returned to Washington, DC. Mother called every week. How was work? Was I watching my weight so that when I came home for Thanksgiving and my dress fitting everything would go smoothly? Then she routinely went down her list of things to do, detailing each task.

I was lucky. Mother's taste was pure perfection, and she was thrilled to take charge. I could continue my work in DC while she made decisions about food, music, flowers, table settings, save-the-date announcements, formal invitations, napkins with our names, and the wedding cake. No detail was insignificant. And, of course, there were the clothes: bridesmaid's dresses, mother-of-the-bride dresses, and the wedding dress. When I became engaged, the hunt was on.

My mother grew up in Midtown Manhattan with the original Bergdorf Goodman, Saks Fifth Avenue, and Bloomingdale's department stores anchoring the street corners near her family's apartment. As a child, walking with her mother and sister, she was awed by the magnificent dresses, shoes, and evening bags featured in the elegantly designed storefront windows. Someday, she could afford whichever designer garment she wanted. The epitome was St. John, the flagship designer for First Ladies Jackie Kennedy and Hillary Clinton.

Our weekly check-ins continued over the months.

In September, she went with her sister to Newport Beach

for the long-awaited mother-of-the-bride dress selection at the coveted St. John headquarters. Even with my father's deep connections with the clothing manufacturing business, it had taken two months to secure this appointment.

My dress fitting was scheduled for the day after Thanksgiving, but, happily for me, had been moved to the day I arrived. Now I could enjoy my Thanksgiving meal without my mother side-eyeing me every time I took a bite of food.

We had pre-selected three bridal gowns and two bridesmaid designs appropriate for an afternoon wedding. I fell in love with a puffy sleeved, detailed bodice and flowing taffeta skirt that made me feel like a princess. There was too much fabric for my 5'2" frame. But, after the third fitting, my mother approved.

The bridesmaid dresses were peach satin, not very shiny. Each of my bridesmaids selected her own bodice and sleeve to fit her individual shape. Groomsmen were fitted for morning suits: gray with a white pin-striped vest.

The last two weeks before my summer wedding was filled with finalizing every detail. Peach roses, without too much orange or yellow tint, ivory chinaware with a scalloped gold rim, peach-colored napkins to be followed by white for dessert, a watercress salad or shrimp cocktail to start, followed by a choice of poached salmon or grilled chicken, moist yellow cake with raspberry filling, Waterford for the water goblets and wine glasses, champagne coupes for the traditional wedding toasts and breaking of glasses at the end of the ceremony.

Daniel was Catholic and I was Jewish, so the service was to be condensed, conducted by my parents' Rabbi. The breaking of the glass by the groom at the end of the ceremony was not up for negotiation. This tradition signified marriage as a commitment through bountiful and lean times.

But there was nothing 'lean' about this wedding. My mother made sure of that. This was my mother's affair where I would show up in a white dress.

Daniel and I married on a warm, sunny afternoon—June 28, 1987. As I stood at the top of the forty-step staircase, my parents in front of me waiting to make their grand entrance, my father asked, "Do you want to go through with this?"

I stared at him with disbelief. I knew he wanted me to marry Moshe, but to ask me this right before I was about to walk down the aisle?

"We can still have a party. I've already paid for the bar and food."

"What?" I was stunned.

"Well, I guess you're going to go through with this, so good luck!"

Everything went blank. I have no memory of making it down forty steep steps wearing a long wedding dress and high-heeled shoes to the ceremonial terrace laced with peach and white roses. I can't remember saying my vows or the end of the ceremony when my new husband stepped on the champagne glass to signify the beginning of our life together. Without the wedding video, I would not recall any of it. Perhaps having no recollection of what is supposed to be one of the most significant days in a person's life was a sign that I shouldn't have gone through with it.

I blocked out my father's hurtful words, not by confronting him, but by burying myself in my work.

19

Green River

*Near Spokane, Washington
Late 1989*

The way we did our work was changing. No longer were teams positioned on dark corners watching their targets for any movement throughout the evening and long hours of the night. Many a local coffee shop was going to lose dedicated customers, as we were now chained to a different type of cell.

The term 'technology' was beginning to enter each citizen's vocabulary. It meant different things to different professions. In my line of work, wireless phones enabled mobility while communicating. Dispatch had the means to locate you and tell you specifically where to go and where not to go.

We each were offered the option to train on the Wang word processor, which was a typewriter on steroids. Gone were the days of using white-out; Selectric typewriters were history. Any old and trustworthy Smith Corona typewriter was no longer the choice for typing reports. I could get more done in a smaller window of time, granting me more precious minutes to eat, sleep, or call home before going out on surveillance again. Carbon paper was being replaced by copiers that made as many replicas of one's initial report as management could ask for. We laughed the day the Xerox machine came to the office: it was a copier and printer in one.

I can still see Mike standing by the old copier trying his best to crank out repetitive reports only to look at Frank Pierce, twenty years younger, coffee cup in hand, waltz by him after picking up three cleanly printed reports from the tray of the new dual-function machine.

Meanwhile, I still wrote out my field reports, waiting for my turn to train on the new word processors. It was then that I learned how much I didn't know about computers and how I wanted to learn more—from the single-drive system, amber-screen boxes that captured information fed to them by rows of typists to the simply tied together terminals called networks.

The more people adapted to the newer, simpler way of doing things mandatory to the job, the more paper flew around the offices. I never understood how one technology could cause so much space to be devoted to files and filing.

In between assignments, we were given the task of either filing reports or typing extracted information from them into fields, named categories inside a larger bank of held data known as a database.

"Name: first, middle, and last," were all typed on different lines and saved to a larger database, stored somewhere below the rows of wooden tables and chairs.

Our supervisors entered the new era with taskmaster

conviction. No longer were the traditional smoke and coffee breaks welcomed in between report filing; now we needed to pitch in and file or type pertinent information into what the department called 'search finders.' Somewhere, agents were being given an opportunity to search these newly created fields to find matches or commonalities between individuals, bullet wounds, or ammunition. Agents were able to pluck specific facts from these fields that could tie together people, places, and events. It was new, it was exciting, and I was going to be a part of it. The way we captured, retained, and used data was evolving right before me.

Sitting at a computer terminal wasn't what I'd envisioned for myself when I was in training back at Quantico, now I realized that many of us had witnessed the digital age transforming law enforcement.

As typewritten fields became more the norm than typing out a report from one's field notebook, I began to see the possibility of how this could fill in the blanks of the older agents' memories or attention to detail. If my fifty-eight-year-old partner could capture the car's description, state, make, model, and year, I could take that information, feed it through the program, and receive results that could lead us to prospective persons of interest. I realized if we could use this information to narrow down the case time of each investigation, we could take on more work with more accurate results. My partner thought I was crazy, until one afternoon when he decided to take me up on my idea.

We had tried combing through boxes of files looking for clues that would tie together a series of rape victims who'd been murdered, some directly after the rape and others within twelve to eighteen hours of brutal torture that ended in strangulation.

All these women were dumped near the banks of the Green River running through Washington and Oregon. Occurring across state lines, this case brought us together with multiple state and local law personnel, each vying for our manpower. It seems that any local district is pleased to have us join in, organize the investigation, set up a common command center, and bring in bodies ready to search for clues. But when it comes to solving the case, each agency is in it for itself, unwilling to share too much pertinent or what is thought to be relevant information.

My idea was to take the written notes of each investigator and extract times, locations, residences, and workplaces of each victim, creating a timeline and looking for similarities that linked them together, rather than treating them as separate cases.

We could work below where the command center had been set up, in the basement of the Federal building just outside of Spokane, Washington. No one would need to know that—while logged reports, systematically filed in a folder, lay in a box, not to see the light of day as months dragged into years—we would be creating a database of the relevant files. We could uncover so much important linkage between these victims that patterns would emerge: where they lived, when they left for work, how they traveled, the route, the bus, the streets they took to catch the bus. It was truly exciting to see how from this seemingly coincidental or random set of deaths, a pattern that the killer employed might begin to emerge.

Most of the victims had young children and needed reliable jobs and transportation, making it common to live in low-income, but relatively safe, areas and take the bus to and from work. Most had jobs on K or M street. Most left for work in the early morning hours before many residents were awake. Many sat at the bus stop for minutes on end, in the cold and dark early mornings, waiting for their day to begin. It made sense that if someone offered them a ride, some would take it just to be out of the cold or to save bus money and get to work quicker than having to wait through each stop before theirs.

And so it went, each part of their lives dissected to look for similarities and reasons to believe someone out there would be able to easily convince them of the good in human nature to accept a ride and not wait for the bus. Unfortunately, the ride led to being bound, gagged, raped, burned, tortured, and eventually killed, with the body being dumped by the banks of the Green River.

We did not volunteer these ideas immediately. My partner, Parker, wanted to test a few theories before running to our agent in charge and professing to know where exactly to look for the murderer.

I gave him several areas within a six-block radius where he should start examining the bus stops. We could ride the route and look for foot traffic, cars, or bicycle riders that used these streets. We could then see if there were people who kept popping up near the stops.

We could then isolate these people and interview them. Had they seen anyone get picked up or any driver offering rides near the bus stops? What type of car was that person in? What time did they notice someone take a ride? This would narrow down perspective suspect much more easily than sifting through rap sheets looking at the hundreds of rapists in the counties these women were from. This would take months, and no agent had that much time, considering this case was no longer on the front pages of the local papers.

No one really cared about poor women, especially if they were Black or Hispanic. They were not the coveted ladies who aspired to be the next Jackie O or Gloria Steinem. Going to work and coming back to get your kids off to school before passing out for some well-deserved sleep and starting all over again did not make for glamorous reading.

No one told us, the young 'inexperienced' agents, that what we were doing would be important in solving a case, let alone become standard operating procedure within the next few years. So we typed. We joked about spilling coffee on the keyboards so we could end the mundane task earlier than expected. That was, until the theory worked.

Sitting across from one of the bus stops, Parker enjoyed a warm piece of sourdough toast and a hot cup of black coffee. He noticed a red Toyota Tacoma truck driving up the street, slowing at the bus stop. A young man, in his early thirties, wearing a mechanic's jumpsuit with a red-trimmed oval patch on the driver's side of his zipped uniform, was eyeing a woman sitting on the bus-stop bench. Then the truck moved on.

The truck came by a second time, and the driver pulled to the curb in front of the bus stop. He rolled down his passenger window and spoke to the twenty-something-year-old woman sitting there.

She shook her head at the young man as if to say, "No." The driver kept talking and then rolled up his window, pulling away from the curb into the two-lane street. This would probably not seem unusual in a small town. People know each other and do stop to converse, but if she knew him, why didn't she take a ride if it was offered? What had he asked her? Did she say anything to make him remember her?

Reaching for a few dollar bills so he could quickly pay his tab before the bus arrived, Parker darted across the street. The young woman moved over on the bench to give him room to sit. He introduced and identified himself. Did she recognize the man? Did she know him? Was he from the neighborhood?

"No," she said. She'd never seen him before.

She was chatty, telling my partner she took this bus four times a week, each workday except Friday when her boyfriend drove her to work. The driver had asked if she wanted a ride, saying he was going into the next town and would be happy to take her near her apartment. He seemed nice, but she had a boyfriend with a temper, and it was a small town. "Not taking a chance for me to be seen with this guy and someone tell my boyfriend. It's not worth it," she explained.

Was there anything different about the driver that she could remember?

"He smelled of grease and fuel. His hands were worn, as if washing all the parts of his trade off had left oil marks and rough skin." She said there was a name patch on his work overalls: Mitch.

Parker thanked her and got into his car to drive back to the station.

Before he left the area, Parker thought to look for any garages that might be the young man's place of work. There were several, but the mechanics were hard at work, and he was driving. It was difficult to see their uniforms, let alone if any were blue with name tags trimmed in red.

We weren't supposed to leave our basement research/search center. What my partner was doing was 'way off the chart' but important investigative work. By taking the information given to him, he was able to reduce the number of bus routes to stage, streets to canvas, and automotive shops to search.

We triangulated six streets and six garage shops, all of

which had potential. It was detective work as done in the new age. While person to person is still important, shaving off valuable time, resources, and mental energy by deploying assumptions based upon data made for more hours of sleep, a complete meal enjoyed over the course of more than ten minutes, or an extra cup of much-needed coffee between 2:00 and 4:00 a.m. We were using this new computerized world based on the yet unproven theory that it would help us get to the suspect before he or she knew we were on to them.

The results of our work validated all the restless hours sitting in front of a dumb terminal, the green characters eventually giving way to amber sentences.

After committing forty-eight murders over a twenty-year period, the Green River murderer, Gary Ridgway, was arrested in November 2001 as he left his job at Kenworth Truck Company in Renton, Washington.

20

The Sinai Desert and the Bedouins

Sinai Peninsula, Egypt
1989

There were many reasons for my joining the bureau, all valid. But it was the allure of doing something different almost every day in a unique environment, away from home, that made me embrace the job.

As much as I loved the small, quiet suburb where I was raised, there was a feeling of displacement when I looked back at my growing years.

It's as if you long to be in a cool pool on a hot summer day. You get excited for the opportunity to swim and then, as soon as you put your foot on the first step to descend into the sparkling blue water, you retract. The water is too cold and sends shivers up your spine to your brain, which immediately demands you remove it from the inviting blue oasis. All you can do is watch while other children dance on the steps in the shallow end and dive off the long board, plunging themselves into the deep end of the massive pool outside your front door.

My interests and my goals had always been different from those of my classmates and friends. The classic suburban middle school I'd attended was filled with Caucasian children: boys, whose ambition was to grow up and become baseball heroes or businessmen; girls, who were short on ambition. Their biggest goal was to get a new dress for the junior high prom or to sell the most Girl Scout cookies. In high school, everyone lived for summer. I was the exact opposite. I loved the structure of the school day, then running track or taking the long way home, getting lost among the maple trees as they released newly golden leaves. Unlike most of my peers, I was never complacent about my future. I wanted to see the world and come back ready to change it.

My job with the FBI was a perfect fit for me. I relished the time in Washington, DC with its renowned art scene and intellectual stimulation. My field agent assignments took me to different parts of the country. CIA and National Intelligence operative work for defined periods of time, although sobering, whetted my desire for foreign adventures.

For the time being, however, I was back in California, married and with my family nearby. But Daniel and I had little in common and were living separate lives. My parents were comfortable with children leaving the nest, checking in now and then, and not being a part of their day-to-day existence. Neither Daniel nor my parents knew that my work (whatever they believed that was) continued when I returned.

I was restless.

I sat in my comfortable West Los Angeles basement office surrounded by banker boxes of case files of forgotten operations. The dust was so thick that we wiped each document down before entering the pertinent data into the file on our dumb terminals.

The phone rang. "Come upstairs. Let's have a talk."

Usually this meant that something was wrong and needed to be corrected. I could tell by my boss's voice that this was not the case.

Long ago I learned that when the boss calls, there is no need to share that information with anyone. No one knows, besides you, him, and Nancy, his trusted assistant. She held all the keys to Director Smith. When others found out that you had been called on to join a team and they hadn't, things around the office could get uncomfortable.

"The boss isn't feeling good," Nancy said, as I walked off the elevator and into her reception area. "Allergies."

"Okay. Thanks for letting me know," I replied.

She waved me through her secretarial office into the formal meeting room, a large room with two big leather chairs, a coffee table, and a round glass table with four chairs in the corner overlooking Wilshire Boulevard and Veteran Avenue. Los Angeles National Cemetery, for veterans, was across the street, where the rows of graves shone brightly in the sunshine, their limestone name placards engraved with rank, name, birthdate, and date of death. Each with a US flag waving proudly in the wind.

We no longer met in my director's office, which was through the door on the left side of the meeting room. That was his room, where he worked, sometimes slept, but more importantly, where he thought, making decisions that literally affected his agents' lives.

"So how is the file project coming along?" he said.

"Slowly. It's hard to concentrate in the dark. We're each trying to do one box of documents a day. It's not very exciting work, and I know we take more breaks than we should."

"It's important work."

I nodded my head in agreement.

He sat across from me in the large brown chair, looking like the weight of the world was on his shoulders. I wondered what he would say next.

"When you were in Israel, did you go to the Sinai?"

"No, sir."

"Have you ever been in the desert?"

"As a family we went to Palm Springs, but no, I've never spent time in a desert, never slept on sand except at the beach."

"Well, then, this will be a first. You will get to go to the Sinai. There are people there who are unsure if they can trust us. I think you'll be able to gain their trust."

Instinctively, I asked, "Who are these people?"

"Bedouins. More information to come, but for now keep plugging away at your box." With that he stood up, signaling that the conversation was over. As I walked out, he held the door open for me.

"Thank you, Boss."

He was a gentleman through and through and cared about his team members. "Go get some sun before going back downstairs," he said, to which I smiled, knowing I needed to do that before facing the inevitable darkness in that basement.

When I got to Daniel's and my home that night, I searched the *Encyclopedia Britannica* for information on the Bedouins. Who are they? What makes them able to live in the desert the way we live in our suburban or city homes? How can they sustain the cold desert nights and, more importantly, the 120+ degree temperatures during the day? What do they eat? Do they live in tribes or families that decided to bond together to survive the elements? And why, now in 1994, do they choose to live in the desert when they could live anywhere in the countries bordering the Sinai?

A Bedouin is defined as "A nomadic Arab of the desert." The Bedouin people have lived in the desert regions of North Africa, the Arabian Peninsula, and the Palestinian deserts, bordering the southern edge of Syria, since 6,000 BC. They're the primary inhabitants of the Holy Land. Abraham, Isaac, and Jacob were considered Bedouins.

In the 1st Century BC, Bedouins moved west into Jordan and the Sinai Peninsula, and southwest along the Red Sea coastline. In the 7th century BC, Bedouins were among the first converts to Islam. During the Muslim conquests, thousands of Muslims, many of whom were Bedouin, left the Arab peninsula and settled in newly conquered lands, later spreading across the Middle East and North Africa.

Camels, donkeys, horses, and sheep were raised for bartering with other tribes and communities. Goats were traded for food and clothing. Traders from around the world depended on Bedouins as guides in Syria and Arabia. Merchant caravans would be lost to the desert if not for these nomadic people. The communities relied on them to bring in goods for commerce and manufacturing.

Many any of these people have settled in areas where their ancestors bartered goods centuries before. Urbanization has encroached upon their isolation. Radio and television have brought them new ideas and exposed them to the outside world. The oil industry has also changed the lives of many

Bedouin tribes. Those who dealt with the oil fields, trucks, and machines in the desert made royal sums that eventually moved the younger generations out of the desert and into towns, but most maintain their nomadic ties through language, culture, and tradition.

Family is the cornerstone of each tribe. Bedouins are especially respected when they become married and have children. There are defined roles for each family member, and their surnames come from the senior male. The extended household ceases to exist when the most elderly male or female dies. The older sons then form their own households, with inheritance being divided in accordance with Muslim law. Children are the Bedouins' most cherished family members. They are raised by the extended family.

Full of encyclopedic knowledge about the Bedouins, my desert story was about to begin. Research doesn't prepare you for everything.

When my flight landed in the early morning hours at Ben Gurion Airport, my guide greeted me. *"Boker Tov.* Good morning," he said, flashing a toothless grin from ear to ear. He was dark, slight, with no outward sign of age except for his missing front teeth and a few small wrinkles around his eyes.

As I returned his greeting, we both felt the warmth of mutual respect. I was giving him work; he was providing me safety and guidance through a desert that was both beautiful and deadly. We gathered my bags and duffel, and I boarded a public bus.

My first stop was the kibbutz where I had stayed many years before. Tzora was still being run by South Africa and still relying on the work of volunteers who came from all over the world. This would once again become my base, where I would participate in assisting with meals and in helping to run the children's camp while I was there. No one stayed for free. Volunteering was a way to pay back to the residents for a clean bed and bathroom, and two meals a day.

Fortunately, my old lower bunk in volunteer house number four was open. It felt good to lie down and close my eyes before dinner time.

The day had been full of my guide's verifying arrangements in Jerusalem and my assisting the office staff with typing out volunteer forms in English that would be used during my interview process. When the head of the office noticed my head bobbing up and down, fending off sleep, she quickly got me up and led me on a brisk walk around the grounds.

"I hear you've been to Tzora before, yes?" Her English was broken but understandable.

"Yes. I loved my time here and am happy to come back."

Never knowing how much the personnel knew of my reason for being in Israel, I tried to show my enthusiasm for the 'experience' of participating in communal living. My assignments were doled out by the group leaders, and I was certain the office head, my contact would come in handy in deciding a toss-up between cleaning facilities, doing laundry, or helping in the air-conditioned office.

She walked with me around the children's week community where all the offspring of the kibbutz members are raised. They see their immediate families on the Sabbath, and their extended family the other six days of the week.

The laughter of children filled the playground and my heart. My soul had felt empty for a long time. I had filled the spaces with work, driving the long way home so I could avoid arguing with my husband who just really wanted his own space. My gut told me to leave all that behind and be present for the happiness on display around me.

"You seem happy here."

"I am. The children are so beautiful. They seek out each other, and watching them play reminds me that there is a time when each person hasn't a care in the world. No hatred, no lies, no betrayal. Just playing in the sunshine."

Perhaps she'd read my mind, as her response strongly reflected the same words that were inside my head. "We all long to get back to that place of pure happiness. Some of us can. Others of us keep searching for a way to get there."

"True," I replied. I could tell she was waiting for me to say more but I didn't. No need to get too personal with her.

We stopped walking. She turned to look directly into my eyes. "Why don't you divide your time between much-needed office work and the playground? I can arrange for you to come here like we are now so you can assist outside and have this time to yourself."

Being young and alone in another country could be an adventure. When people help you, it's a gift. I know this now. I should have been kinder then. My parents taught me manners. I said "please" and "thank you." I lacked the maturity back then to understand that people don't need to be kind or helpful. But strangers helping me, nursing me back to health, showing me how to survive would get me through this mission.

About two weeks into my stay at Tzora, I was just getting into the groove of being part of this well-run community when the phone at the manager's desk rang. I could see her peering over her typewriter, looking in my direction. She hung up the old black phone with its circular dial and called for me. I knew my time at the kibbutz was up, and that the real reason I'd come back to this part of the world was now going to reveal itself.

I listened as she told me that I would be picked up that same evening after supper. I was to come to her office where she would sign me out and store my things until my return from the Sinai. I could take only one backpack, and in it a few pairs of socks and underwear, one pair of jeans, a lightweight jacket, a few shirts, a hat, brush, toothpaste, toothbrush, and most importantly, a compass and water bottle. "The desert is not easy to navigate if you get separated from your guide. Stay close," she advised. "Be careful. We will talk more once you return."

I packed up my things, separating the few personal items into my backpack and the rest into my duffel bag, and concentrated on what needed to be achieved and how I was going to make that happen.

I tucked Moshe's picture into the corner zip pocket of my pack. He'd lost the Star of David I'd given him years before and was lucky enough to find it in the desert. I wanted his luck to be with me. He was still my real love; I needed his presence in some way.

It felt good to lie down my cot. I should have been more grateful then for the comforts the kibbutz provided. I would learn to value the kindness of strangers.

My driver was a small Arabic man in his fifties. He sang to the radio as we drove, first through Jerusalem, the Jaffe, and then the border of Jordan and Israel.

My teeth chattered as I rode in the truck through the cold toward the Sinai Desert. I tried to close my eyes, but the wind blew through the uneven creases where the worn rubber seal met the passenger window. *Try to sleep, try to get some rest*, my mind kept trying to counsel my body, but to no avail. I wanted to absorb each noise and each barely visible image, knowing it could be the last time I saw 'civilization.' I fixated on the dim lights periodically coming from the roadside homes or from a vehicle passing us going in the opposite direction.

This was to be a lesson in survival. My kibbutz contact told me during our last conversation. "Stay focused on where you're going, not where you've been." Those words resonated as we pushed through the darkness toward the border.

Being Arabic, the driver would have no problem crossing into the Sinai. I, on the other hand, had a fake Jordanian passport, so there would be no telling what would happen. If I were asked any questions, he would answer for me, as traditionally men spoke for the women in their company, especially if they were family. We looked similar, even enough to pass for relatives if one didn't look too closely.

The darkness of the early morning would help. We timed our arrival just as the guards would be serving their last five to ten minutes before leaving their post to get some much-needed sleep. If we kept our pace, we would make it to the border without being too fearful of the guards.

"ETA fifteen minutes and counting," the driver said.

I nodded my head up and down, so he'd know I understood.

The border was simple. A single policeman lifted the metal guard gate. Nothing was automated. We handed our passports through the driver's side. A flashlight shone through that same window to illuminate the front seats and dashboard: coffee cups, a pack of Chicklet gum, and my jean jacket that was covering me as a poor excuse for a blanket were all that were visible. Nothing else was asked or said. The guard signaled for the policeman to raise the gate and let us pass.

I wondered when we'd see the desert, when the city lights would fade to the point where we'd only see a black sky pierced by the twinkling light of stars. Could we get past the guards so we could breathe and, perhaps, lighten up our darkening conversation? I wanted to get past all the police and roadblocks. Once we got past them, we could collectively catch our breath. However, two more guard posts loomed in the distance.

We had an uneventful drive with little road traffic in either direction before sunset on the second day. As we approached the last guard post, my driver smiled his warm, comforting toothless grin.

"We will be fine. You have work to do, and Allah will take us to where it's safe. It is written."

I smiled back and nodded in agreement. I didn't know Arabic. Speaking English or Hebrew would draw attention to us if someone heard me. Best to be the docile, female companion of a kind, older Arab who looked like he could be my grandfather.

The beaten-down Mercedes Benz truck in front of us looked suspicious. No windows, no brake lights. It was bound to be pulled over, if only to figure out what was in the back.

I held my breath as we came close enough to see the driver being asked to step out of his truck. Now was the time to act and get past all of this. The two guards positioned themselves on either side of the truck, and another stepped out of the concrete bunker to speak to the driver, guns loaded, ready to fire. The driver was now on the ground, hands palms up, spread out like a cross. My driver knew not to look. He drove slowly by the scene unfolding to our right. He gave me a quick, but very stern look, knowing it wasn't something I should see. No one wants to recall those images right before a gun fires and someone dies. But just like viewing a car accident after the people have left the scene, we still hold up other drivers just to rubberneck at the mangled steel, wondering how it happened and who was at fault.

I had to count in my head and avoid thoughts of looking back. Anything to discourage my mind from what I really wanted to do. I sat on my hands to keep them warm and closed my eyes as we pulled away from the area. I counted from one hundred to eighty-eight, and then the sound of gunfire came and went quickly. No words were exchanged between the driver and me. We just continued down the road, each of us anxious to put distance between us and the shooting. I closed my eyes and tried counting backward again. When I got to sixty-five, my mind let go and I fell asleep.

At 0400, we pulled up to a small concrete structure. Outside in the dirt yard, two boys were kicking a ball. They looked younger than they were.

"These boys, my brother's sons," the driver said as we pulled into the makeshift driveway loaded with a broken-down four-wheel-drive truck and too many chickens to count. An old woman stood in the doorway waving to us.

"Your mother?" I asked. He looked so happy as he nodded yes. Hopefully, they would share a part of this homecoming with me. It would ease the anxiety of not knowing what was to come and lessen my homesickness that I felt reflected in my eyes, now full of tears.

He became caught up in the simple joy of the boys running toward us, gleeful and excited to see their uncle as his mother busied herself shooing the chickens away, clearing a path for us to quickly come to her. The boys hugged their uncle, asking in Arabic who this stranger was who was with him. "A friend" is all he said. Children understand the simple, direct answer and looked for no more. "A friend" was sufficient for them to go about playing their ball game, forgetting us altogether in the fury of their game.

He held his mother, hugging her tightly. She buried her face in his shoulder, crying. Then, pulling gently away, she waved her hands in front of her burka-shielded face. Her Arabic was fast, full of the marvel of a mother who has found a lost child. She was curious why he was so thin, why his hair was not kempt, why his shoes were untied. She then stopped her chatter and grabbed him closely, holding him near her, not wanting to let go. At that moment, our eyes met.

She didn't look happy to see me. I represented the outside world that had brought her war, loss, and mourning. She would comply with her son's request to feed and house me for the night, but there was nothing about this act that exhibited welcome or kindness; it only showed respect to her elder son, who was clearly a favorite.

As we made our way through the chickens into the small modest home, the air was filled with the most wonderful scents. Turmeric, saffron, cooked eggplant baked in pine nuts, braised lamb that must have been smoldering overnight in the firepit hole in her backyard. In this world, the outdoor yard is an extension of the kitchen. It's where the animals are slowly cooked, while the laundry dries under the powerful sun. Children play in the front. Women work in the back of the house.

She motioned us to the back of the small home toward the water well to wash our faces, feet, and hands in preparation for the meal. The ride had been long, and we were hungry, but not to the point where we didn't prepare for the gift of food, eating together as a family and recognizing the beauty of the moment. Gratitude filled the air. It was palpable. I felt a warmth that I would not take for granted. None of it. In my best Arabic, I asked if I could help, as I was the only other woman in the home. The mother looked at me in surprise. I wondered if it was from my offer or my broken Arabic. Her tumult of words came loud and quickly. I was a guest. I was not to help, not to offer, not to take away the responsibilities of her family members who were here because they each had a job to do within this family.

That morning I learned just how proud a person can be. She would see that all family members knew their jobs and their place within their unit. This responsibility would not be taken away by a stranger. I would not make that mistake again while I was here or at any time I was among these people in this land.

My eyes filled with tears as I watched her reaction to what I had meant to be a kind gesture; yet I pulled back the waterworks, not wanting my driver to think I was weak. That would have been disrespect on an entirely different level.

He explained to his annoyed mother that, in my land, sharing responsibility was a sign of respect. Not sitting back and being served, but to "pitch in" (my wording) was what house guests did when they wanted to show their gratitude. Although she heard him, she wasn't going to change her mind.

The quicker I leave, the better for everyone, I thought. Let them get their lives back to normal. That would be the best show of appreciation, gratitude, and respect I could give this tireless, overworked matriarch.

I finished my meal and waited until she'd taken her last bite. Then before I could say anything, my driver asked if I wanted to freshen up before we were on our way. I most wholeheartedly did. It was soon time to leave again, but, before I could properly say thank you to the driver's mother, we were out on the road again.

"You can sleep if you like. My family," he said after a long pause, "are simple. They only know what they know."

I listened, not saying a word, then said, "Maybe that's a good thing." I leaned my head back into the torn bench seat in the old truck.

Hours later I felt the sun on my face and left shoulder. Opening my eyes, I could see only sand dunes, miles of peaked hills with shadows of all shapes playing in the crevassed canyons. The light changed from white to pale yellow to golden bronze, depending on the angle at which I positioned my head. I felt as if I was in a dream, covered in warmth. We had arrived. The Sinai loomed in front of us. The road back to civilization was far behind me.

"Here it is. Time to move forward," my driver said.

He unloaded supplies and I stretched my arms toward the sky, trying to shake off sleep while breathing in the surrounding beauty. My mind was clear. I was ready to meet my guide and start to gather the information I was sent here to receive. And what was that? I had some idea but it would be up to me to figure it out: one element of intelligence that is unspoken.

Just as he did on our drive, the driver sang to the wind. As if harmonizing with the way the breeze swayed, his Arabic chant was peaceful and soft. The sound was mixed with a clanging of bells. In the near distance I could see several silhouettes bobbing up and down. The bells must be attached to their camels. We shielded our eyes as the sun was still high in the sky. I squinted and tried to make out more of the moving group. My driver exchanged words with them. Though still a distance away, I could hear their words clearly.

The desert's quiet makes every sound more exaggerated. There is no background noise except for the soft wind. The sky was now a soft blue, no clouds, no breeze. What I couldn't stop looking at were the rolling hills of sand that spread for as far as I could see. There were no mountains of dirt here. It was all sand. Nature here was clearly in charge. If you came to terms with that, then perhaps you could live through this. If you fought the power of the environment, surely you would die.

The sky burst into purple, orange, and red. It was so vibrant that it captivated even the camel brigade who had come to lead us to the camp where we would spend the night. I was the only woman. At this point, my suspicion and trust level were about the same. Would my driver protect me or let these four nomads do what they wished with me if that was their intention?

The tallest man dismounted his camel and embraced my driver. The friendship and camaraderie they had for each other was comforting and quieted my fear. The camel gave out a loud shriek as if to say, "Enough. Time to go." The two men exchanged small leather pouches. I believed this was money, as the other three Bedouins looked on with pleased expressions on their faces.

We gathered our two backpacks out of the beaten-down truck, and my driver mounted the camel as his friend held the intertwined red-and-blue rope reins. He held out his hands for me to use as a stepstool. I placed my left foot between his interlocked fingers and hopped up onto the midsection of the camel, behind my driver. No saddle, just a worn wool blanket to separate me from this creature. I held onto my driver's jacket as the animal swayed side to side.

The sun was setting lower now. Our guide walked back to the truck and started the engine. Was he leaving us out here with these three men who were not friends like he and the driver were? What was happening?

My driver said to me, "We are safe. We will start through the sand to their camp. He will meet us on the other side of these dunes once we are done."

"He" was whomever I was supposed to meet, the person who would make clear what my role was in the Sinai.

"How do you know he'll be there?" My fear level rose with each word. I was trying to be brave, but I felt as though this wasn't going to be easy. My feelings were showing, which is never good. We'd been trained to deal with whatever situation we encountered. I held myself in check, wanting to take back my question.

"Of course, he will be there."

Off through the countless dunes we went, sharing the movement of the camel. Up one sandy mound, then down its backside. Each step of the animal felt like a cross between a swaying, rocking kayak going through a strong boat wake and a horse's trot. Just hold on and look forward. You need to get to where you're going and then you can figure out what to do next.

The sun was at the lowest point on the horizon, the sky a deep red and fading into a rich blue. It was one of the most beautiful sights I had ever seen, something I knew I would never forget. The colors were seared into my brain. The stillness of the sky was etched into my heart. This was peace, this was surely what it felt like to be one with nature and probably as close as I had ever felt. Moments like this are never assumed; they are created by something outside of ourselves. The four men seemed to take it in stride as if scenes this magnificent happened every day.

As we proceeded toward the camp, the wind began to pick up, blowing sand into our faces. "Take this," my driver said. "Wrap your face so no sand gets in your mouth."

I tried to look ahead, but at that point the sand covered us, cutting off sight and sound. The only noise we could hear was the wind. I lowered my head, closed my eyes, and prayed to whomever was listening that we would be spared. The night sky turned from dusk to dark. My mind was blank.

We approached the top of a high sand dune and saw lights flickered in the distance. It was like being on top of a mountain and viewing the valley below. I knew it must be the camp. The fire would be our beacon in the night sky. My driver knew this world. He was calm. He steered the camel up and down the sandy terrain, making use of our bodies shifting side to side to help balance the load of supplies that were attached to the sides of the animal.

An hour later, we arrived within walking distance of the heat of the campfire. My driver dismounted the steady camel. He wanted to give the animal a break from carrying the two of us, plus our supplies.

When we got close enough to see the elder men around the large fire, my driver and the three elders greeted one another with arms open. The exchange was brief: *"Salem."* The figures wrapped in blankets quieted.

I sat on top of the weary camel who became restless and ambled closer to the group. I grabbed the reins, and the rope cut into my left hand. The animal wanted nothing to do with being stopped. Its determination to go where it wanted was winning over my failed attempt to halt him. I shifted hands and pulled back with all my might on the rope. He raised his head upright, then back toward me, letting out a nasty belching sound. The men looked up and laughed.

What was so funny? Was I going to let this beast take me off into some unknown direction? Was this going to be the end of me? No. I had to let it know who was in charge. If I didn't, how could I expect these nomads and whoever else we were to meet here know that I was someone to contend with?

The laughter stopped, and from the far end of the camp I saw a woman holding a tiny bundle. She was swaying back and forth to calm the baby. One of the men we'd ridden to the camp with approached my defiant camel. He held out his hand with some vegetable treat. As he fed the camel, I carefully hoisted my right leg over and around the back side and lowered myself down. Not knowing how far the ground was, I stepped from the blanket, falling squarely on my behind. The camel didn't budge. He was too busy enjoying his much-deserved treat. My driver rushed over to me as I sat awkwardly next to the camel trying to figure out what had just happened.

"Are you alight? Can you move?"

"I'm fine. I didn't realize how far down it was."

He grabbed my hands, seeing the gash inside my left palm and pulled me upright. "Come with me, slowly. You fell from high. You need to be looked at."

"I'm fine," I said in a matter-of-fact tone. This was not the time to be treated as a defenseless woman.

A woman, young and dressed in robes of burgundy, blue, and black appeared from the corner of a tent to my right. One of the elders was telling her where to take me and what to do. She seemed frightened, hesitant to come near me, as if I were something alien that she hadn't seen before. Maybe it was how I was dressed that confused her. Blue jeans, army boots, t-shirt, and jean jacket were not the normal attire of a woman in this part of the world. My head was uncovered, and my hair was disheveled from the long trek. I certainly looked like nothing she'd seen before. I tried to lock eyes with her so she would understand that I meant no harm.

My hand throbbed from my camel encounter, blood dripping down my fingers and onto the ground. Extending her hand, she touched my jacket. It must have felt foreign to her, the material unfamiliar. She pinched the fabric, pulling me toward her, then released my sleeve and turned toward the tent behind us. I followed, trusting that it would be a place safe from the sand dunes, warm enough for the cold desert night, and that I would be welcome.

Inside, oil candles lit up the vibrantly colored walls and floor. Velvet, wool, silk, and cotton rugs and drapes lined each area. It was exquisite.

I looked from the top of the tent to the floor, soaking up the colorful interior. Pillows of all shapes and sizes covered the floor. Small benches made of rich brown wood lined the back wall of the tent. On the benches sat fruit, meat, vegetables, and flat bread. The young woman motioned for me to sit. I carefully lowered my tired legs to the soft pillow-covered floor. The young woman turned toward the opening and disappeared.

When she returned, it was with an elderly woman who carried cloth that was pure white, oil, and water. She knelt next to me and took my wounded hand in hers. Dipping the strips of cloth in the water, she washed my wound, careful to get the dirt and sand out of the open skin. Then she took clean strips and dipped them in a copper bowl filled with warm oil. I no longer felt the pulse pounding away in my hand. I started to feel calm, as if the incense from the oil was taking over my body. I began to fade and, at some point, fell fast asleep on the soft, luxurious pillows.

I woke to the sound of the wind beating the outside flaps of the tent and sand wailing against the outside walls of the strong, fortress-like tent that protected us. I was thirsty.

The elderly woman saw that I was awake. She brought fruit and water. I sipped slowly from a leather bowl, the liquid soothing my parched throat. I took a bite of a dried apricot, then another, followed by dates, figs, dried apple, and more water. Each bite brought me back to life. I was feeling stronger and tried to focus on my surroundings. I drank, ate, and fell back to sleep, not remembering whether I thanked the kind woman for bringing me back to myself. I wanted to show my gratitude, but how?

In the morning I woke to several children peeking into the tent, their faces darting back and forth through the opening. I rubbed the sleep from my eyes and smiled back at their inquisitive faces. Two older women chased the children away with stern voices. I didn't need to understand their language to know these grandmothers' warnings. As they made their way toward me, I bent my head in a gesture that I hoped they would understand as one of thanks. I was drawn to their warm faces.

The women sat on either side of me, gesturing for me to remove my jacket. I tried, but my hand was stiff, and it was difficult to remove the worn material as I had to bend my left arm.

One woman removed my clothing from the tent, the other started to unwrap my hand. As she got closer to the last few strips, I noticed there was no blood on the pieces of cloth. She removed the last strip, inspecting my palm. Pleased, she smiled at me as if to say, "See, you are no longer hurt." I looked at my palm: the skin was pink and tender, but the wound was no longer open.

"Thank you. *Toda*."

She nodded and took the pieces of greenery from the water and pressed them to my healing flesh. She closed my fingers around the leaves, held her hand over mine, then sang an unfamiliar Arabic tune. She hummed, and her soft melodic tones filled the tent. When she finished her song, she released my hand, holding it up so she could inspect my fingers, wrist, and arm. After wrapping my palm again with something that resembled cheesecloth, she helped me into the makeshift tub made from wood and leather basins, then sat down next to me and took my blistered feet into her hands. Using the oil, she massaged my tender feet with her soft touch. She took her time, making sure to apply pressure to the forming blisters. Afterward, she helped me out of the tub, and wrapped my feet as she had my hand and left the tent.

I was lost in thought when the young woman from the previous night appeared. She held a beautiful, purple robe, a soft, linen-like undergarment, and a long flowing scarf. I hoped that I would be able to dress myself. But she helped place the linen-like gown over my head and arms, took my right arm under her shoulder and lifted me to my feet.

This small young woman was strong, stronger than anyone would expect. After adjusting the linen-like gown, she helped me step into the beautiful robe. It felt soft and shone in the sunlit tent. My hair was damp from the bath. She took the scarf and expertly wrapped it around my hair, head, and face, leaving my eyes exposed. The bottom was open so that I could feel the warmth of my own breath.

She looked into my eyes, and I tried to smile, before realizing she couldn't see my mouth. She giggled, and I returned her soft laugh with a hearty hoot. The elder women must have been nearby, as they both came swiftly into the tent holding their worn fingers to their covered mouths. It was not the time to be loud. We lowered our eyes, knowing what we had done was somehow wrong, but each of us felt it was appropriate at the time.

We sat, the young woman next to me. It was the first time I felt some sort of friendship from these Bedouin women, who were steeped in traditions about which I knew nothing. The quiet around us started to fill with the familiar chanting of prayers coming from outside the tent.

Men's voices raised in unison, praying for themselves, their families, and their tent-mates to enjoy the blessings and bounty they deserved. I closed my eyes and silently prayed for these kind people: the women around me and the men who brought me here safely. I was lucky to be among this nomad tribe of watchful people. I was safe, and my thanks to God was for that and my family back home.

Prayer time ended, and we got up and left the tent. The sun blazed down on us. The men were gone. Only the elders, children, and women remained. I counted thirteen people, including children. I watched from outside the tent as the organized makings of a village came together in front of me.

Children took water in small jugs to the women, who sat around barrels much like the one I'd bathed in and systematically washed undergarments, wringing them, and hanging the garments to dry. Wanting to help, I walked to where two young girls were hanging the clean clothes. I offered to help by handing them the wrung-out clothes. They took each piece from me without looking at me or the others. They just accepted my small contribution of handing them the clothes so they would not have to bend down into the barrels and grab the items themselves. Six barrels lined the tents, each needing to be tended to. I rose after emptying the two tubs and went to the next barrel. Here, I hung them myself.

I could sense the children watching me. I kept working,

since of the women stopped me. The children went back to what they had to do, not paying any attention to me. I was a part of this working group. This is how I could show them my thanks.

As I tended the last barrel, I noticed the children rolling the empty containers away from the tents. Every action here had a purpose, a part of what these people did to survive. Nothing frivolous, just necessities. I thought about home. How much we had in our world, and just how ridiculous it all seemed. More than we would ever need, and yet never enough. How many times did I buy new jeans, shirts, and dresses when I already had plenty for the small amount of time that I wore them? Most workdays, I wore the same three blue suits I'd owned since college and my first paycheck from the bureau.

I got in line with the other women, waiting to receive the next task for preparing the afternoon meal—now the priority before the men came back from the dunes that surrounded us.

The afternoon was quiet. When we finished the main meal of the day, the men retired to their respective tents. The women visited among themselves. I sat on the edge of the campground, content to enjoy the entire scene—although still awaiting the reason I was here.

The sky turned from light to dark; the colors were magnificent. Blues turned into purple as the light passed, streaking the evening sky with lines of orange, like shining pieces of glass that pierced the black background of the early nighttime. It made for a spectacular show. The first burst of pure white starlight exploding onto the black arena drew me in as if lured by a carnival barker, and wondering if the show would be magical, captivating, or completely breathtaking? No one knows until the show itself.

What was evident was that this warm-up act of the first constellations appearing in front of me was something I'd never forget. The moon rolled to the far-left side of the sky, clearing the stage for what would come next. The stars poked through the dark, dancing their time away. I wanted to stay up all night, enchanted by this celestial show, but it was getting cold.

I grabbed my army jacket and pulled the sides close to my body, hugging my legs. The wind began to swirl the sand that surrounded our camp. I kept searching the sky for a shooting star. How badly I wanted this nature show to end with a monumental bang. I looked upward, a swish of crystalline pieces spread out in front of me—from the right to the left, swishing against the black canvas. It was the curtain call. I was so fixated that I didn't realize the firepit had been extinguished by the wind. The dust and sand were fiercely spiraling all around me.

The Bedouins were asleep except for the few sentinels that guarded our campsite throughout the night. "Ma'am, please go inside," said the guard. "A storm is coming."

His voice startled me; I thought I was the only one awake in the vicinity. Sleep was very important, as each person's body labored throughout the day, helping sustain this community, enabling it to thrive in this hostile climate of dust and sand. The stars were disappearing before my eyes. I had to struggle just to get up and walk back to my tent. I tried to block the tent opening with my body as I slid through, careful not to let the sand in. The canvas and heavy rags heaved in the wind, then fell into position, pushing me inside.

An older woman was awake, tending to a child. I felt bad, hoping I hadn't disturbed her sleep. While she rocked the child in her lap, we exchanged smiles and I moved closer to her.

She was captivated by my jacket. I guess it looked odd to her to see a woman wearing what to her was a man's clothing. I took the jacket off and laid it near her feet. She looked down on the green camouflaged garment and then straight at me. Studying me, she didn't say a word. Then she pointed at my watch, a simple silver Timex that I'd hastily grabbed from my belongings before making the trip to Ben Gurion Airport. The ticking seemed to interest her. I slipped it off my wrist and held it out for her to take. She seemed reluctant, so I placed it at her feet. As she leaned over to pick it up, the child stirred but remained asleep. I was fascinated by her reaction to a modest watch.

She held it in her hand and brought it to her ear, listening intently to the tick-tock of the works. She must have never seen a watch before. I reached for my jacket to use it as a blanket. She got up and put the child back on the luxurious rug used for sleeping. Then she came close to me and extended her arm. I sat up and fastened the Timex on her wrist. She grinned from ear to ear.

"Keep it," I said to her. Knowing she didn't understand, I placed my hand on hers and pointed to the watch, then to her, hoping she would understand that I was giving her the watch. I lay down and fell asleep, knowing she was watching me.

In the morning, I awoke to find a beautiful necklace on my chest. A soft, golden chain from which hung the most beautiful black-and-yellow disk. It was handmade of glass. I don't know how, but it captured the light between the colors. She had offered me a part of her in return for the watch. It was unfair, as the necklace was one of a kind.

I shucked the sleep out of my eyes and stared at the unique piece of jewelry. No one was in the tent. Alone, I washed my face and hands, changed my shirt, underwear, and socks, and placed the chain around my neck. This was so special that the only way to guard it was to wear it. And I did so, with pride.

21

Yemen Secrets

Sinai Desert, 1989

The morning sun bounced golden light off the sparkling necklace as I greeted the elders. They seemed to notice a new energy in my step. Each looked up as I walked by, acknowledging my strange presence in their world. They weren't bothered by my visit, but certainly wanted to know when I would be gone and their life would return to normal. As if reading their minds, three of the guards walked through the camp directly toward them.

"They are a hundred feet outside," one said.

An open dune buggy roared up a dune and coasted down the backside. It appeared that the reason for my time here might become clearer, but I had no clue exactly what. Who were 'they?'

My gaze tracked the guards as they positioned themselves

in front of and on the sides of their leaders, forming a barrier between them and the arriving outsiders. I considered going back to my tent and retrieving my gun, but there was no time. If it was a violent confrontation, I would move toward the tent, avoiding any women or children who might be in the way. They didn't consciously consider this world of outsiders with guns, bullets, and positions of hatred based on religion or nationality as they went about their daily routines. My mind returned to my training with the Hebron. The Israelis trained for surprise attacks in public places. Could this be that?

Then I heard the familiar sound of the English language in the distance. I moved toward the sound, but one of the guards stood in front of me, blocking the way. I realized by his shielding stance that he was treating me as one of their tribe. I wasn't on my own, as I'd been most of my life. I was part of their community now and would be protected as one of them. I felt the concern, and as one of them, I would protect them as well, even if it was for one day, one moment in my life.

We watched the dune buggy approach as it crossed the last sand dune before entering the camp. The occupants—two Americans, both wearing desert military fatigues and flight jackets with US patches, and their desert guide—disembarked. Our elders would be the first to speak to them. The two sailors—one a naval officer, the other a Navy SEAL—spoke perfect Arabic in addition to English.

But I didn't understand Arabic. Did they have information to share with me? Or were they just going to take me to another place where I was to wait and wonder all over again?

One of the Bedouin guards stood tall and described something to the elders, pointing in front of and behind us.

At that point, the elders withdrew into their tent. No voices could be heard. The area was quiet, completely still except for the random cry or giggle coming from the children's area. The guard motioned for me to enter the tent. I followed obediently.

Once inside, I saw five Bedouin men sitting in a circle. Each had a single stone in front of his folded legs and seemed to be in some meditative trance. Two other men sat in the back of this luxurious tent. Perhaps one of them would become the next elder, once one of the five departed this earth. I wanted to know what they were thinking and why. What was the significance of the small, shiny, and beautifully worn stones in front of them, and why was I so fortunate to witness this tribal collective?

The first elder placed his stone, solid white, in the middle of the circle. He looked up after bending his head in prayer or deep thought. Then the next looked straight ahead but didn't move his stone. The third looked at me, then straight ahead, followed by the fourth, who placed his gleaming gold nugget in the circle. There was one elder left.

He was still deep in thought, eyes closed, head bent, as if he knew he would be the deciding vote and that the stones were for or against the issue. His stone was deep blood red, as smooth as I had ever seen, and gleaming just the same as the other four. He held it in the palm of his left hand and recited some type of Arabic chant, then placed it in his right hand, holding it tightly.

One by one the remaining two men left their luxurious tent, and I studied the jewel-like stones left neatly on the rug. Probably not what I should be doing, but they were mesmerizing, and I wanted to pick each of the stones up to examine exactly what they were, but I didn't dare. Bedouin guards, each with one glove on, extracted the stones quickly, putting them back in their proper place, a drawer of a very heavy-looking dresser. The guards were there to keep a close watch over these precious artifacts of their Bedouin tradition. I assumed that these plain stones were markers for their voting process and wondered what else they were used for. It seemed that everything had more than a single use in their culture. I watched the guards, waiting for them to guide me as to what came next. Silence.

Minutes went by, and my sense was to leave the tent, to see what was happening outside. I started to take steps toward the entry flap of the tent when the guard sharply addressed me. "Stay," he said, as if he knew the meaning in his native tongue but was not confident saying it in another language. I halted mid-stride as if a gun pressing into my back. In front of me, where I thought I was going to exit, stood the two American sailors, cleanly shaved, dressed, and eyes wide open.

"Let's talk," said the officer, the older and taller of the two.

"Talk to me? Why?"

My time with the US military was limited to Quantico training, where we exchanged time between instructors, and when I was on base as part of my bureau training. I didn't know why these Americans were here. I had nothing to share and could only listen if they were here to pass information to me.

The officer introduced himself as Taylor. He and I sat on the floor, cross-legged. His 'partner' stood by the tent opening. The two Bedouin camp guards positioned themselves at the back of the tent.

I waited for Taylor to speak. What came out of his mouth next was a total surprise to me. The Yemen Army, known to be an unorganized group of thugs funded by Al-Qaeda, had attacked a US battleship.

"The *USS Cole* has been hit, potential loss of life undetermined, but we need to go in and we need reinforcements. If you can get assurance from our government that our troops can come across the international waterline so we can retrieve them, this will make our jobs easier and prevent unnecessary loss of life."

Now I understood the task, but I needed to verify some facts, as this kind of situation can change by the minute.

"When was your briefing and who gave you the information?" I asked both sailors directly. My questions were clear and precise. If information given to me was not corroborated by our folks back home, then my purpose for collecting the information would be considered 'non-relevant' meaning not to be used or not actionable. This was something like playing a game of telephone where the message starts as one set of details and ends 180 degrees from where it began.

Taylor held a scrap of paper up to the light that filtered through the cracks in the front entrance and holes on either side of the tent—where the leads came through to hold the structure upright.

"Ground informants, Yemenite, sympathetic to our holding the seas at bay from pirates and helping certain imports/exports come and go. On paper, their economy would tank without what the US achieved on the seas. We owe much to those brave men and women and don't want to see them hurt."

On the scrap of paper were the longitude and latitude coordinates of the targeted ship coming in from the US to Yemen. When he finished reading, he took the scrap of paper and neatly folded it into the small triangular shape it had once been in, then put it back into his shirt pocket.

"Is there more? A name, address, any identification as to

who wrote that note?"

He gave me the name of the dock manager where our naval ships were held before they were churned back into the open seas.

"Did he write this?"

"Not sure, ma'am. But he would know who did."

"I'll need that paper and the coordinates of the next ship coming into the dock. When can we get a message out so I can start researching what you've shared?"

"The Bedouins say a storm is coming. We should stay here tonight and leave early in the morning. Is there a way we can stay here tonight?"

"I'll ask on your behalf. Wait here," I said, as I rose from the softly padded pillowed floor of the elders' tent and into the world of the Bedouin troops.

This culture was extremely respectful of their elders. I was uneasy requesting permission for the Americans to stay since I hadn't given anything to the leadership in return for asking the favor.

As I approached the elders, my watch-wearing friend came up beside me. She took my arm and led me away from the older men. I explained to her my plight, trying to act out my words so she would understand my request. Hand to mouth to show food, lying down to show sleep, and rising early to leave the group by showing her the time on the watch we now shared ownership of. She understood me, if not completely, then at least well enough, and she sat me down, holding her hand in front of me as to bar my getting up until she returned.

About ten minutes later, she stood in front of me, smiling, holding her arms out on either side of her wide body. I rose to my feet and hugged her. It was spontaneous. A reaction of gratitude and happiness that she believed me and knew I was trying to help these two Americans just as she and her tribe had helped me survive in this unforgiving desert. She stood, arms to her side as I held her to me, feeling her heart beating quickly through her many robes. Friendship in the strangest of places was forged by trust.

I was there to receive a message from these US contacts because someone they worked for knew my group could be trusted with the information. Vet it, then bring the details back to the agency that would covertly plan an attack separate from our military action. The only possible way I would be able to be here to do my job was because of a network of Arab and Israeli contacts, all of whom were trusted by my command. Each person played a role in any mission: the individuals who make things happen and those who protect them.

Today was no different. I was being protected, and now these two Americans would be given a place to rest until early morning when they could leave the Bedouin camp and begin their journey out of the Sinai. I would remain here until my trusted guide returned with provisions for my hosts and my passage back to civilization. My worry turned to the time it would take for me to get back to civilization. If it was that hard to get here, how long would it take to get back and would it be in time for me to vet the information on Yemen and get the details back to my command? Would I be the bottleneck, or could I truly help?

I returned to the tent. A fierce storm was brewing outside, sand was beginning to swirl, and the camp was starting to close in preparation for what was to come. Was my guide out there in the middle of this or did he know that there was a sandstorm coming in the distance? Was he safe? Could I get through the night without thinking about all these things depriving me of sleep?

My backpack! I had to get back to my original tent and retrieve my notebook. I'd then be able to unload all my thoughts and get them out of my head. I went to the inside flap of the tent. The wind was so strong it pushed me to the side, making me grab onto the canvas siding with both hands. This was not going to be easy, but, somehow, I'd have to make it two tents to my left. I'd barely exited the tent when my sweet Timex-hostess blocked me.

We didn't speak the same language, but I knew a disapproving look when I saw one, especially when it was directed at me. I tried to explain with hand gestures what I was trying to do. She just looked at me as if to say something bad will happen if you choose to leave this tent now. I felt the turmoil of trying to satisfy my need with the discontented looks and feeling I was receiving. Was it worth risking the friendly relationship I had with these incredibly giving people? No. It was not. They knew much better than I did what to expect when a storm came through the desert. I'd had one brief experience on the way to their camp, and it was scary.

I knelt and crawled back to the side of the tent. My hostess seemed relieved. I held my jean jacket over my chest, took one of the worn blankets and wrapped it around me. Instead of counting sheep, I would systematically list each question I'd need to vet once I was back in the States and that would clearly take most, if not all, of the night. Would any other intelligence come my way before it was time to leave the camp? How would we know this information was timely when we were so far from the real world? No radio, no television, and no papers. I'd have to get back as soon as possible, but without my guide there was no way. I needed to slow down and keep my frustrations to myself. Things would look better in the morning. We would regroup and if I just prayed for my guide to come get me tomorrow, or as soon as possible, I'd be able to get this information back to Director Smith, who would know what was real and what was not.

Early the next morning, the two Americans met with me. The Bedouin guards, again, positioned themselves at the back of the tent.

"I have some questions," I said to the sailors. "Did you verify Russian arms or soldiers in the area?"

"We did, but we need to verify the artillery."

"Do you have serial numbers? Can we get a grouping so I can submit that with the information you already gave me? It will help us know whether the Russians were involved or if the neighboring countries were sponsoring any of the warfare going on. I need more information before we leave, so think it over and when you're ready to talk I'll be sitting right here waiting."

There had to be more, or why would they come all this way? What were they holding back? Why would they risk the trek through the Sinai just to give some and not the entire story? It didn't add up, and since we had another night, I'd be patient and wait them out.

I remembered when I was in bureau training standing in the back of a Quantico training room where the Washington, DC director addressed us newbies.

"Few create change," he said. "That's what we must do: upset the status quo, evoke chaos; simply put, create change."

Sometimes it's best to just do what comes naturally, not knowing how it will affect others. Just being yourself, doing you. The group I would join after coming back from the Middle East pitted people and groups against each other. We did this across countries where our interests were challenged.

Change affords conflict; whether political, religious, person to person, and nation to nation, the conflict results in change. The question is: was the change worth the conflict? Did it make one's life better, easier, more fulfilling? Or did it break down society and make a person start over? Life redefined by worldly change can result in a person's best life if one accepts the new normal and moves forward.

Another day passed with the unrelenting sandstorm, and, still, no returned desert guide.

Overnight, I'd determined that the only way to get the sailors to give me more information would be for me to not let them go. If I could make them stay, I could use their getting out safely as the catalyst to create that change.

There was much to be done before Taylor and his companion awoke. I searched out my friend, the proud owner of my Timex watch.

These nomads of the desert may not have the modern conveniences of the twentieth century, but their creativity and work ethic far surpassed many of my colleagues back home.

I needed to find out when my guide would be back. There was no one in this working circle of women who would understand me. I had to ask one of the elders. This would need to wait, as work had to be done before any of them would be available. I kept my eye on the tent where the two 'visitors' were sleeping and started to rake my own blanket.

About an hour later I heard Taylor and the younger American talking to each other. They were trying to figure out when to leave. Both knew there was no possible way of surviving in this desert without a proper guide. They also had to be able to pay that person, but with what? Information wasn't a currency to the Bedouin people. Food, coal, wood, water, donkeys, and camels were all valuable commodities that would result in producing a guide that would get them back to civilization. The idea of going out on their own would surely be their demise. I sat back, waiting for the precise moment when I would strike a bargain.

Taylor got up and announced that he needed to go to the bathroom. He communicated his urgent need to one of the guards. As he left the tent, I knew this was the time to start negotiating with the younger man, the Navy SEAL—probably in his twenties, probably no older than I was.

"How do you plan to get back to the border?"

After a few seconds, he replied, "With you."

"That depends. I need more information from you and your superior or that won't happen."

He looked at me blankly. "What do you mean, that won't happen?"

"You will not come with me and my guide. You'll need to figure something else out."

"But we gave you important information. What? Do you need more?"

"You're a smart guy," I said looking at him without emotion. "You know more than you're letting on. I want facts that you have, and if you want to leave here with me, write out all you know and give it to me before the morning. Once I've read what you've provided, then we can discuss whether you two can leave with me."

"I can't. I would be disobeying a direct order."

"That's for you to work out, but the longer you wait, the troops you're trying to protect are in harm's way when we can help them. Seems to me that's disobeying a higher direct order, don't you think?"

He sat back, leaning on some ornately embroidered pillows. Time to think. Time to choose smartly. Now I needed to do the same and see how this would unfold. My gut told me that here was a young man who was idealistic. He'd want to be able to tell his parents he helped save his fellow sailors and protected our assets in Yemen. He would be very proud of himself, knowing he participated in thwarting capture and possibly death there, as opposed to playing the role of delivery man. So how could he earn his stripes conveying information instead of eyeing the enemy and taking them out?

Sit back, I told myself. *And wait.*

The young man kept his eyes fixed downward toward the jacket he had wrapped around himself during the night. It was now tossed on the floor as if it didn't matter. I felt it was the opposite of that. It must contain something important. I knew he was trying to get me not to think about him or his jacket, but he couldn't have been more unsuccessful. People are obvious if you let them be. Watch, listen, ask questions, and be prepared to interpret responses in words, body language, and facial expressions.

"Do you mind?" I asked, as I reached for his jacket. "I'm cold, and yours looks a lot warmer than mine."

I reached for the sleeve of his black-leather flight jacket and pulled it close to my chest. What could he do but watch, hoping I wouldn't feel around in the pockets or put my fingers in the center top flaps? I started to curl up with the sheepskin inner lining draped around me; he looked unnerved.

"Do you want it back?" I asked, innocently.

"Uh, no. Not now," he replied in an overtly detached way so as not to be obvious, which it was. *This guy would never hold his own in the field*, I thought, clutching the warm lining around me so that I could feel into the pockets when the time was right.

A few minutes passed and I could feel his eyes on me.

This had to mean he was going to ask for it back despite how unchivalrous the act would be. I had to work fast.

Moving from my right side to my left, I reached my left hand into the pocket, keeping my right arm visible. I adjusted the heavy jacket across my right shoulder. Nothing in that pocket. The front was folded inward. I went through the top and bottom flaps. Nothing in these. I started to curl up on my left side and saw a zipper in the lining running from the top near my shoulder. This had to be it. There must be something in the jacket liner, not in the pockets.

My mind raced with ideas on how to get to what secret was hidden there, but how to avoid giving away what I was planning to do? His partner wasn't back yet, but he might be any minute.

The two camp guards moved past the young sailor toward the flap leading outside. I clutched the inner-lining zipper and tugged. It was right there underneath the zipper. A piece of paper. The jagged edges were rough against the fleshy part of my fingers. There wasn't any time to search for more. This had to be something, and I prayed it was what I needed.

With the guards now outside, the Navy SEAL looked at me, trying to determine whether I really was cold and needed his jacket. He couldn't take it anymore. The guards were gone, and his immediate commander wasn't back, so the timing was right for him to talk to me.

"Excuse me. Might I have my jacket back? Looks like you warmed up some."

I didn't reply. Was he just trying to make conversation? I wanted to see him squirm, knowing that would mean there was something inside his jacket that he wanted back. It's funny how easy it is to make another person uncomfortable. A stare, a look of disgust or of curiosity all can create an air of discomfort between two people. It's much harder to make someone feel at ease, especially when that person is trained to be cognizant at all times. "Never let your guard down" was a saying I'd heard throughout my Quantico training.

Time to create a friendly environment. All I needed to do was give him his jacket, or, at least, I hoped that would be the result. I shifted my position, nestling further in the pillows, and there he was, holding a blanket out toward me. An exchange of sorts was my immediate thought. I rose to a sitting position, smiled, and said, "That's so nice of you. Thank you." I took the blanket and handed him his flight jacket.

No time wasted. The guards returned to the tent with Taylor. The two sailors spoke quietly, and though I couldn't hear their exact words, I could tell that Taylor, the ranking officer, was annoyed. With a stern posture and voice to match, he told the younger man to get up and get moving. Where were they going? The guards looked uninterested, which made me believe they didn't understand what Taylor said and weren't involved in his plans.

"You." Taylor pointed at me. "Get up. You're coming with us."

Now I quickly tried to get the guards to understand what was going on.

"I'm not going with you," I said firmly, as I planted my behind squarely on the pillows underneath me and my newly procured blanket. But he came at me as if to pull me up to a standing position. I rolled to the side, and he grabbed my legs, trying to twist me back to a front-facing position. The guards jumped on him: one from behind, while the other grabbed his legs, lunging directly toward the back of his kneecaps. Taylor got one guard off his back, but he couldn't grab him from his position. His face had smashed directly down into the pillows where I'd been lying.

Taylor had released my leg sometime between his jumping on me and his latest efforts to lunge at me. I climbed to my feet ready to help, but instead of getting into a fight that the guards were winning, I focused on the younger American.

He hadn't moved. Sitting with his jacket pulled around his chest, he watched his superior try to fend off the two Bedouin guards. Never had I seen a sailor not help his fellow sailor, especially an officer. Clearly there was more to this situation, but what was it? Perhaps there was more to this guy than I'd originally thought. He wasn't acting like a military man. Maybe he wasn't one after all. None of his responses, verbal or physical, lined up with what I believed would be a true military action. I saw defiance in his eyes, generally not a sign shown to a superior.

"Come with me now," Taylor blared. He tried to pull me toward him, aggressively grabbing my sleeve. The guards reacted quickly, pushing him to the ground.

My heart beat faster than I wanted to admit. Who was this American officer flailing on the floor and who was the young man who had so graciously given me his jacket?

As the guards pulled him upright to his knees, Taylor directed his anger toward his comrade. "Why are you standing there? Leave now. I am ordering you to leave."

The resolve to disobey was evident to the point that Taylor, despite being restrained, said in a steady voice, "I gave you an order."

The young man looked directly at his superior and said, "I don't take orders from criminals."

I was watching a mutiny of sorts, a "there is nothing you can do to me, but there is much I can do to you."

Now, not controlling his sudden change into power, the

young man said, more to all of us in the tent than to Taylor. "You won't get away with any of it. Not now."

The guards hoisted Taylor to his feet, one on either side, and marched him out of the tent. He gave one last look to his subordinate and to me, and drew up a huge wad of spit and fired it toward the young man. Disgusted with Taylor, the guards dragged him through the flaps to the outside and, my guess, directly to the elders for guidance as to what to do next. The young man and I were in mild shock over the repulsive act of the now-captive officer.

"Let me help you," I said, reaching for a cloth and wash bowl kept in the corner. We used this to wash our hands before and after eating and before going to sleep. He pulled his shirt off, then his undershirt, trying to get away from the soiled clothing. I handed him the bowl and wet the towel, placing it in his open hand.

"Thank you," he said quietly.

"No problem," I replied.

I took the clothes, rolled them into a ball, and removed them from the tent. When I returned, he was still washing his face and hands, methodically, as if he couldn't wash away the revolting act that he'd just endured.

"Are you all right?" he asked.

Why would he ask me that? Then I noticed his eyes were on my shirt. The sleeve had been ripped from my shoulder.

"I hadn't noticed, but I'm fine. You're the one who needs another shirt." I handed him my sweatshirt.

He fought with the collar of the shirt. The opening was too small for his head. He handed it back to me. "It's too small, but thanks anyway." He slipped on his jacket, then, after an awkward pause, asked, "Who are you?"

"What do you mean? You two came here to see me. You

know who I am."

"No. I don't. Maybe Taylor did, but I don't."

"I'm the one person who can help you now. The people I work for, that's your country and mine. Tell me what the plan was, and I'll get you home."

He shifted his weight and rocked back and forth.

I stood motionless, silent, waiting.

"That's what he told me. Taylor said if I helped him, he would get me out on an honorable discharge and home before Thanksgiving."

"I'm not Taylor, but I'm telling you the truth. Why else would you be here if he didn't know who I was and that he would give me information to pass along? I'm the person who can make that promise and fulfill it, but it's your choice."

The elderly woman who now proudly wore my Timex entered the tent.

"Let me show you something I gave to her." I pointed at her wrist. "She's my friend. She trusts me without speaking the same language; we trust each other. Let me help you."

Silence.

The Timex lady handed him a long robe-like top. He gently took it from her hands. She left as quickly as she'd come. It was back to the two of us in the tent.

His name was Campbell. He was a Navy SEAL/Special Ops deep-sea diver and trainer. I was now going to hear his story: where he came from, how he got into this situation, and what Taylor's plan was.

22

Campbell's Story

Sinai Desert, 1989

He tried to fight emotion, but clearly there was a sadness to him. Campbell left an alcohol-fueled home to join the navy as soon as he turned eighteen.

There was no joy in his childhood memories except for the junior dance at Stephenson High School in Wichita, Kansas, with the girl of his dreams. "One more dance, even if it was the last," he said, as his mind trailed back to the memory of her face and the smell of her light-brown hair as she rested her head on his shoulder, swaying in time to the music. The song was Lionel Richie's "Just to Be Close to You."

He lowered his head as he described the last time he saw her, when the dance ended and her father picked her up to take her home safely. All that would change. They didn't make it home. If he'd been able to drive her, maybe they'd both still be alive, and he could have the life he dreamed about.

He didn't even know what had happened until he took the bus the next morning to his weekend job at the 'Savemore' on Blecher Street. The smashed cars were still on display. The tire marks fresh on the asphalt. Yellow tape surrounded the corner where the car had jumped the sidewalk, and the downed light pole, bent like a hunched back. The other car's front end pushed halfway through the passenger door of their car.

No one knew any details until later that afternoon when one of the church ladies came in to grab some staples for her Sunday dinner. That's when he learned about the victims. He then walked out of the store and never looked back. A one-way bus ticket to the neighboring town, a short visit to the navy recruitment office, and a signature in exchange for a room, hot shower, and warm meal.

Nothing from the past would prepare him for naval life. The discipline was necessary, but far from what he understood. As a child and teen, he'd been left alone more than he'd been supervised. He had what he thought was 'self-discipline,' but that barely registered on the navy scale. Knowing you had a place to sleep, three hot meals a day, and were run physically to the point you didn't have to think of anyone or anything but getting through the next drill was what Campbell needed. Not to think. Not to remember.

At night he slept soundly, but only because he was completely exhausted. The time had come to push past all the 'what if's' and go it alone. The drills tested his strength past what he thought he was capable of accomplishing. He was named "Drill Lead" because he'd rank number one or two in most drills on any given day. This gave him an opportunity to voice commands to the group. He tested his leadership skills and realized that others wanted the strength and perseverance he embodied.

"How do you do that?" he was asked by multiple sailors in various drills. The hundred sit-ups, hundred squats, fifty push-ups, all without taking more than ten seconds between sets. The many miles run when he'd hold the American flag at the front of the group, setting the pace for the five, ten or fifteen-mile cross-country drills. How could he explain to the others that he didn't think of anything except the task at hand? He had no friends among the kids he trained with. All were competition to him. All could replace him on the list of able-to-fight sailors, preventing him from leaving to wherever his corps would be deployed. My heart ached for him, but it was not my place to say anything nor to comfort him. I was there only to listen.

The hard work and consistently high scores afforded him many coveted assignments. This was where he found peace. During the first three years of deployment, he met many different types of soldiers and sailors: hardworking but not smart, smart but lazy, lazy and not smart. He also met black sailors, which was a first.

No one he knew in his hometown was black. Campbell had never known a person who looked different from him. Sure, he'd known people with brown hair and eyes, quite the opposite of his fair hair and bright blue eyes, but those folks were just as white as he was.

His bunkmate, Moses, was black. Though similar in build, his hair, eye, and skin color were foreign to Campbell. He marveled at how Moses picked his afro instead of brushing his hair. The stories from Campbell's youth prevented him from accepting Moses as his equal.

"They have tails like Jews," his grandmother explained to him when he was young. "Their blood is blue, not red like ours."

It wasn't until the night that Moses came from the shower holding a piece of toilet paper up to his cheek where he cut himself shaving that Campbell learned any differently. The white paper glistened with bright-crimson blood dotting through it.

"Your blood is red," Campbell blurted out.

Moses looked at him strangely. "What did you expect?"

Campbell felt ashamed of his thoughts. Clearly their blood was the same color. He'd been told all his young life that it was not the same, the marked differences planted firmly in his mind from the one person who supported him, nurtured him, and made him feel loved. Now he felt tricked. Another betrayal. It was difficult for Campbell to answer Moses's question. The shock on his face said it all. There really wasn't any way to hide his surprise.

"I just thought it was different."

"Different?" Moses asked, "How?"

"The color. I thought it was a different color."

Moses shook his head in disappointment. "You were probably told that. You think I have a tail too?" he said as he moved off his bunk and back to the bathroom to tend to his face.

Campbell lay there on his bunk, not wanting to face the fact that his past was going to keep him up for another restless night. More bad dreams. More haunted images. He decided since he wasn't going to get any sleep, he'd take someone's place standing guard at base camp. One lucky guy would get to sleep in his own cot tonight. This sort of action increased his likability with the troops.

It had taken some time, but everyone loved Campbell. He was a sailor's sailor, always volunteering to do more than his share. Little did his fellow sailors know why. The thoughts in his head would quiet down with his focus on the task at hand, but they never completely went away. It was days later that the sergeant called his name, pulling him out of the mess hall. Campbell was irritated. There were few breaks in the daily routine when soldiers could rest and eat; his time was being cut short. He entered the commander's office, annoyed, and sat in the narrow hallway on a cold metal chair waiting to be called in. The minutes felt like hours.

I get it, I thought to myself as he described his anxiety. My mind raced back to when I longed to be loved by any adult. Foster parents, nurses, teachers, even the abusive ones, it didn't matter. The feeling of constantly trying to prove myself to adults who might change my future course. Didn't matter if it was providing extra help in the house, doing extra-credit assignments in school, or outperforming my classmates at the bureau academy, I needed to be the best so that I could get out, move on, and move up.

My heart really did hurt for this lost young man. I wanted to make his pain subside, knowing all along that couldn't be done. We just must push through our personal hells, no matter what they are. There's no other option. We don't go through the hurdles to reach the other side thinking there's a reward.

"Campbell." The commander walked out from behind the door to his office and stood in front of him. Campbell stood at attention. "At ease. Go take a seat inside. I'll be back in a minute." Campbell felt as if something special was happening. Getting to sit before a meeting with military leadership was out of the ordinary.

When the door opened once again, he again stood at attention.

"At ease, sailor."

The commander sat down and rummaged through the paperwork on his desk, looking for his file on Campbell. "We have an assignment for you. Have you traveled to the Middle East before?"

"No, Sir."

"Then you'll find it of interest. I spent years there helping our friends develop core skills. We have some friends and many enemies over there. Not too many folks are in between. One side or the other. Our Seal teams have done a great job protecting our interests at sea and fighting off pirates who roam around looking for unprotected ships, but we need more assistance on land. There are times you'll want to come back, but it's going to help change the course of your career." He looked up from the open file and into Campbell's eyes. "It did for me, and it can for you."

Campbell had many questions; none were appropriate to ask here. "Yes, Sir. Thank you, Sir."

The commander got up to dismiss him. One last salute and Campbell was back out on the training fields.

About a month later, he was called out of a drill and told to pack his bunk. He was being reassigned. He was relocated to Coronado, where he trained with the Seals for eight months. He wasn't joining that elite unit but was one of five to be trained in underwater body retrieval and combat. Not understanding, never asking why, he just absorbed the training, adding more successful drills and record-breaking completions to his list of physical accomplishments, such as staying under water without air for eight minutes, without getting any signs of deadly bends or hydrophilic brain activity. It was as if he were inhuman.

The instructors had no explanation other than mind

over body. "Sometimes, we get these kids who can perform incredible physical acts, but not consistently. Campbell is not that person. Each time he drills, he does something we think can't be done twice."

The end of training spproached without any sign about when he would be deployed and to what part of the Middle East it would be. Patience was a virtue few military have until their first time in combat. Most then want to retreat to boot camp, never again to hear mortar fire, the last breath of their brothers, the loud crashing inside their heads from the concrete reverberating as the buildings implode around them. He waited it out, trying to better each drill time or master each physical feat until it became an unconscious reflex that he knew he would need in order to get out alive from whatever situation they placed him in

He was stationed near Yemen. In late October of 2000, the incident that would bring him into my life occurred, the attack on the *USS Cole*—one of the deadliest against a United States naval vessel since World War II.

But Campbell had experienced this sort of drama before. In 1987, during the Iran/Iraq war, the *USS Stark,* an American frigate in the Persian Gulf, was hit when an Iraqi jet fired two Exocet missiles at the ship, killing thirty-one crew members: twenty-nine from the initial explosion, and two lost at sea. Campbell was one of the divers who found those lost remains so families could have the closure they so respectfully deserved.

At that time, Saddam Hussein said the Iraqi jet pilot was not acting under orders from his government when he 'mistook' the *Stark* for an Iranian oil tanker. There was very little press on the *Stark* compared to the *Cole*. News was muted on the subject, reminiscent of the Vietnam War, when our leaders tried to hide the number of soldier casualties from the American people. No one wanted to see death on their television before or after dinner.

It was in that vacuum that Campbell and the others who were selected to retrieve their dead compatriots from the *Stark* went about their duty.

When it came to Yemen, he was the person that others in his unit came to for advice on the terrain, the people, and the sea. He would once again advise divers when the *USS Cole* was attacked, and more bodies needed to be recovered. Until that happened, he spent his time learning the language and customs of the different Yemenite tribes.

Campbell gained the trust of the local fishermen and became aware of the Russian arms-dealing that transpired on the docks where he liked to mingle when he was off base. Through these exchanges with the locals, he got involved with Taylor.

People from other countries dealing arms with Russia and trying to curry favor with United States Air and Naval authorities was a normal practice in Yemen and a risky proposition for any serviceman. As much as Campbell liked to upset the status quo, he didn't want to start befriending the men who were brokering these deals.

The problem was that he had a habit of pitting himself against others. One such confrontation ended in a fistfight where he was pulled off a local by several off-duty sailors. Campbell had to 'cool down' in the brig, and that's where he met Taylor, who was already a troublemaker.

Campbell and Taylor stayed up that night talking about their commissions, American interests, and where they were being challenged. Both men had different opinions about the armed forces and where they should be serving as peacekeepers and where they should not be. Both men wanted to help fight political unrest but steer clear of religious conflicts. It was also here where Taylor pitched his 'brig mate' on the notion of setting up the dockworker who had gotten Campbell arrested and help secure arms and ammunition to sell on the black market.

"The details will be saved for another time, but just say I got caught up in a scheme that I knew I needed to undo. I …" Campbell stopped in mid-sentence. "I knew when I met you that now I had a way to get out of this mess, and that you could help me come clean."

I'd heard his story—or most of it.

Campbell and I sat outside the hexagonal-shaped tent, close to the outdoor fire that helped keep the sentinels warm between rounds.

How and when would I be able to help Campbell? When would my guide return? I'd have to negotiate with him to take another person back to civilization with me. I reflected on Smith's words at my first training course at Quantico: "Figure out what is important to your target. What makes that person do what they do, who benefits and why?" Immediately my thought was that Campbell would benefit by breaking away from Taylor. The obstacle here was how to convince my guide that Campbell was worth helping.

My perception about almost everything since childhood was shaped by the need to survive. I focused on what could go wrong, always cognizant of potential danger. "Don't be surprised by anyone" was ingrained in me from the orphanage.

I told myself to look at what the situation presents itself to be—not the risk, but the outcome—to take control. I needed to control my apprehension, not to let it control me. When I made my way back to my tent, I was no longer consumed with the 'what ifs.'

Morning came with the usual routine of washing, rolling up my sleeping blankets, and waiting for daily work orders. But no wife or young woman appeared with instructions for me. Instead, my 'friend' with her Timex watch came into the tent with fruit and tea. I ate the dates, apples, and apricots with gusto. They were so sweet and delicious, I thought I was having dessert instead of breakfast! She smiled as she watched me eat, sharing in my joy at the appreciation of this simple, yet tasty meal. I felt so fortunate to have had this time with the Bedouins: to experience their kindness and willingness to help one another and the strangers who came through their camp.

I let her lead me outside the tent. She stood in front of me, apparently to shield me from the powerful wind. I had to trust in her sight; I couldn't see in front of me. But I could hear a distant yet familiar noise. The grunting of camels, the clinking of metal Turkish coffee cups and pots, the faint sound of men's voices spurring the camels on. It was time to go home. My guide had returned, and she knew. She smiled at me and pointed to the north. I smiled back, nodding to let her know I understood why she brought me outside. "Thank you," I said as I attempted to contain my excitement.

The group approached the outer perimeter of the camp. I could make out the silhouette of two tall men and three camels.

"We really need to talk to these guides and decide how we'll make it," Campbell said.

So now it was 'we.' If he came along, I would support it, but I wasn't going to stay here longer just to help him get out and back to the real world. There would have to be more to what he knew in Yemen to make it worth taking him. My guide would know what was best. He had to have an idea of the timeline for getting back to the town where he'd parked his old, beat-up truck.

***

How we got out of that desert alive was a miracle. Because of the extra person, the camel carried more weight than had originally been expected. This turned out to be very dangerous.

The legs of the eldest 'work horse' buckled under the hot sun. The painful sounds coming from the camel were like mourning for a loved one who had passed too quickly, unexpectantly. After several mournful wails, followed by a buckling, then stumbling from an animal that was too tired to take another step, she landed, front legs bent in a kneeling position, on the warm sand and closed her eyes.

The guide placed his gloved hands over her eyes and gently closed them. He held her neck steady with one hand and began to chant. As in Western civilization, an owner of any working animal truly respects what service they have performed for that person and his family. This was no different. The guide thanked her for the years of hard work by chanting and stroking her forehead. Then he shot her between the eyes.

Finally, after ten hours through and out of the desert, I lay safely on a cot in the familial home of our guide. I couldn't sleep, so I got up and walked to the doorway leading to the adjoining room where I could hear Campbell's drawn-out snores. The sleep of a hard day. Why hadn't I seen him as a man before now? I looked at him with a longing to touch him, and feelings of heat rushed through my legs toward my stomach, but I stopped myself. I had a job to do and couldn't get involved with him in that way. I returned to my tiny cot and tried to get a few more hours of sleep.

The next day, we would be heading back to Tel Aviv through Jerusalem, where parts of the highway were heavily patrolled due to the Arab Spring—the series of anti-government protests, uprisings, and armed rebellions that had spread across much of the Arab world.

The Israeli Army stayed on high alert, as bombings had occurred throughout the city—on buses, in marketplaces, at cafés on the clear clean beaches of Bat Yam, and in the densely populated old city of Jerusalem. People tried to ignore the signs that they lived in a place where ownership of the old city had been fought over since Christ's birth in Bethlehem. Men, women, children, and the elderly all had to stay aware; yet, as I'd witnessed before, most people accepted danger as routine.

There would be violence, untimely deaths, and unnatural loss, but life had to move forward, and people had work to do. Parents tried to smile at their little ones when they walked with them to school, not knowing if the stranger on the street or next to them on the local bus would pull the cord on a homemade bomb, annihilating them all. I felt a sadness for them as I had for Campbell, mixed with an admiration for being able to go on another day even if your heart is broken and your mind is fighting to keep the face of that person you lost alive in your head and heart.

I tried to go back to sleep, but still awake in the early morning, I couldn't stop thinking of how Campbell would feel inside me, kissing me, and holding me. I envisioned the school dance where he held his first love so tight and placed myself there as his partner, resting my head on his chest as we swayed to the innocent love songs played during that time. Could I bring joy back into his life? Into my life?

That was what we had together. The unspoken bond of our youth leaving too soon. People like us need to grow up fast to survive.

As he slept, twisting and turning, trying to make himself comfortable on the short, narrow loveseat, I wondered what Campbell was thinking—perhaps how nice it would be to lie next to the person who gave his life back to him or thinking he would be indebted to Taylor for the foreseeable future. Was his mind drifting in and out of their plans of setting up those innocent sailors for death, his pushing back on Taylor, and wanting to get out of the situation he knew was not for him? And now here he was on this small couch—out of the desert—Taylor exposed for the thief he was?

Could he be thinking of the young woman who knew there had to be something more under the surface he'd built to protect himself? Who was able to get it out of him? Did he see her as a mix of soft caramel, buttery beauty with strong nerve, unwavering resolve, and bravery that made him feel undeserving to be with her? Why would he want to be with this woman he barely knew?

I watched Campbell get up from the couch and pace back and forth. He looked out the small window across from the wooden table where the six men had eaten the night before. He could see the sun begin to light the sky. It was time for us to make our way back to civilization.

Our guide's family started to prepare for the day, and we began to gather our few belongings to continue the trip back from the Sinai. As common as kissing each other goodbye, the guide and his mother embraced, she shed a tear, not knowing he felt the same way.

He didn't know when he would return and worried for his sister, her husband, and their son. How much his nephew had grown in the five months since he'd been home, and now they would spend more time apart from each other.

"He will be walking by the time we see you next," his sister had said before going to sleep the night before. He hoped she was wrong and said that, after delivering us, he would turn around and come back home. He had no other assignment to make him go back into the desert before being together. He could really help his mother at home and sleep in his bed that he'd had since he was a teenager. Neither money nor work were important to him now, knowing his mother was getting weaker, not able to keep up with the daily demands of keeping a home, cooking, cleaning, and chasing after her beloved grandson. It was time for him to be a part of their daily lives and to be there for the expected daily drills that each community had. The bombings were becoming more common, even in remote towns like Kfar Sava.

It was time to get on the road. The clock read 5:40 a.m. The guide was still getting used to driving on streets again after navigating the ups and downs of the sand dunes. The truck was loaded up with tomatoes, rice, water, three sheep and one goat that he could bargain with along the way if he needed to. Getting to Jerusalem was a trek, but now it was dangerous in parts, which made for an adventure.

He and I climbed into the cab, and Campbell rode in the truck bed for the first leg of the trip, giving us some elbow room and a place for the lunch our guide's mother had made for us. Our guide looked back one more time at the small home where he'd grown up, and the hurt he felt leaving was almost unbearable. I could tell something was bothering him, but my instincts told me to listen if he spoke, but not ask any questions. The guide had been through many hours of travel the last few months, especially hard when he came home from the desert to learn that his mother was sick and had been hospitalized. The pain he must have felt, knowing he had to leave to take us back. Best to look out the truck's dirty window and try to figure out where we were based on the landmarks that I'd tried to remember from the trip out to the Sinai.

The sun was still rising, creating a bluish hue across the mountains. There was a calm in the air, and the road was clear, as most of the people were preparing for their day. We traveled eastbound through the small but heavily populated Arab outposts on the way to Jericho, where we could stop and stretch our legs before having to get back into the small vehicle and begin the final leg of our journey.

I tried sleeping, but the road was too bumpy. Each time I drifted off, my head was jarred from one side to the other. But I had no way of knowing just how badly Campbell was feeling in the truck bed. No matter how strong or manly you think you are, no one wants to be wedged between containers and livestock in the back of a truck. He barely had room to move with the boxes and sacks surrounding his small crawl space. I tried to wave to him through the cracked rearview mirror. No response.

About two hours into the ride, I thought we should check on him. "Can you pull over so we can check on Campbell?"

The guide was lost in his own thoughts, so I tapped him on the shoulder and asked again. He gestured yes, and we moved to the side of the road. I got out and walked toward the back of the truck. Being five foot two I couldn't see above the boxes, so I climbed up onto the back of the truck and tried to hold onto the rope in front of me.

The boxes started to move, and Campbell yelled, "Hey, don't move those. My head is right next to that box, and I don't want it crashing on top of me."

I laughed, knowing he was all right, just agitated due to his lack of space and mobility. "We just wanted to make sure you're still there," I said, trying to raise my voice so he could hear me over the makeshift barrier.

"Thanks, I'm good. Let's get back on the road."

My idea to check on him only added to the time he had to spend in the back, so I guess it wasn't such a great idea.

"We'll get back before it turns dark," said our driver. "But we can't stop again until we get to Jericho and refuel."

No one back home would ever think of my being here. My college friends and San Fernando Valley neighbors would never think that I was working for the government, collecting information that kept them safe. Being in a faraway country, not speaking the language fluently, but enough to get by, the image of me as a perfect student, quiet daughter, people-pleaser was tucked into the back of my brain. My thoughts of being two distinct people were swirling around in my head when we started to slow down.

I could see a line of trucks and a few cars. A traffic jam. Something that rarely happened here, but the line was at a stop. No one in front of us was moving. We tried to look out the windows on either side of the truck, and our driver started to swear in Arabic. He became quite heated, but over what I wasn't sure. It seemed like any holdup was an annoyance to him today. He wasn't in the mood to have his plan go awry.

The delay was caused by a camel train. These four-legged creatures, ten of them, ambled across the highway. A young Arab boy held a stick longer than his height and waved it back and forth while calling for the lead camel to follow him. His father, or maybe uncle, was at the rear with a brother or older son driving the tail end of the train.

More car and truck drivers yelled in unison, not happy with this lag. No one seemed to care that these animals were the mainstay of the economy. From agriculture to transportation, without the camels these desert people wouldn't be able to survive.

By the time the last camel cleared the pavement, more horns were blaring, the drivers shouting colorful words with fists raised at one another and at the old man shepherding the animals. The scene seemed to represent the transition between the old school way of life and the modern present-day realities.

The path finally cleared, and we started to pick up speed again. We cleared the city limits of Jericho and saw a flashing neon sign in the distance. This was strange to me as it's not a typical sight in this part of the world. The sign became clearer. "Gasoline, Petrol."

We'd reached the spot the driver had designated for fuel and food, and to let Campbell take time to stretch his legs and walk around, hoping he would regain sensation in his feet.

We pulled into a small two-pump gas station. Two older Arabs were sitting outside the concrete storefront, shelling pistachios with their broken teeth. They talked intermittently about their families, the weather, and whatever else came to mind as they spit out the shells.

I couldn't wait to get out and walk, although I felt guilty; I wasn't the one holed up in the back of the truck, surrounded by boxes and grain bags. I stepped onto the dirt, stretched, and looked around the station for a restroom. *Probably on the side of the building*, I thought, so I wandered over to the old men and asked. They pointed to a side door on the far end of the white cinder-block structure. "Back in a few," I shouted to Campbell and the guide and sauntered along to the can.

On shutting the door of the restroom, I thought I

should've asked Campbell if he wanted to go first, but he hadn't emerged from the truck bed yet. As I sat down on the toilet, a huge explosion rattled the block walls. I held my hands over my ears, realizing that a bomb, some type of improvised explosive device (IED), had detonated. I sat in the bathroom, paralyzed, not sure exactly where or what had exploded or if it was safe to exit.

I didn't know how long had passed since I'd heard the deafening sound. Everything was foggy. I cleared the few pieces of cinder block that had fallen after the explosion and pried open the door a few inches. The smell of burning fuel and flesh overpowered me. The smoke was so thick, it stung my eyes. I tried to turn on the faucet, but nothing came out. The only water left was in the toilet. I figured it was clean enough, so I wet some paper towels and covered my face, leaving a few inches open so I could see. I covered my hands by stuffing some more of the towels under my long-sleeved sweatshirt. I hesitated to leave, but I had to assess what had happened and find out whether Campbell and our driver were hurt.

The ground was dotted with burning pieces of wood, metal, and torn flesh. No sounds emerged from the side of the building. I hung close to the block walls that were still standing, trying my best to see through the dense smoke, blacker than I'd ever been in before. No sounds, no screaming; nobody made any noise. I tried to call out their names, but the smoke choked back my words. I was standing back against the wall trying to shout out again when a hand touched my shoulder. It was Campbell.

He had a torn shirt, stained with blood, but he was in one piece. "We have to run," he said as he grabbed my hand. "Run!"

I ran as fast I could, knowing this was life or death, but from whom or what was I running? We passed the fence that had been torn away from the blast and down the highway where red lights approached from the distance. The farther we could get from the station, the better.

We got to the other side of the road and were just starting to catch our breath when the ground shook and fire blew up into the sky. The fumes were overwhelming. I grabbed the wet towels stuffed into my waist and handed a wad to Campbell. He took half of them and covered his face so he could breathe through them and put the other half under his torn t-shirt. We would have passed out from the fumes without them. I slumped down onto the side of the road, exhausted from running and the shock of the explosion. All I could make out was the stream of fire rising in the sky.

The fuel tanks had erupted, making it too dangerous to go back and look for survivors. My heart beat so fast I thought it would jump out of my body. Campbell stood next to me shielding his eyes and trying to figure out how far we were from the station and whether we should keep running. We'd run at least half a mile. My eyes were burning through the damp paper towels. I could barely see.

"Take my hand," Campbell said with a sense of urgency, and he pulled me further away from the burning gas station. "We need to get up aways. I see red lights."

Cars would be up ahead, maybe we could flag one down. I had no idea how Campbell was. The tears in his t-shirt revealed the bloody wounds on his chest. Once I saw how badly hurt he was, I couldn't believe how far we'd made it from the site. One thing about him I understood was that he had no quit in him. Anyone who was lucky enough to get to know him, earn his trust, and be a part of his team said the same. He always figured out a way to survive. Not just him, but any person on his team knew that, if they waited it out, he would find them and bring them to safety. Later, my admiration grew when I heard these stories, knowing I'd spent time with a true hero.

The lights ahead got brighter and bigger. I could tell we didn't have far to go before we could flag down a car or emergency responder. Campbell had been right about running toward the red lights. An army transport blocked the road, making it impossible for vehicles to approach the bomb site.

"Help!" Campbell let go of my hand and started waving his around, showing that he wasn't armed. One soldier heard us and turned around. I was crouched down, knees on the hot pavement, head foggy as I tried to catch my breath after running with Campbell toward the red lights.

"Help. We're hurt!"

The soldiers ran toward us. I looked up just in time to see Campbell, my teammate, collapse into their arms. He'd lost a lot of blood and was unconscious. They called for a medic. One of them lowered him to the ground, and the other soldier got close enough to me to notice I was a young woman.

He backed up like something was wrong and yelled for another member of his platoon to come over. It was a young female, who gently told me in a heavy accent, "You're safe. I'm here."

I remember being lifted onto their transport along with Campbell. The female soldier never left my side, watching every move the medic and other males in the vehicle made toward me. It was interesting how the army handled women even back then. We were given different, but not special, treatment by the IDF.

My eyes watered uncontrollably. I tried to raise my head to get one last look at the burning location. The two old men sitting outside of the storefront were gone. My guide, our driver, was also gone. No way would he have made it. It broke my heart thinking of what his mother would experience once she was told her eldest son was dead, killed in a bombing while taking us back to the city. I prayed that night, lying in the King David Hospital on the far west side of Jerusalem, that her daughter, son-in-law, and grandson would give her the strength she would need to go on. Not knowing how many others had died, I tried to get the image of my guide's face out of my head.

The next morning when I opened my eyes I saw a nurse tending to my IV.

"Do you know where the man is who was brought here with me?" She looked quizzically at me.

"Wait, please," she said, leaving the room.

She returned with a male soldier. "Hello. The nurse does not speak English, but she understands you. When you are more rested, I'll take you to see him."

"Is he okay?"

The soldier looked at me, now realizing I had no idea how bad Campbell's condition was. "He's lost much blood. At this point, the doctors don't know."

I sat up immediately. "Take me to him. Please."

He looked at the nurse.

"Please," I said as I looked back at them, trying my best to hold it together.

The soldier left the room and returned with a wheelchair. The nurse positioned the IV bag on a mobile cart and untangled my tubes leading to and from the two bags of clear fluid I was being administered. The soldier told me to put my legs over the side of the bed and roll onto my side. The nurse then lifted my head as he helped lift my left side until I was sitting up.

My head was heavy; it was a true burden keeping it upright. I'd never felt like this, struggling to keep my head up, as if it wasn't attached to my body. It was the strangest feeling, having to make a conscious, concerted effort to keep my head from toppling to one side or the other.

"You have a severe concussion. The doctor needs to examine you before I can tell you if you can see your friend."

I followed the doctor's instructions, looking directly ahead at the white wall as he checked each of my eyes for signs of dilation. Then he checked my ears to verify that no blood was coming out or going into my inner-ear tubes. He asked me how many fingers he was holding up.

"Two, four, one," I answered. My patience grew thin. I wanted to wheel myself down the hall to where Campbell was but knew I could not. I tried to quiet my mind, thinking I'd see him soon and figure out when we'd be getting out of here.

"Okay. She can go have a short visit. Five minutes, no longer," the doctor instructed the nurse and soldier. "

Toda," I replied, shaking his hand to show my gratitude.

We wheeled down the hall to the elevator without seeing any other patients. One long sterile corridor led to another with no people around. That was strange. We turned left at the elevator, not using it, and went down another long hallway, nobody but the three of us in sight until we got toward the end of the hall. Two armed soldiers stood at the entrance. No windows, no sounds, just us wheeling across the gray-and-white-flecked linoleum flooring. Soldiers were standing guard outside his room. Inside, Campbell fought for his life.

Machines monitored his heart. A thick bandage covered his head and right eye. Not a good sign. He lay motionless. The sound of the respirator, the ticking of the electrocardiogram machine, and the slow drip of the single IV were the only sounds that came from the room. They wheeled me closer to him, but I could tell they were trying to position me far enough away so I couldn't get a real view of his face. "Closer." I needed to get to where I could talk to him. They pushed me as close as they could to the side of his bed clear from the equipment he was hooked up to. Then they left, leaving just the two of us in his room.

Something compelled me to take my right hand that wasn't hooked up to my IV and wheel myself. I was determined to get next to him. I tried to conceal any emotion for fear he'd pick up on it, even though I sensed he wasn't present. The respirator was working overtime. Could he feel me near him? I got as close to the side of the bed as I could, but the wheelchair made it difficult; it kept striking the cold metal bar that prevented all the wires and tubes from tangling up.

My hands were cold. I tried to warm them up before reaching out for his fingers. He didn't move. My mind raced, trying to recall every moment since I'd met Campbell.

"I can tell you're listening," I whispered. My heart hurt. He wasn't moving; no response. I once heard that when people are in a comatose state, they can hear.

"I'll be back as soon as I get us some help. We've got to get out of here," I said, squeezing his right hand hard, trying to get him to open his eyes. There was no reaction.

I looked around for a telephone, but the only things in the room were medical equipment. I scanned the devices and saw a long cord originating from the back of the bed. A call button. Perfect. I bent forward, trying to grab the cord, but my head felt as though it would explode. I couldn't move as quickly as my mind told me to. I sat back, eyeing the cord, then closed my eyes, trying to visualize a solution. There had to be a way to get that buzzer. Then it occurred to me that, even if I did, would someone come for me?

I opened my eyes and let my left hand move down the wheelchair seat toward the footrest without moving my head too quickly. I found the brake and released it. Now I needed to let go of Campbell's hand to lift the other brake. My fingers unclasped his hand, and I tried sliding my hand from under his heavy palm. He moved his fingers as I removed mine. Trying not to alarm him, I said, "I'll be right back. I won't be long." With that, I held my head upright and pushed the wheels back so I could turn around and face the doorway.

I rolled into the hall. No one was around. There were no windows and only a few doors ahead. I wheeled up to the first door. Locked. Then the second and third. Both locked. Time to pick another hallway. Back I went until I got to the middle of what appeared to be a laboratory. The glass jars and bottles had many different plants inside. Liquids bubbled in tall, wide vessels. I looked around the room. The doorway was open; no sounds came from inside except the gurgling of colored liquids. No human noises. We needed someone to help us, but no one was around.

I slowly got up from the wheelchair and steadied myself by holding onto the solid tabletop, trying to hold my head in alignment with my body. I hadn't stood up in a while, but for how long I wasn't sure.

Time to act. If I approached the bubbling containers, a camera must see me or a motion detector would go off and then somebody would have to come. I reached out to the glass tube closest to me and gave it a shove, spilling its golden-green contents across the white Formica tabletop. An alarm immediately sounded, followed by blue-and-red lights flashing over the doorway and splashing their colors on the blank white walls.

I sat back in my wheelchair, took a deep breath, and counted backward from ten. I hadn't reached seven when two guards burst into the room. They looked disappointed when they saw me.

"You need to go back to your room," one said with a thick accent.

"I will when you let me make a call."

"You don't tell us what to do; we tell you."

"I need to make a call, please."

Just then, the doctor who had given me permission to see Campbell arrived in the lab. "I will take her back," he told the guards as he commandeered my wheelchair, steering it from the back, pulling me out of the room.

"Thank you," I said to the doctor.

"Don't talk; just stay calm," he said.

We moved quickly down the hallway to an area near the loading dock. He opened the doors, one after another, revealing laundry trucks coming in and out of the facility. There were very few people, mostly trucks. No soldiers were present. I stayed silent and tried to count the trucks, the doors we went through, and the number of workers I saw. Nothing made sense, my head felt like my heart, both beating fast to two different irregular pulses. Would he help us out of there?

This question went unspoken. At the end of the loading dock, stood a van, side door open, with Campbell lying still on a gurney beside it. No tubes attached. I wanted to yell and scream out loud, but I knew it wouldn't matter. He was dead.

Now my only thought was that we were leaving this place,

but not the way we'd come, not how I'd promised him. As the doctor helped load me into the van, he whispered to me, "He was dead before he got here, understand?"

No words came to mind that I wanted to say to the person who was supposed to help us, heal us, save us from the damage caused by the Arab or Yemeni terrorists who blew up my guide along with others in Jericho. I knew he was only trying to help me let go of Campbell, but I'd seen Campbell's tears, had felt him fighting to recover, and had promised we'd leave here together.

Now we would be going home, but just one of us would ride in an airplane seat. The other would ride where the military transported our fallen heroes—in the cargo section, his coffin draped in an American flag.

23

A Mother's Son

Los Angeles, California
1993

One year after returning from the Sinai, I was pregnant. I'd left one kind of desert for another—back to a married life that was dry, without any joy. Daniel's and my beautiful baby boy, Evan, brought happiness into a home that previously had none. But then the real estate market crashed—the beginning of a recession, where mortgage interest rates were 10 percent.

Daniel lost his job as a residential architect. He spent his time sitting on our couch staring, expressionless, into the television set while his mother stepped in to help take care of her grandson. My days were spent working at the West Los Angeles Federal Building. Waking up at 5:30 a.m., feeding our son, driving thirty miles to work, then putting in the full day of any typical worker. Driving back home, making dinner, feeding and bathing our baby, holding him until he went to sleep, and then passing out from exhaustion only to wake up and repeat the same routine.

My body wasn't the same. I was hormonal, agitated, unhappy. I resented my husband's laziness. He knew my job (as he knew it to be) provided insurance that covered all of us, so he lacked the motivation that most responsible husbands and fathers innately feel to provide for their families.

Most families didn't have two incomes. My college friends stayed home rearing their children. That was their job, just like my mother had raised me. But I'd always had some type of job. At eleven years old, I was babysitting, then working downtown for my father's friends who owned clothing stores and needed help on the weekends. By the time I was in high school, evening babysitting was a regular thing; throughout college I worked on campus, or at night as a word processor before being recruited by the FBI.

Fortunately, Daniel's and my home situation improved as the spring turned into summer. Eventually, Daniel got some surveying jobs, which led to architectural supervision and to a point where he was so busy that he needed to hire a few people and could create his own company.

One summer afternoon, when Evan was nearly two years old, the three of us went to Disneyland with some friends who had a daughter just a few months older than our son. The temperature was approaching 100 degrees, and the children became cranky. As we stood in line to ride "Dumbo's Flying Elephant," my hot, sweating son started having a fit, wanting to get out of his stroller. He cried unconsolably. I suggested we leave, but his dad wanted to stay. He raised his voice and told me to do something about our son's screaming.

"He needs to get out of this heat," I said, trying to control my voice in public.

"If he stopped crying, he'd be fine," Daniel snapped back, not understanding that the heat was probably why the boy's crying had grown to a fevered pitch. "Once he's on the ride, he'll be fine."

"I doubt he knows or cares about this ride," I said while trying to hold onto a screaming, squirming toddler.

Daniel pushed the stroller right into my shins, the force of which almost made me drop my son. Below the left knee, my skin started to swell. I limped off holding on to Evan, trying to find a shady place to sit.

I sat down under a tree with Evan, but Daniel stormed up to us, commanding me to get back in line because he needed to cool down in the shade, not caring that he'd hurt my leg or that I needed to cool down, too, since I'd been holding our child in the hot sun for the past half hour. Daniel sat down, pushing me out of the shady spot under the tree. Since I didn't want to cause a scene, I got up, and it was then that he kicked me from behind. I fell, scuffing my right knee and elbow. Bleeding and embarrassed, I went to find a bathroom.

There was no way our friends, as well as the other people who were around us, didn't see what had just happened. So much for visiting Disneyland, the 'happiest place on earth.' As I was washing off my elbow, my friend came into the restroom.

"Are you all right?"

"I'm good."

But we both knew that wasn't true.

Too many times I'd fought off the warning signs that I was in a bad marriage. I'd pushed them out of my mind, not paying them the attention they deserved. That day at Disneyland I should have walked away with my son, but I didn't. Instead, I did what I usually did—I buried myself in my work. Would we need to put him in daycare, or would my mother help fill in so my son wouldn't feel a void as I had as a child? One of my greatest fears was my son's safety. Maybe that's because I saw the world differently from most because of my job. I wanted to keep Evan home where he'd be taken care of by someone who loved him.

Daniel's mother worked as a bookkeeper and helped us on weekends or at night after her workday. She was incredible with Evan. Knowing exactly what to do before it was needed, she rocked him, fed him, read to him. Shortly after he was born, she crocheted a baby blanket for him. I loved coming home and going upstairs to find her with him. Watching her lull our boy to sleep in the rocking chair, the green and blue blanket draped on her lap to keep them both warm, was an image I kept returning to when I was away working. My mother, on the other hand, had little time to spend with my son or to be concerned for his wellbeing. Her own son kept her plenty busy. My brother.

When it came to being a 'handful,' Jeremy was all that. Adopted at birth, he exhibited signs of restlessness as a baby. Back in the mid-1960s, no one thought to test mothers for drug consumption while pregnant, so who's to say why he had the issues he did? We grew up with the same opportunities, same schools, same home, same supportive parents. For me, school was a haven, a positive experience that I embraced each day. For him, it was torture. His only goal was to figure out how to ditch class differently each day without getting caught. The kids he gravitated to were troublemakers. Then the pot smoking started, followed by getting kicked out of two local high schools.

College wasn't in the cards for him, not even community

college, where he would have been able to learn a trade. He could take apart things and reassemble them. This talent was either self-taught or innate. I could read a Shakespeare play and write about its theme, but putting together an engine was something I couldn't comprehend. Although I was three and a half years older, we'd played together, eaten together, swam together, slept in the same home, and shared the same parents. But we were worlds apart from one other. Our connection was incomplete.

While Jeremy was content to play with his GI Joe action figures, I read. While he enjoyed having his toys fight, I consumed books: everything from Nancy Drew to biographies about Martin Luther King, Queen Elizabeth, and Helen Keller.

When we were both children, my mother kept her disappointment about Jeremy inside herself and focused on me—her first adopted child—as her conduit to achievement.

The orphanage told her that my IQ was higher than the average eight-year-old, so the books I read, the music I listened to, and the puzzles she encouraged me to piece together were far too advanced for my age. But competition fueled me, and she rewarded my efforts with praise: "You can do this." And I did it to please her.

I didn't worry or think about Jeremy when I was living in my dorm room at college or once I moved to DC. When I called home, I'd get the inevitable report that there had been another issue at school, another fight with a neighbor's child, or a run-in with authorities.

It got worse. Counselors were enlisted and therapy initiated, all with the goal of finding answers for his behavioral problems. Where did the anger and defiance come from and why couldn't they control him? Why couldn't my parents have two smart, well-mannered high achievers as children? Why was it so difficult for him to be good? No answers came from the thousands of dollars spent in search of the reasons for his destructive actions toward others and himself.

Most eighteen-year-olds would have loved moving from our quiet San Fernando Valley suburb to the cool beach community of Santa Barbara. Here was a local school that would be able to assess Jeremy's skills and position him for a job where he could make a living. Not low-income, but a respectable blue-collar profession that would offer him the opportunity to be self-sufficient.

The answers came slowly. Maybe that's why Jeremy fell into the biker world and became absorbed into another family unit. A world with countless violent acts toward those outside the 'family' or those who threatened their incomes, usually derived from illegal activities. If that wasn't enough, there was a harboring resentment toward our parents for 'not understanding' him.

As we drove home in the early morning hours after my bailing him out of the Los Angeles Men's Jail for the second time, he told me, "Mom and Dad never treated me right. They just care about themselves. They wanted us so they could fit in with their friends. We were never a family."

Jeremy's words stung as painfully as any feeling I'd felt since I was an orphan in Kansas. He went on and on about how much he hated our parents. Part of me wanted to scream at the top of my lungs in anger and condemn his words, but the other and stronger part of me was about self-preservation. If he could talk that way about two caring people who turned their lives upside down to help him, what did he think of me, and what would his new 'family' do to me? Would they think I was a threat? Would they come after me or just use me for money and a free ride once he was out of jail? I wanted to remove myself from the situation and give him the space to lead his new adult life away from me. Without me. So I listened while I drove down the 101 and exited at Topanga Canyon where I was to drop him off at some buddy's bike shop where he'd meet up with his new brothers.

As I turned onto Ingomar Street and toward the mechanic shop, I felt an overwhelming sadness. There was no hug, no brotherly kiss, no thank you.

"I'll pay you back when I get a job. Are you good with that?"

"Sure," I replied, knowing I'd never see that money again and wondering whether staying in touch with him was good for me and my son. He shut the passenger door to my 1990 Cherokee, turned away from the car and walked into the motorcycle shop where he was greeted with back slaps by his fellow Oxnard 'Angels.'

I backed out of the driveway, wanting to see him in his element. He moved to the front of my car, holding up his hands, signaling me to stop. I rolled down the window.

"Don't tell Mom and Dad where I am. I don't want to talk to them." As I rolled up the window, he came to the driver's side and leaned into the open space between the glass and the molding.

"Do you have some money? I can really use a beer."

I reached into my purse and pulled out a folded ten-dollar bill and handed it to him.

"Is that all you have?"

"That's all, sorry."

Driving away, I was relieved to be out of his environment and that he was with his chosen family. I had no love for him, only pity for the bad choices he continued making.

Weeks later, I brought my son over to visit my parents. As I held Evan with one arm, trying to push the screen door open with the other, I overheard my mother talking to my father.

"I don't understand why he doesn't call us," she said, as they sat at the dining-room table still sipping their morning coffee after breakfast. It was a Saturday, and my mother's birthday was right around the corner.

"He will," my father said, trying to reassure my mother. "Probably later this week, knowing it's your birthday."

I couldn't help but hear the uncertainty in his voice. Too many birthdays, anniversaries, and significant life events had occurred where no call came, no card, no acknowledgment of them as his parents or that he even considered them part of his life. Unless he needed money. Then he'd call, and they would be grateful that all was forgiven. No mention that he had forgotten them all year until he needed help. For them, any connection with Jeremy proved to be so emotionally great a good that it overrode all the sadness and hurt that he caused leading up to those one or two calls per year.

He called while I was visiting. My mother answered the phone.

"Are you close by? Why not come over and I'll make you lunch? Oh. That would be fine … see you on Monday at the bank. Okay, honey."

It was too hard to listen to, so I pretended to be busy reading a book to my son in my old bedroom.

Jeremy always showed up to get money. Most of the time he'd meet my parents at their bank. Then he'd leave, ungrateful, and be out of their lives until his next problem arose and he needed their assistance.

When I left my parents' house, I realized my mother's time, however misspent, was going to be focused on her son.

She was determined to bring him back into their life. I knew I would do the same if it were my own son. I couldn't fault her, but I couldn't witness the pain that eventually occurred.

The next week I found a suitable daycare halfway between work and home and enrolled my son.

24

Arghandad District: Testing of a Team

Kandahar Province, Afghanistan
1999

In my line of work, each team was assembled by the director, each member having special skills needed to accomplish the mission. Teams were united with one common goal: achieve the objective with no casualties.

Teams didn't just take the place of family; they were family 24/7. It was imperative to be completely transparent with one another, to build the type of trust that could save your life or theirs. I had to build bonds with any team family so I could increase my odds of safely getting back home to my son. The importance of finding the right mix of team members and of bonding was tested and validated again on a mission in Afghanistan.

Other assigned members and I were joined by nine Special Ops members to influence the takeover of a village critical to our troops. We were to take out the water tower outside the base used to store water for the Arghandab District's villagers.

When we first arrived in Kandahar Province, none of us were sepaking to one another. We were not happy campers. All thirteen of us were fresh off spending time with our children, spouses, and extended family. Our heads were back home, and our bodies were in a forsaken desert with an enemy that didn't negotiate, listen, or back down.

Robby, one of the team members, wanted to make a name for himself. He wanted to place himself in the first-shot position. The problem was that he was 6'3" and could be seen over the extended lip of a rooftop or behind desert shrubs. He was just too tall. But that didn't stop his eagerness or his drive to be regarded as the best sniper and to be given the privilege of the first shot. That was my position, earned over eleven years of being part of and eventually leading our core team.

When we discussed strategy and positioning, he lobbied each member for a vote to be first, with backup being called by him when or if he felt the need. We didn't work this way. Backup was called by the team leader and not by the sniper, who had to be completely focused on the target and the surroundings.

As we approached the tower on the designated day, we knew there was only one clear shot and that was from a nearby Kandahar Province pickup truck depot. The shot had to be clean, precise, and done in a way that the soldier guarding the water tower would fall on the opposite side of the fenced-in area. We would need to remove the body quickly before the other guards had time to notice one of them was gone.

To reach the tower, a modified L115A3 rifle would be used. This was the type of weapon used to eliminate a Taliban machine gun team in 2009 from 1.54 miles away. At that time, it was the longest sniper strike on record. This weapon used a .338 magnum caliber shell that combined the range of a similar .50 BMG round with the maneuverability of a smaller .51 cartridge. These rounds lacked the impact of a .50 caliber shell, but the weapon used to fire them had less recoil and muzzle flash when fired. This would serve to keep the sniper better concealed. Don't let the modifications fool you into thinking this wasn't a powerful firearm. The rounds were strong enough to penetrate armored glass.

In perfect conditions with no wind, mild weather, and clear visibility, I could rest the bipod of my weapon on a compound wall surrounding the truck depot and aim for the gunner on top of the tower. But Robby wanted to take the shot. He pushed his way past me and knocked my arm, causing the bipod to fall forward. "I can do this," he said. These were his last words.

He'd been towering over the wall where the two Afghans on the tower could clearly see his head and shoulders. Blood sprayed everywhere. Brains and blood. Tissue and bone. Before I had time to think during the brief second of trying to comprehend what just happened, I lined the sight of my scope toward the tower, wiped my cheek clean and squeezed the trigger, hitting both guards. As one slumped to the left of the gun turret, the other lurched forward and fell sixty feet to the ground.

The others and I quickly picked up our gear and crouched down, putting Robby's decapitated body in front of us and the wall. "Count," I said to myself. By the time I got to five, one of the men was dragging me back toward the road cleared for our departure. We both scrambled to get into the back of the jeep.

"Too damn full," he said.

"Too damn eager," I replied.

We both knew that being ready to shoot and wanting to shoot were two different mindsets. No emotion. Just a part of the job. We were able to get back to camp, shower off Robby's remains, and walk to the mess hall, ready for and in need of a hot meal.

It's one thing to be thrust into life-changing events with others. It's another when that's your job, and changes that affect your target or your team happen daily. It's an act of trust to get through the many missions and another to actively stay friends when you're out of job mode.

25

A New Assignment: A New Team

Washington, DC and a Bunker in Maryland
2001

My excitement level rose as the plane started its descent into Dulles International Airport. I couldn't wait to get off the plane, even though I didn't know exactly what I'd be doing.

I thought of all kinds of possible assignments. Maybe Yemen, or back to Israel or Iran. I did have a love for the Middle East and felt at home in the countries I'd worked in so far. There were also many projects occurring in parts of the world I hadn't seen. Nuclear plants were being inspected in North Korea, where tensions were ratcheting up. The civil war in Rwanda was ongoing. Serbia was continuing its assault on Bosnia. our personnel were there at all events as part of a greater effort invested in creating political change.

We needed different skill sets for each mission, and teams were being formed throughout the office with very few folks repeating their current or past partnerships. Everyone wanted to be on a team with members who worked well with each other.

The year ahead would change my life. Back in DC from Afghanistan, my job moved in a different direction. I worked on a collection of data that would be used to search for potentially hostile political groups. The United States government had stored this type of information for many years in random files throughout the country, but not in one comprehensive database until now. We were tasked with organizing and digitizing boxes of files, each having information to be combed through and entered in a database comprised of fields like last name known by, last known location, group affiliations both past and present, and so on. This was worked on at multiple levels, but the basic information still needed to be transferred from paper to a digital data file, and the boxes never stopped coming.

I'd never been one to sit for long periods of time and found the work tedious. We were told how vital this project was and that everyone had to participate, but no one enjoyed the process. We just had to endure it and hope to be placed on a team as soon as possible.

My time in front of a dumb terminal started to take a toll. My mind wandered as twenty of us were left to decipher poorly handwritten triplicate papers coated in a light but persistent coat of carbon. We all felt as though we'd been passed up for more exciting assignments, and our fears started to show in the way we treated each other and the work.

Then I finally heard from the one person I constantly relied on to chart my course. "Phone for you," my supervisor said.

I got up from the terminal and went into the small coffee room where a phone hung on the wall between the round table where we ate lunch on bad-weather days and the small refrigerator surrounded by old linoleum cabinetry.

I picked up the handset and was asked to identify myself. Everyone had a code. Not a code name that was given by your team members, but an employee code or identification code needed before, during, and after employment, and certainly before being able to speak on a secured line.

"Seven-seven-eight-six," I said into the receiver. After a pause I heard the familiar dial tone that one heard before a phone call was made.

"It's Mike Smith. I can't go into too many details, so just listen."

"Okay," I said, surprised by Director Smith's businesslike tone. He was usually friendly and wanted to chat about what I'd been doing before going into information mode.

"You have an opportunity to become part of a very strong team. They've been together for four years, so you'd be the newbie. You will also be the only woman. I want to give you the best chance to return unscarred and successful. You'll be briefed in the morning at headquarters. Do you trust me to make the decision?"

"Yes." I hung up the phone and looked at the dial. That small piece of clear circular plastic reminded me of my mother's yellow kitchen phone. That phone got more use than any other device in our house except the fridge and stove.

I knew the familiar feel of the wall telephone in my hand, remembering all those teenage hours laughing and talking to classmates, as well as the sting from the silence of the phone when waiting for a call from your high school crush. There was no joy or remorse for either memory. Just a new anticipation that stayed with me for the remainder of the afternoon and throughout the evening. That evening would turn out to be one of my last times in that small Georgetown apartment.

It snowed for two days. Our makeshift apartment—a brownstone duplex where the landlord lived next door, occupying all four stories—had six steps up to the front door. The landlord rented three of the four stories of the adjacent apartment to various graduate students from George Washington and Georgetown universities, and government workers like me and my five roommates.

Focused on tomorrow's team news, I shuffled from the Dupont Circle Metro station down Connecticut Avenue to turn onto "O" street. I held my coat and tote bag filled with snacks, a book on manners, and my work shoes close to me, and I wasn't watching where I stepped. While going down the bumpy sidewalk toward the duplex, I stubbed my foot against a raised section. One foot stepped forward while the other was firmly planted against the concrete. I went down face first, throwing my arms out in front of me like I was preparing to dive into the deep end of our swimming pool back in LA. Fortunately, my face was protected by the softness of the worn-cotton tote bag and the thick cardigan stuffed inside that I wore inside our very cold offices. But for the tote bag, I would have done some serious damage to my mouth and nose. My body ached when I got into bed that night.

The morning came with the anticipation that occurs when questions have been unanswered. Who would I be teamed with? Probably all men, which wouldn't be the first time.

My driver pulled around the corner where "O" connected with Connecticut Avenue. We had more than an hour drive ahead. That's all I was told. All agents choose their pickup time. I tried to calculate for unexpected traffic, car problems, or anything else that could make me late. First meetings, like first impressions, only happen once. If you're late, that will follow you through the course of your time together: no one saying anything out loud to you, but inside, thinking you're unreliable.

We pulled up to the concrete bunkers that overlooked the Potomac. I wondered why there were no cars, trucks, or lights on. The facility had been used to shelter House and Senate representatives in the 1960s and '70s. Now it was a row of gray, weathered low-lying buildings hugging the river's banks. Multimillion-dollar mansions dotted both sides of these eight or nine buildings. Each had a large vessel anchored to a private dock. I wondered who lived in these homes and wanted to be one of those people who could look at where I stood and know they lived in view of a piece of US history.

We came to the fourth structure, its door slightly ajar. A dim light hung off to the far side of the room, and a long fluorescent light stretched the length of the rectangular table where we would gather for our briefing. I thanked my driver and surveyed the number of chairs surrounding the table. Thirteen cold, metal, uncomfortable-looking seats. I didn't want to sit down first and endure the tortuous-looking seats for any longer than necessary, and I debated whether to sit to the left or right of the head of the table.

A figure stepped into the wood-framed doorway. "I usually take the chair to the right of the director," a low and commanding voice said to me. "Hello. I'm Mike Simmons. Some people call me Big Mike."

He was average height, about 250 pounds, bald head, deep-chocolate skin, and a smile that lit up his entire face.

Looking back, I think it was his smile that immediately made me feel joy. His voice, deep and resonant, was soft and kind.

"Logistics?" I asked, figuring by his size that he was clearly not running bad actors down streets or jumping from roof to roof, a mandatory exercise for field agents working abroad.

He smiled again, nodding his head up and down while slowly saying, "Uh-huh."

I was about to speak, but a loud, twenty-something-year-old interrupted me and commanded our attention.

"No coffee. Shit. How am I supposed to wake up without some damn coffee?"

Where did he come from? Clearly, he had no clue that these meetings weren't corporate with a breakfast cart full of pastries, fruit, tea, and his coffee.

"Isn't it early not to have coffee?"

Big Mike looked at him matter-of-factly. "Next time get up earlier and make your own coffee so you can drink it on the way."

"Who are you?" the young man asked in an obnoxious voice. "The organizer of the group, or are you just the old guy that knows everything?"

At this point, I felt we might need a referee, not because of Big Mike, but because this young, overly agitated man was wanting to fight.

"Hey, punk. Shut it before I do it for you," said another man now standing in the doorway. He was half Mike's size in weight, but about the same height—5'9" or 5'10". This guy was pure muscle. Short hair with the top sticking straight up, like the crew cuts of old, but his was prematurely gray, which, along with his thick mustache and goatee, gave him an air of immediate authority. "You're right, man," he said, acknowledging Mike's comment. Then to the young guy, who I learned later was called Jason: "Make your own for the ride next time, and don't expect someone to take care of you. We're not your mother."

Jason looked at the new guy and retorted, "Nope, you're anything but that." He was trying his best to get a rise out of a fourth person in the room.

"Not gonna happen, kid." The muscled guy pulled a metal chair out from the table and took it to the far corner of the room. He sat directly on it, facing the door, almost parallel to the chair at the head of the table. He looked directly at me, not sizing me up with his bright-blue, steel-like gaze. "Sorry to be rude. I should introduce myself to the lady," he said with a slight smile.

I could tell he didn't smile much. Way too serious for taking time to laugh and entertain people. He was all business. Just the type of teammate you want. No bullshit, no games, just pure attention directed toward accomplishing the mission.

"Whitney's my name but call me Whit. Everyone does, even Director Mike Smith." He knew that would grab my attention.

"You and the director are friends?" I asked.

"No. Not friends, but we've been through things together, and he's got a good group of folks that I've worked with before."

I nodded in agreement, not thinking about my being part of the group, but of my past teammates and how we, too, were no BS, no games, business/mission driven.

"Good to know" was all I could reply.

He didn't intimidate me, but he did interest me. This was the kind of guy who would create the strategy, write the game plan, and execute it. Whether he worked alone, which I think he preferred, or with others, this was the group's brain trust. Taking directions was not for him. I wondered if he would collaborate while working out the plan. Would he listen to others or, more importantly, would he incorporate their ideas into the plan or be dead set on his strategy being the plan. *Guess I'll have to see,* I thought.

There were four of us now, looking at each other, sizing each other up, with an awkward silence falling over the room.

"Who are we waiting for?" Jason asked as he fidgeted in his chair next to the door.

"At least two more people," Big Mike said. "Probably one more team member and the director's liaison."

"One more highly intelligent, can't-live-without moron." Jason was full of comments, all of them equally annoying.

"We need at least two more team members," Mike said. "Unless you can drive and be obnoxious at the same time," Whit added to Mike's comment, but directed it toward Jason.

"Why you sweating me, old man? What's your problem?" Jason replied.

This was going to be a long morning.

"No problem here." Whit wasn't going to lower himself to Jason's level. That was easy to see, but what I didn't understand was why this jerk would be on the team that Director Smith said was chosen for "safety first" reasons. What had he achieved and how many missions had he been on prior to this morning? What was his skill set that made him so valuable? Whatever it was, it must be off the charts because enduring him was going to take more patience than I believed I had, especially if we were going to be in close quarters or under any cloak of silence needed for the mission's success.

Big Mike decided to ask the looming question. "What is your specialty, Jason?"

"Mine?" he said in a clear voice as he straightened his back against the cold metal chair. "I blow things up."

"Perfect. Just what, exactly, do you blow up besides doors, windows, or cars?" Whit inquired, looking up at the ceiling, probably not wanting to hear his response, but knowing there would be one.

"Mostly people," was his reply.

None of us looked surprised or moved from our positions around the table. We now figured out where we were probably headed. The Middle East was the focal point for creating untimely deaths of political leaders no longer friendly to the United States. No Ph.D. was needed to understand we were going to the land of sand, heat, unclean water, and often, untimely death.

The doorknob turned to the left, signaling someone would be entering. Hopefully, it was the last member of the team, so we could begin the briefing. It was the liaison. Tall, with dark glasses covering pale skin. Short, light-brown hair cut perfectly around his angular face. Lean, almost skinny, with faded medium-brown shoes in need of a shine. But well-suited in a dark blue wool overcoat covering the dark indigo-striped suit and blue, green, and black silk tie: the green being just as dominant as the black dots covering the front part of the tie down to the fourth shirt button. When he took off the coat and suit jacket, the green turned to a light blue from that point to the end of the tie, still covered by black geometric-looking dots. By the cut of his clothing, he made enough money to be working for a higher level within the Intelligence Agency. This would be significant in terms of why we were being asked to meet outside of any official building. The fewer people seeing us together, the better.

We'd been waiting on the person with the intel to show

up, and now he was here, but still no other team members, so more chatter from the guys.

"Anyone else coming?" Jason asked in his 'put-out' manner. The tone was somewhere between sarcastic and annoyed, with a touch of petulant child thrown into his teenage-sounding voice.

"No one else is coming, so let's get started," the liaison quipped back, letting everyone know without saying aloud that questions would be permitted when he asked us if we had any; perhaps he wouldn't ask us at all, which does happen. These government workers showed up to deliver a message from our leadership. They said only what they were told to say, not to answer questions, whether or not they were related to the information.

Clearly, Jason hadn't been part of this level of briefing before. I was getting uneasy without even knowing what we were about to be told. I couldn't shake the question of why this guy was part of the team. I thought to myself that I needed to focus on the briefing and not waste mental capital on that guy. Easier said than done.

"The four of you will be going to Ramadi. You will be met there and taken to a temporary shelter so you can prepare."

He took a penlight out of his left pants pocket and pointed it toward the far wall of the small room. An image of a map appeared on the white concrete.

"As you can see, we have a visual on the area. This was taken eighteen hours ago, 8:00 a.m. Here is the target."

He projected a long, narrow image to make certain we could see the person's face. We all assumed there would be one person who came into view, but two faces appeared. Neither caused any reaction from my new teammates.

The liaison went on to say, "The issue between these two

guys is this."

Another picture appeared. It was a bridge linking an unfinished road to a finished road on the other side.

"Both of these men were paid by us to complete this four-lane road enabling our troops to traverse from the depot to several base camps. One village leader shown here completed his portion four months ago. The other leader, from a rival town, still has not. Our cash built this bridge, but it turns out it's not stable. We want the bridge gone and this man terminated. The message it will send means more than the ease of the makeshift alliance between two factions. Let me be clear: both men must be there to watch the bridge come down. Only after that do you take down the target. We want the leader to witness the shot. He needs to know we are thankful for his service to our country. He will grasp just how appreciative we are, as he will then be able to take over the rival township if he so chooses. He will need to either rebuild the bridge or complete the road, that's his choice, but we'll allow him to make it." He shut off the penlight, making the map and images disappear. The room was silent. No response from anyone.

The liaison said nothing else. He closed his suit jacket and began to put on his overcoat. Just as he slipped his right arm into the coat sleeve, he looked directly at me and said, "Make sure he sees the shot. If by chance the demolition of the bridge takes him out, the mission will be considered a failure. Our preferred leader needs to see his rival fall and not from some rebar impaling him or the explosion blasting him to bits."

I returned the look and decided to respond. "Understood."

"Thank you, all. That will be it for now. You know the objective—develop your plan. You will be contacted with instructions within forty-eight hours of your pickup, when we're ready to deploy. Be ready and good luck."

He stepped out of the bunker and all I could think was that this wasn't going to be easy.

***

Maryland became home for the next month. The team barely left the bunker except to eat and sleep, which, as we found out, wasn't something any of us needed or wanted until we could get a plan together without killing innocent citizens. We tried to gather intelligence in a part of the world where no one trusted outsiders, especially if those outsiders were American.

From the bunker where our intel briefing had been held, I could see the Washington Monument in the distance. The lights over the Woodrow Wilson Bridge that connects Alexandria, Virginia, to Oxon Hill, Maryland, danced across the waters of the Potomac River.

I wondered how the river would look from up on the bridge. How it would feel to be as close to the water as I could without plunging down into it. This bridge could rise up and down like a drawbridge, allowing larger ships to pass through. I wondered if we could construct a blast that just took out the middle of the bridge in Ramadi, leaving both ends somewhat intact and effectively creating the ability to rebuild it as a drawbridge. It would better serve the communities by allowing trade to increase, as larger ships would be able to traverse where they couldn't at the time. For all that we do to destroy our enemy's cities, perhaps this could be perceived as an improvement and would be considered a token of goodwill. What if we created change that was for the better? Instead of demolishing towns, leaving the people who have suffered at our expense to regroup and rebuild, we could provide an opportunity for them to become stronger and more independent than they were before.

I felt good, positive about my idea and excited to share it with the team. Not being an engineer, I had no idea if the plan was feasible, but I did believe it had legs and I could sell it to the others for a real chance of making it happen.

"It's too impractical," Jason started out after I explained my idea to the group. "Attempting to only take out the middle decreases my ability to kill any of the leaders."

"You don't have to kill anyone," Whit stated in a stern, direct voice. "You only have to take out the bridge, middle or as best as you can."

"I can do both," Jason retorted. "I just need some time to determine how to compact the blast material."

I got up and drew a vertical line down the middle of a chalkboard. Being more of a visual thinker, I did my best work by writing or drawing it out. On the right side, I wrote "task," and on the left, "person accountable."

We spent the next few hours going around the table, naming each part of what we believed we needed to achieve to accomplish our goal. The hard part wasn't listing the mission's steps; it was debating with Jason what we needed from him, not what he felt he could provide.

"I get that you think you can do it all, but that's not your role in this group. We're a team for a reason. If we hadn't been called to do this job, and they'd asked only you to execute this, then why are we here?"

He looked up from his seat, not saying a word.

"Let's get this laid out so we can all get a hot meal and get on with our lives," said Big Mike, as he rocked back and forth in his uncomfortable metal chair. "I don't think my ass can take another day sitting on this torture device."

We all laughed, knowing he was right. The room was probably designed that way so people wouldn't get too comfortable and forget why they were there.

Another three hours elapsed with all of us working individually on our assigned and agreed-upon tasks. As we went around the table, starting with Mike's logistical plan, I could feel the team's cohesion developing; we began working more in unison than before.

By that night, we'd reviewed all aspects of staging (Whit), logistics (Mike), kill-shot approach (me), and partial explosion tactic (Whit), leaving Jason to develop his IED recipe. Each of us encouraged him to take his time and create the perfect explosive main device and three secondaries for backup.

"You're the only one who can do it," I said to him, as we got up to end our nine-hour session. "It will be great to see what you come up with."

"I got this" was all he said.

Whit responded, not looking over his shoulder as he led us out of the bunker: "You better, kid."

My thoughts were on firearms; specifically, which to use to take out the designated target. From where we thought our cover would be, the shot was no more than sixty feet away. It had to be simultaneous to the blast so nobody could accuse us of an assassination. It would be an unfortunate accident, a casualty related to the bridge coming down. According to a Department of Defense study authored by Sartori in 1983, a human body can survive a high blast of pressure without experiencing extreme physical trauma. If we were in a physical structure, most buildings would collapse at five PSI, meaning we would be too close at sixty feet away to survive.

Later in the week, we submitted our plan with a

recommendation that the Corps of Army Engineers design plans for building a drawbridge.

Weeks passed with no response. We all stayed busy back in DC working our desk jobs, waiting for further instructions. We avoided talking about the Maryland bunker and the upcoming Ramadi mission.

Still, while sitting at my desk, people I'd worked with in DC earlier in my career dropped by to shoot the breeze. Uneasy as it made me feel, part of my desire to fit in or be part of the office group was now being satisfied by the newfound attention.

"What was it like?" said the passersby.

"What do you mean?" I'd reply, not wanting to get closer to the conversation for fear of giving away information that I shouldn't. My desire to fit in wasn't going to outweigh my goal of moving from desk duty to intelligence in the field.

Finally, nine weeks later, it happened. I'd just begun to look at getting a night job so I could afford to move to a small one-bedroom apartment on my own, one without bureau roommates. I was almost out the door when the phone at my desk lit up, and, inside, so did I.

"Time to pack and be ready by 5:00 a.m."

"Yes, Sir."

"More instructions in the morning when the driver will pick you up."

That was it. Back to field work.

By the time I got to my apartment, snow was falling at a steady pace. Looking out the window as I packed the first of my three bags, I wondered what season it would be when we returned to Georgetown. Would it still be winter or could we skip the cold, wet snowy season and be lucky enough to arrive back in springtime, just in time for the cherry blossoms to start blooming?

Sleep was fleeting that night. Some field agents drink and stay up all night, not wanting to waste time sleeping before they leave. Others relish staying at home with their kids and spouses, trying to embrace their surroundings and family, making a mental imprint of each voice, face, and poignant conversation so that in the still of the night before going into the kill zone, they can pray these memories back, quelling their fear of the unknown.

Then there were people like me who just wanted to go. Even if it meant leaving my two young sons. I would never have abandoned them. I couldn't let go like that. I don't let go easily when I love, probably because it takes so long to get to that place. Still, I needed to go to Ramadi, to meet my commitments, to complete the mission. I was still proving myself to myself. Still much the child at the orphanage in Kansas.

Finally, 4:00 a.m. came. I stepped outside my room and looked back at my sleeping roommates, strewn around the apartment. I shut my door to find Tom in the hallway, his silhouette reflected by the bathroom light behind him. It brought a smile to my face.

"Come home safely. Don't take any shit."

"Will do," I said as quietly as I could, and then before shutting the door, I looked right at him and said, "See you soon!"

26

Ramadi: The Mission

Ramadi, Iraq
2001

When I woke up two days later, I felt the heat of another desert. My senses heightened every time I saw its expanse; my eyes watered, and my throat closed. Sleep-deprived and dehydrated, my back ached from lack of any cushioning on the makeshift seats of the plane. Transport flying is fit for nobody, not soldiers who will see battle, not for young women, and not for older field agents pushing forty; their bodies aren't the same as when they were fresh out of Quantico.

When we got to the base in Ramadi, we were hot, smelly, and cranky. We needed real sleep. We wanted hot food, and all I could think of was a hot shower. That would be no easy feat. Imagine an army base full of young men stuck out in the hot desert with little to entertain themselves except for the occasional United Service Organization (USO) tour that breezed in and out once in a three-year stint of duty. The officer's quarters were separated from the long line of khaki tents that made their way down the middle of the base. Outlying bunkers, PX, classrooms, and latrines separated the roads that were created by the three long rows of buildings and tents.

They couldn't figure out where to house me and exactly what area of the base would be safest from the prying eyes of the young soldiers. Even those given the platoon duties to watch weren't to be trusted when it came to the idea of sneaking a peak when I was wet and soapy. My goal was to get into the shower and out quickly.

That didn't happen. On my way to the officer's shower, I was stopped several times by soldiers questioning my destination. They were inquisitive to the point that each offered to escort me to the showers. I declined, knowing that at least one of the four would probably come by in ten-to-fifteen minutes and offer to hand me soap or shampoo or try to help me out of the shower. Men are so predictable, especially when they're starved for female attention. My thoughts turned to how I could make this a win-win situation. Partially showing my less than full breasts wouldn't bother me. If I gave the inquirers that, what could I get in trade?

My last obstacle to entering the showers was the soldier, Dennis, sitting at the front of the officer's bunk. He was filling in for a colleague who'd fallen ill. He normally worked in procurement. This was my lucky day. I was only too happy when, about two minutes into the shower, there was a knock on the stall door.

"Just making sure you have warm water," he said in an anxious voice. I pulled open the metal stall door just enough for him to see the side of my right breast and a partial front view of my left.

"Thank you, Dennis," I said in a very appreciative tone. "I feel like I'm in heaven. The water is perfect. You're very kind to check on me."

I slowly closed the door, watching him fidget with his uniform hat, fixated on my chest. I let him take it in long enough to smile at him, so he knew I understood he had the luck of working the desk that day and meeting me.

As I dried off and changed into fresh clothes, I heard voices outside the locked facility. Dennis had visitors: two of the young soldiers I'd encountered along the way were at his desk trying to confirm my location. Dennis held them at bay, not letting them pass. I walked out fresh and clean, smelling like Pond's cold cream and Herbal Essence shampoo, and smiled and thanked Dennis for watching the door. I'd be back tomorrow and wondered if he'd be there filling in for his sick peer.

My thoughts quickly switched to my immediate surroundings. "Lunch will be served in Mess Hall B today, 1100-1300 hours. New members to the base report to Building for instructions." It was 10:48. I hurried my pace and counted the building numbers as I quickly walked by. At least the numbers were declining. 10:56. I was now in front of Building 2. Big Mike had beaten me there.

"You look fresh," he said, as he hoisted his five-foot-nine-inch 5'9", 260-pound frame off the concrete steps leading up to the front door.

"Feeling fine!" I said.

"You're looking fine, too!" said a young voice from behind me. It was Jason, eyeing me up and down. I glared at him and tried to quiet my temper before addressing him.

"I know this may come as a shock, but guess what? I am your teammate, not some bar chick, wannabe date, or pickup. Do not speak to me that way again. Got it?"

He looked shocked, as if no woman except his mother had ever dressed him down. He was the type of young man who had no innate manners. You know, the type of guy who believes women are second-class citizens, especially black women; he probably was raised thinking someone biracial like me belonged to an extra disgusting class of people. His glare reminded me of the janitors at the orphanage, eyeing any girl at least twelve years old as they pretended not to care about them, but were mentally taking notes as to which young girls would be easy prey once the lights went out at bedtime.

I can still remember their soft screams, the crying, and then the silence. Before I was old enough to really understand what was happening to these girls, I was in foster care. No one talked about it, but everyone old enough to know understood that these wards of the state were being molested. Some were being raped. I knew the look Jason had shot me all too well.

In the second home I was placed in, the caretaker had a brother. I was about six years old. He was in his late twenties. One day while I was on my cot napping, I saw his big frame leaning against the doorjamb. I'd been sick with the flu, so I was home from school. It was hot. I'd gone back and forth from being awake to sleeping throughout the afternoon.

Have you ever had the feeling that someone was staring at you even though your eyes were closed? That's what I felt. Someone staring through me, not just at me. I remembered wanting to run as fast as I could, but he was blocking the doorway. I had nowhere to run. The room was small, no windows or closet. Just two cots vertically placed up against the side walls facing the door as you were lying down.

He walked closer to me, and I drew my knees to my chest, pulling the sheet over my legs up to my chin. He moved slowly, quietly, and started to put his hand toward my face, but the caretaker came through the door and slapped his head from behind.

"Idiot," she yelled, as she pulled him back from me. "If you hurt her, we're done." I didn't understand what she meant by "hurt," but I knew that feeling of being looked at by a predator.

I tried to shake off that memory, and Big Mike helped pull me back to reality. "Stand down," he instructed Jason as you would a dog that had just peed on a new carpet. Mike's hands were on his hips, eyes squinting, his toothpick flicking in and out of the left corner of his wide mouth. That look became his signature. So was the dress down.

I couldn't contain my laughter.

As we walked away, Jason, head sideways and lowered, was trying to process what he'd heard. I think he really hadn't been put in his place for some time. Certainly not by a woman or by a man he truly respected. New territory.

"That was rich."

I couldn't think of the right words to say except, "Thanks for the backup."

"Always. You're my gal." He continued, "I originally didn't want to do this mission and fought it mentally, but each morning discussing and then formulating our plan, I could see that you and Whit really knew how to draft and execute a strategy."

He continued to chat as we walked back to Building 2, thinking the door would be unlocked by now. "I knew then to stop second guessing myself and became part of the team."

I completely understood what he was saying. Knowing

when to look past the negatives and to start focusing on a solution.

The door to Building 2 was wide open. Not wanting to deal with Jason right now would have been all over my face.

Mike looked at me and said, "Let me go in first and see what's going on."

"Great!" I replied quickly to his offer, probably too quickly, but I was starting to form a friendship with him and wanted him to know that my initial guard was coming down enough to let him help me in this kind and chivalrous way. It was a nice gesture. It was only seconds before he stood in the door frame motioning for me to come inside. Whatever the reason for coming to Building 2 before lunch was, the coast was clear.

I walked up the stairs and into the building. Inside four soldiers stood at attention. The general was walking by them, saluting each as he passed. I'd never been present in front of an armed forces general. Our troops' lives were in his hands. One bad order and soldiers die. That's a lot for anyone to shoulder, let alone the fact of winning a war versus losing and the impact that would have on our lives as well as those of the enemy.

It was very evident that a general was in the area. Through the doorway, I saw armed guards on top of the building across from Building 2 and at each door. The front and side doors were visible from the hallway. Rifles were locked and loaded, ready to fire if need be. General Raymond Odierno was the commander of Multinational Force (MNF-1) in Iraq. He was the twelfth American military officer to command at the division, corps, and army level during the same conflict and only the second in history since the Vietnam War.

Whit and Mike were standing with their backs to me. I

could see the general looking my way. He motioned for me to join them. The line of soldiers was 'at ease' as I walked by. They never changed their forward-looking stares. I joined my teammates and introduced myself to the general.

"Thanks for joining us," he warmly responded. Since the troops didn't yet know he was on site, he suggested we eat inside the air-conditioned building. Tonight, after he watched several military exercises, he would eat with the troops, with the men and women who would be front and center when there was action.

We followed behind the guards as the general led the way through a side door left of the hallway. The room was simple but pleasant. A circular table set for five awaited us, surrounded by pictures of the base on the walls. Five yellow roses sat in the center in a round vase with the place settings forming an outer circle around the flowers. The deputy general who lived on base came through the door as we were about to sit down. That made five. I was relieved that Jason wasn't the fifth person; yet I wondered why he'd been excluded, and whether that would intensify his wrath.

"Let's get to the point," Odierno stated as soon as the pleasantries had ended and the salads served. "I want to hear your plan from start to finish. I want the details. My guess is you have little information on the two opposing factions, and I want to determine our risks as they pertain to your mission."

The lunch lasted for over two hours. We discussed our plan in detail, from logistics (Mike) to the architect's drawings of the future and current bridge (Whit). We detailed where in the building he would set up the Hollister I would use to take out the target. The one part we couldn't describe was the explosion. Those of us invited to this meeting didn't have Jason's final mixture nor did we have his detonator information. This was a flaw. We were all concerned that we couldn't explain that part of the plan.

I ended by explaining the calculations about how the rounds would take out more than the leader with the amount of force needed to hit a target half a mile away, careful not to lecture. These men knew warfare, they knew weaponry, and I was no expert on either, but I knew how to sight a target, stay calm and silent, and ready myself for the right moment to pull the trigger. People handle themselves differently when it comes to their shortcomings. Some describe their assets to the point where the listeners feel they're among aliens. Others start out with all their flaws, building up to the peak of their abilities. I was a fish out of water in this new military world. Working the streets as a bureau field agent was my comfort zone. I was given this assignment because of my expertise in shooting a target.

Being a young woman on a US foreign military base made me apprehensive. I was a guest on a base that had few women, in a country that had little respect for females. *Just get me out of here as soon as I can,* I thought.

Perhaps I was thinking about this the wrong way. What if the power to change how they feel about women was inside me? Getting this mission over with, successfully, would show others what I as a woman was capable of. My early years had instilled more self-doubt than confidence. Many adopted children feel that sense of insecurity. Perhaps being sent here as part of a team assigned to pull off this risky mission would finally silence the voices in my head telling me I was nothing.

After offering details about the mission, I watched the general, waiting for the questions to begin. He paused before he said anything. "From what the three of you have shared with me, I believe this is solid. I'll leave you with my deputy.

He will ask for more detail. You can sort through it with him." At that, Odierno stood up and shook our hands as we all stood to say goodbye. "Godspeed." He gestured with his hand over his heart like a priest praying over soldiers, knowing they may not return.

The plans were more involved than the deputy had known. What hadn't been described was the explosion. My sense was that they had a different plan. Why else was Jason not here as part of the team?

Most military campaigns were led by commanders who empowered their troops to act as they must to advance their agenda. We were given the authority to develop a plan that would fit our skills and accomplish the goal, but also to help the community improve their lives. Mike was particularly passionate about this part of the plan. The rest of us, although somewhat altruistic in thought, weren't driven by what would happen to the people after we left. If we fulfilled our directive, we would return to our lives until called upon again.

Feeling like we'd passed some test, we went back to our respective bunks until 17:00 when we would reconvene to review weaponry, ammunition, and vehicle transportation. Satisfied about things, I decided to cool down by taking another shower, provided the same soldier was manning the desk. As luck would have it, he was on duty. His counterpart was still in the infirmary with the flu. I decided not to press any reciprocity on him, but to ask if he would watch the door like before.

"Yes, ma'am! Let me know when you're done, and I'll make sure you have enough towels and some water to drink."

"Thank you."

He left me to walk down the hallway to the shower area by myself. I closed the door. It had no lock. Maybe I should put a chair that was to the left of the shower under the doorknob, so, if someone tried to come in, I'd have time to react. It was 110 degrees outside, and I was relaxed from a super delicious lunch and just wanted to cool down. Screw it, I thought, and turned on the cool water.

Five minutes later I was about to step out when an arm reached in and pulled my hair, snapping my head back. I felt the heat from his naked body as he pulled me backward out of the shower and slammed me up against the wall. He was erect, but not huge.

"Suck it, bitch!" he ordered as he held both of my wrists tight against the gray, cool concrete wall. I couldn't move, so getting near his dick wasn't an option. "Hold it!" He started to ejaculate.

I wanted none of him near me, so I took my right knee and pressed his small, wet penis against his own leg, letting him moan freely as he felt the coolness of my skin. He lowered his head and moaned even louder. That's when my knee moved smartly under his scrotum, and, with all my strength, I kneed him directly, facing forward. First his balls, then his nose as his body crumpled to the floor.

I gathered my clothes and unused towel and got out of there as fast as I could, running down the hallway, holding the towel up to my chest and around my naked body, my other hand trying to hold my clothes, shoes, and hat, as I made it to the front desk.

"Where were you?" I screamed at the young man who I thought was my shower security.

"What do you mean?"

"Go look and see," I said in disgust. I needed a place to change. I was shaking. When on base, there is never a safe place for a woman who's not a soldier. *Just get me out of here* was all I would think about for the rest of the day and the remainder of my time in Ramadi.

Getting through the munitions tour, into the evening, to the next day, my head was somewhere else. I just lay on my cot thinking that at any moment someone might break through the door to try and hurt me again. I skipped dinner that first night and breakfast the next morning, not wanting to leave my little room, the door of which I barricaded with the foot of my bed, pushed up to the little cubby that I shoved in front of the door. No person wants to live in fear. I had to get with the living and stop obsessing about the shower incident. I had to kill the fear, or it would take over and prevent me from doing my job.

"I know you're in there," Whit said in a low voice.

He understood something was wrong, but I didn't know what or how much he knew. I snapped myself out of the cloudy haze of my own thoughts and answered, "Okay. One minute."

It would take me some time to push the furniture away from the door. I slightly opened the door. He looked inside past me then right at me. "Come outside so we can talk."

I was glad to do that, as I thought his coming into my room wouldn't be a good thing at this moment. Eyes are everywhere when you're on a base. Nobody should go into my room except me. I grabbed my hat, still dressed from the afternoon before, and followed him outside to the area in the back of the mess hall. Soldiers who had worked the morning shift were sitting around shooting the shit, smoking, and relaxing before they began preparing for lunch.

We took a seat at the far end of a group of picnic tables. The makeshift mess tent was thrown on top of two trees, giving shade from the desert sun. It was hot. Everyone dealt with that. Part of being here.

"I know what happened," he began. His tone was low, as if to avoid attention to us or to display emotion that anyone could pick up on. "You got him good." He cracked a slight smile, looking at me with pride.

"I should have head butted him, but I didn't want a huge bruise on my forehead."

"Having to wear the hat 24/7 would ruin the look," he said. "Just so you know, you broke his nose. He can't hide what he did because he's got to walk around with those bandages and bruises for a while. Guys like that will talk. Eventually he'll tell some guy he thinks is his buddy. That guy will tell someone who will tell someone who will tell someone until it gets to his CO."

"As long as we're gone by then" was all I could say. I looked off in the distance, not wanting to discuss it anymore.

"Here's the thing," he said, looking straight out onto the training field that was in the far distance from where we sat. "No one is safe here, especially women. Personally, I don't know what they were thinking when they sent you here, but here's what I'm thinking." He paused, raising his left hand to his goatee, stroking the salt and pepper hair on his chin. "I think you'll do a great job, and I'll back you up so you can."

"What do you mean?"

"I'll make certain you can sleep, eat, shower, and work without worrying about your safety. Just work your magic when the time comes and get out of the building in one piece so we can get the hell out of here. Can you do that?"

"I can do that."

"Okay. We have a deal then."

The proper part of me wanted to thank him. The child in me wanted to cry and release the anxiety I'd been feeling. The fighter in me wanted to push forward, past the incident, past this conversation, and move on.

"Let's get some grub and go figure out what ammo they have here."

We got up and walked into the already busy mess hall.

"Where's Mike?" I asked. He'd been quiet during the munitions tour, and I could tell he wanted to get to the car depot, select our transportation, build the road maps verifying where the IEDs could be, and navigate us to the airfield for exfiltration.

"He's at the car depot. He wanted to go yesterday, but no one could drive him there and back before the curfew."

Big Mike was on it, getting ready for action. And so was I. Time to eat, reach clarity, and get back the business at hand.

We ate chicken sandwiches with lettuce and mustard, pickled carrots, and fresh potato salad with little bits of green onion dotting the top of our scoop, washed down with ice-cold lemonade. It was better than traditional army food. I looked beyond our table at a variety of faces: some with full, thick hair, no hair, some with glasses on pointy and flat noses. These soldiers defined the melting pot that America is. I had one duty to perform, and staring at the sea of noisy, food-inhaling troops, I knew I had no choice but to be my best me and get this mission done without error: make the shot.

We took our time looking through the array of long-range rifles to choose from. X-Bolt Browning, Ruger Predator, B14 Ridge, and Howa RDG Bravos. This place had them all. My mind was made up to use the 6.5 Grendel cartridge, which I could vouch for the precision of out to 1,000 yards. My comfort zone was the ammunition I'd used the first day Director Mike Smith pulled me out of basic field agent training and asked me to take a walk with him.

I remembered holding my scarf over my face to block the cold. Tears formed in my eyes as we walked. The puzzled look on my face made him laugh.

"I thought this was a test," I said as he opened the door to the gun range.

"Well, maybe it is."

He went on to explain that he'd heard from my instructors that my target practice scores were the highest each had seen in their seven and thirteen years teaching at Quantico. It wasn't about the actual scores as much as it was being consistent day after day, month after month. Anyone can have a good day striking one-hundred rounds into a target at seven and fifteen yards. The difference that he felt was unique was my ability to do it repeatedly with little variation in scores. From seven yards and fifteen yards, the numbers were plus or minus two for five months.

Now, here at the base, Whit looked at me and smiled. He knew whatever fear had gotten to me, I was now pushing past it, ready to practice until my eyesight started to strain. Six hours a day, then seven, then eight. Our drills were early in the morning and late into the night. People would get angry with us. We did take up more than enough time and resources, but it was important if we were going to get this right. We had one opportunity when the two local leaders would be called by our intelligence to meet and then we would get our signal to go.

Nine days into training, and no one knew what Jason was planning to do. I was anxious and wanting to get this mission underway. Each time I closed my eyes, I no longer thought about the soldier forcing himself on me—I thought about Jason. Where was he? What was his plan? When was he going to share the details with us and why had he been gone for eight of the last nine days that we'd been training on that hot desert base? Everyone wanted out, but I couldn't help but think he was done with this difficult assignment.

Waiting around for training times was a tedious routine. The range and simulation bunker were used by others almost every minute of every day, so just getting on the list was hard enough; actually, getting to use the areas took an act of Congress—unless the general assigned you, as he had both Whit and me.

The base commanders didn't like us. We used up too much ammo, and we took precious training time away from their troops. I tried to avoid eye contact with the army leadership when standing in the entrance line for the bunker. We'd been guests on their base for ten days, and it felt as if we'd worn out our welcome.

We headed to the dining hall and made our way through the line to a table. I heard a noise growing outside. I wondered what was causing such a commotion when the door flew open. It was the deputy general's secretary. He had a presence. Shoulders pulled back, his stride up the center walkway between the mess tables caused even the most disinterested soldier to look up from eating his lukewarm meal. He caught me glancing a few times until I realized he was coming directly toward us. Whit, Mike, and I tried to deflect his gaze. We knew this would only further alienate us from the guys and few gals that were legitimately here. We just wanted to pass through with very little exposure. This wasn't helping our cause.

"Team, we need you in Building 10 at 2000 hours."

We all nodded and figured we could get a few more bites in while separating us from the secretary, which was exactly what we needed. Jason would have run after him, the exact opposite effect that we wanted at this time.

"Why the urgency?" Mike chuckled as he watched Whit try to shove a few more bites of potato into his mouth before getting up to go to Building 10. Stuffing food down wasn't my thing, so I got up and moved toward the back of the table, reaching for Mike's collar to get him up from his seat.

"Let's go before we must see Whit shove more of these disgusting potatoes in his mouth. We don't want to draw more attention this way."

But before we could make a clean getaway, we got flagged by another commander wanting information on why the D-Sec was summoning us.

"What's with you guys? You're not part of this unit, so what are you doing here?" Generally, we would diplomatically respond and deflect the question.

"If you get out of our way, we can tell you!" Whit blasted in the commander's ear. I couldn't tell if the guy was shocked or scared, but he stepped aside so we could make an early exit and get the hell out of there. We walked past the never-ending line of soldiers waiting for their hot meal, avoiding eye contact with them.

My mind was made up. If Jason wasn't part of the intel we were about to receive, we needed to regroup and pick a new time to carry out the mission. If not, this mission was doomed. No support where we were staying, coupled with a lack of intelligence on the ground and incomplete game plan, wouldn't make for a successful outcome. So, with wings on our heels, we hurried to Building 10. Nothing was going to get in our way. We all wanted, no, needed to receive the complete plan.

Little did I know that the base commander was attempting to subjugate us. Apparently, he wanted to subvert the game plan and get the credit if we were to get the green light to move forward. My teammate was not impressed.

"Everybody wants their fifteen minutes in the spotlight," Whit said, as he shook his head side to side, still walking at a brisk pace, but looking deep in thought. I was trying to keep up with Whit, and Mike tried to keep up with me. The three of us powered through the five-minute walk like we were running the last leg of a relay race.

The only person not winded was Whit. He was in great shape for his age. He could outlift, outrun, and outmaneuver guys half his age. Whether in the gym back home or on the base, the guy would turn any normal workout into a competition. Someone was going to lose because he was all about the "win." With his team or by himself, losing wasn't an option.

The door leading into Building 10 was slightly ajar. That was unusual, certainly not the norm. Generally, one or two military police guarded the entrance. Why they weren't around was anybody's guess. Mike pulled me back by my right arm, spinning me around in the process.

"Don't move closer. Something doesn't look right."

I tried to keep quiet as Whit started up the stairs leading to the door. Mike was between the first step and me. Whit quietly ascended two steps, keeping as far to the right as possible. No one made a sound.

A light was on inside the door, probably from the front desk in the reception area. Still, no one came to the door, and no sounds were heard from inside. When he got next to the door, Whit moved out of the direct path of anyone who might be pushing to open the door or to charge at him. His military training kicked in. He could determine who was about to round the corner, their plan of attack, or what weapon would be used and how.

To Whit's surprise, the door pushed open slightly, and a cat sprung out like it was escaping from someone or something inside the building.

"That damn cat!" yelled the deputy general. "Every time I try to catch it, it runs away."

"Guess you're not a cat person," Whit replied.

"Negative. Never was, never will be."

A television was positioned next to a small table across from the deputy general's desk. Anti-government demonstrations in the Al-Ramadi province were taking place. America had begun placing troops in Afghanistan and Iraq. Most areas were not hostile. Al-Ramadi, situated about seventy miles west of Baghdad, was different. It was on the Euphrates River.

This area formed a rectangle situated on the Tigris River and the Iranian border on the east. To the west was desert. The highway and bridge were located on the eastern side, transferring across the desert to the Mediterranean Sea. This land was vital as a stop for the caravans that traveled between Baghdad and the cities called "the Levant."

This large area in the eastern Mediterranean separates Lebanon, Syria, and Iraq. The neighboring towns were clashing over a dissident who'd been killed by an Iraqi intelligence agent. Everyone wanted justice.

We stood around the television watching the people in Al-Ramadi taking to the streets, their fists raised, shouting for justice. I said, "We need to get this wrapped up before it becomes impossible to leave."

The men just stared at the television.

"In case you didn't hear me, I said we need to wrap this up."

Mike turned to me and said, "I heard you. What I didn't

hear is how the bridge will remain functioning when we take out the end of it."

That was the issue. Had been since we left the bunker in Maryland. I looked back at the TV. Now citizens were running as the crowds were breaking up.

The DG said, "Your guy is ready."

"Jason? Ready?" asked Mike. "Did you see what he's devised?"

The DG looked at Mike as though he was about to dress him down. After a long, measured breath, he calmly replied, "No, but not because he didn't want to show me. He was eager to. I don't want to call attention to the plan. You think setting off an explosive around here is a good idea?"

None of us answered.

"I want to run down the plan with you three. Jason will stay off base. Better to keep him where he is until we move out to the location. He's a hothead, a rookie. Best to leave him be until he's needed." No one disagreed with this either, so we stood there awaiting the briefing. An hour later, we heard what we needed to execute the plan with minimal damage.

As we left the DG's office, each of us had one thing on our minds: Would Jason be able to pull his weight? None of us really understood him, because none of us took the time to get to know him. Mike, Whit, and I had bonded quickly, but Jason was cocky, just as the DG had said he was. We'd been around these types before, and the one thing we all agreed on was those types get killed. My goal was to stay as far away from Jason and his bravado as possible; yet we all knew that if he didn't feel like he was a part of the team, then we were putting ourselves in danger. I couldn't let that happen without trying to connect with him.

"Let me see Jason," I said to the DG. "I'll stay with him,

and we can be picked up and transported to the site together."

Whit and Mike looked at me as if I'd said something completely outrageous.

"Look. You guys know if we don't try to befriend him, he'll have no sense of team. If that happens and he screws up, we could all die, and he really would have no sense of fault. I must try to make him feel part of the team." They got it and gave up their protest.

The DG, who'd stayed out of the conversation, now piped in: "Go grab your gear and meet me back here at 1900." I acknowledged and started back to my barracks when Whit hollered from behind me, "Don't try to save him from himself."

"Duly noted," I said. "I'm not Mother Teresa, okay?" That made all three of them laugh. *Good way to end being here on base*, I thought as I walked away, not looking back.

***

"Let's get out of here."

My backpack and I were now in the back of the transport truck going to wherever Jason was being kept. It was a long ride through desert terrain. The stars were out and shining so brightly that streetlights along the two-lane highway weren't needed. It reminded me of the Sinai. Those stars were magical.

As we bumped along, I thought about how to approach someone like Jason. Deep down inside, he wanted to belong to a group, to be a team member, but he sent all the wrong social and verbal messages. One encounter and you immediately disliked him. How could I connect with him so he didn't feel judged? So far my time spent with him was all group interaction. *Maybe some one-on-one conversation would be helpful,* I thought, as we pulled off the highway and traveled down a dirt road that seemed to have no markings except a few rocks on either side.

Please let me connect with this guy, to open a dialogue between us that will help Jason understand that all we want is a successful mission—executed swiftly, with precision, and all teammates back home whole.

The transport stopped abruptly.

"What's happening?"

"There's a roadblock ahead. Looks like we'll need to wait until they check the entire vehicle."

As we waited, I sat back and closed my eyes, trying to picture home, my family. Was it worth being gone for so long? How were my sons? Would anybody be there to come back to? Realistically, for me, existing in this mission-bent world was home. The time spent between assignments was the unfocused, uncomfortable space that I tried to avoid as much as possible. Maybe Jason could relate to that feeling. I thought that could open a conversation if it didn't happen naturally.

Glaring lights surrounded the vehicle. The driver and I both held our hands up so the military police could come in and check the cab and rear area of the 4x4 truck. Those of us who'd been through a security search knew the drill. Nevertheless, the idea that some incendiary device could be planted in or under the steel truck was always at the forefront.

Flashlights beamed into each compartment. I wanted to yell, "Hurry the hell up," but I had nothing but gratitude for their work. Being diligent is a lifesaver. One missed device compromised our lives and, certainly, the sad, unlucky souls around us.

Once the underside of the truck and inside was cleared, passengers had to go through the process. My only regret was not saying thank you at the end of the twenty-minute inspection. We should, as women, be able to speak our minds, but, in this part of the world, our headdresses cover our faces except for our eyes. Certainly, our voices should've been heard, even if muffled by the thick burkas. Now wasn't the time to change history; it was time to be silent, downplayed, invisible to the male guards who'd just cleared our transport to continue down the bumpy, dirt road. Say nothing, just breathe.

I did just that, and about ten minutes later, we found ourselves in front of US Army trucks. Behind the trucks were ten tents, some large, most small. About twenty soldiers stood around the trucks, armed, smoking, and conversing. It looked like a bunch of guys hanging out, discussing the latest sports scores or the incredible plays that'd been made during a game. The driver asked for some directions in Arabic. We were directed to the tent last in from the left of our vehicle.

When I stepped out of the vehicle, the MP closest to the truck grabbed my hands and yelled in Arabic, which I didn't quite understand. He looked past me to the driver and began berating him. Clearly my presence there wasn't the norm. I'd broken some unspoken code, like women shouldn't be here. Period. Did our communication fail?

What now? What was going to happen? We were out in the middle of the desert with no telling who knew exactly why we were here. The driver was US Army, so he should have been clearly following orders, but what were these orders? Did the DG get the proper approvals before we left the base? Nobody wants to sit around an active military site. The feeling of being targeted, like a sitting duck, makes moving and having a purpose the preferred option.

About ten minutes later, they waved us through, with a

reprimand toward me. In a tense voice the driver spoke to me in English while staring straight ahead, not wanting to make eye contact with me, "Keep your head covered and don't talk to anyone but your fellow Americans."

Women were considered bad luck on a base, and there should be minimal contact with any woman, especially American women traveling with and being protected by the US military.

I didn't want to make matters worse for the driver, whose demeanor suggested he was only guilty by association. "I understand."

This was going to be a long night.

"Here," he said, wanting me to exit the truck as quickly as possible. "Last tent is yours."

I jumped out of the transport. *"Salem Merci,"* I said, and went to grab my backpack.

He held it for a moment. "Do not stay long here. It's not safe."

"I understand."

I didn't look back as I walked past my tent and directly to the guarded bunker in the middle of the circle, where I found Jason. He was hunkered over a long metal table with many cords, wires, and various electric tape rolls spread out around him.

"Working hard?" I said in an uplifting voice. He didn't raise his head. "How's it going?"

No response. Jason took his time, and when he looked up, annoyance was written all over his face.

"They sent you. Figures."

I wasn't sure what to make of that comment, so I chose to answer him from a different tack. "I offered to come. I wanted to see you."

He again took his time before looking up from the wires he'd separated out in front of him.

"Don't flatter yourself. The reason you're here is to check on me. Not because you wanted to come here. You just want to make sure I'm good to go and won't blow all of you up."

I sat on a crate next to the tent opening. He'd placed it there to prop open the flap, allowing the cool night air to breeze through now and then.

I looked outside the tent up at the stars. They lit up the entire camp. "Do you ever just look at where we are? The stars are incredible here. After a few nights I stop looking and then realize in a few hours I may not get to see this sight again."

He kept busy with what was in front of him, but did reply in a quiet voice, "I stopped looking up a long time ago."

My thoughts were stuck in the past. Too many of the young men I'd known would've said the same thing. Why were there no positive feelings coming from so many of these young guys when they had everything going for themselves?

"I don't get it," I shot back at him. I usually don't get mad from the jump, but this guy pushed my buttons. "You're smart, you're young, you have a chance to be part of a team that others would give up family for and you sit here complaining, at first when we met you, then showing off without having any experience, and now you sound like the best part of your life is over. What made you so unlikable?"

He finally reacted. "Me? Unlikable?"

I replied, "I'm the best person to team with because I care about everyone making it out alive. You can't even get out of your own head long enough to get to know someone else, especially if that person wants to help you."

No comment. Just the body language of someone who really wanted to disengage from the argument and not offer any explanation for his behavior. "I took a chance coming here to talk with you. Do you get that? Do you even care that I risked myself to come make sure you knew we're counting on you to do what you do best? What did you say when we met you? That you blow things up. Right?"

He stood up and seemed to give me the once over. Then he motioned with his hands, directing me over to the table. I got up deliberately, wanting to see what he was going to do next.

"Come here. I want to show you something. Have you ever held the lead line of an explosive device?" I shook my head side to side. "Don't you want to? Nothing will happen. There's no juice to this wire." He pointed to the tent and to the table. "No electricity here, just the stars and my headlamp."

I knew if I didn't participate willingly in this little test of his, I was never going to get him to open and trust us as teammates for this mission.

"If I do, what do I get out of it besides showing you I'm willing to trust you not to blow me up?"

He laughed. "That's good," he said, holding back his long hair. "I'm usually the one asking what's in it for me, not the other way around."

I stood there waiting for his answer. "What's in it for you?"

He took his right hand and ran it through his straight brown hair looking at me as if his next words would call out his self-consciousness. "I guess a teammate."

I smiled and said, "With less attitude?"

He laughed again. "I can't promise."

"Fair enough."

I walked to the other side of the table and waited for instruction, praying if he was going to do something bad, it would kill me instantly, so I wouldn't have to remember him every day for the rest of whatever life I might have left. I looked right at him and said, "Here's to all the people who said I can't trust!"

He took my hands in his and watched them, waiting to see if I was going to shake loose, if my palms would sweat and whether I would show any fear or nervousness. I looked directly at him, hands clasped together, waiting him out. I'd learned not to show emotion or any sign of being scared from a young age. This wasn't unfamiliar. I wondered if he wished they'd sent someone else who would have tried to fight him and make him realize he was insignificant in their eyes. Replaceable, not important. "Fight for what I feel" was what I used to say. Now I felt an overwhelming sense of self. *I can help him figure out who he is.*

"And now, what's next?"

He was surprised. He couldn't hold it in. The idea that the 'girl' in the group could see him, see through him and his bravado. It was just the two of us in the tent. No one else seemed to care or even wanted to acknowledge that we were there. So why not share something he'd always held inside. Why not share what he felt with this stranger who asked, "What's next?"

Jason released my hands, looked at me and said, "Let's build this mother and go blow something up!"

We both laughed and proceeded to build two backup devices that he felt were needed just in case we had to move to plan B. I started to say something but held back.

He waited, then asked me, "Do you have a plan B?"

"Not here. We need to get some sleep," I said. "A driver will be here soon to get us, and we have to rest."

I surveyed the tent for a blanket. There was a deep-blue and purple throw in the corner next to his backpack. It looked handmade.

"Is that yours?"

"Yeah. My grandma made it for me."

"It's beautiful. May I?" As I reached down to pick it up, I heard something drop and looked down to see a tiny picture frame that must have been tucked away within the keepsake. It was tilted on its side. I could barely see the face and figured it was his grandmother.

"Yeah. That's her. She was the only person who believed I could do well." I handed him the picture frame, and he put it in his shirt pocket.

"Let's get some sleep." I sat back against the hard, cool tent canvas. My eyes closed. What would tomorrow bring? Would there be time to let tonight sink in once we were out of this country, safely flying back to the States?

I was asleep when Mike's timer/beeper went off from within my backpack. I jumped to grab my pack and find the noisy device, my eyes locked on the beautiful throw covering me. Jason must have put it over me as I slept. That's probably why I slept so soundly; being warm and cozy wasn't a state I associated with this place.

"It's our ride," I said—Jason had jumped to his feet when the beeping began. "Time to pack up."

My idea of getting ready to leave was three easy steps: grab the backpack, stuff it with irreplaceable items, and run to the transport. Jason would need some schooling. He took five minutes compiling all the extra wire and then another three minutes packing the miscellaneous parts.

"Let's go!" I said excitedly. "There's barely time left to grab your personal things."

"I never really unpacked," he said in a calm and steady voice. He took his right hand and placed it over his shirt pocket. "I'll be ready in a sec. I've got everything right here."

I remembered his grandmother's picture that he'd placed in his shirt pocket. I envied that relationship that I'd never have. Yes, I was adopted and was grateful for my parents; however, their parents were deceased, and I'd never had a grandparent relationship. He was one lucky guy.

No time to relive thoughts that never go anywhere pleasant. "It's 0323. Time to get outside." Pickup was 0330. "Let's roll."

Jason seemed to be in another world.

"Hey, give me that device now," I shouted, not caring who might hear me. I had no idea whether the people outside this tent understood what this guy had been doing, but I didn't care at this point. We had to go, and today was going to be our exit day after a successful mission.

He carefully loaded the main device into a duffel while I grabbed the backup IEDs, shoving them into my backpack, then stood wedged between the tent flap and the outdoors. "Time to go, now," I said firmly.

I saw two guards approaching the tent. Both looked annoyed as they could see it was me and not Jason in the entrance. "Our hosts prefer to see you, so get out here," I barked over my shoulder, without taking my eyes off the guards. I told myself: *just hold onto why you're here*. One of my instructors at Quantico had given each member of his class a card upon graduation. I kept that card tucked away in an inner pocket inside my backpack. It read:

> *Do not question your worth.*
> *Ask, what is your purpose?*
> *Stay focused.*
> *Lt. Donnelly*

Each time I needed to regroup within my own head before a mission, I pulled out that card and read it, re-read it, and committed myself to the words.

Getting out of the camp was easier than getting in earlier that evening.

"Daylight is not our friend," my driver said, which I knew was correct. Getting in and out before first light was imperative. Now it was 3:28 a.m. We had approximately two hours to perform this mission.

Jason and the guards walked a foot in front of me. I struggled carrying my backpack, now ten pounds heavier than it had been. My shoulders felt each step as I tried to steady myself on the makeshift dirt road strewn with ankle-twisting pieces of concrete. If I ran and stumbled, the devices could be damaged. I couldn't let myself be that person who compromised the mission before it even had a chance to unfold.

Finally, at 0330, we boarded the transport. Our other team members were already on-site canvasing the surroundings for the right place to set up our detonation area and the best location for me to take the shot.

Jason sat with his duffel between his legs, his grandmother's picture still in his pocket and the blanket tucked away inside his personal bag.

"Thanks again for the blanket," I said. "I got a few good hours of sleep."

"It can do that," he said, looking down at the duffel. "I think it has some kind of magical power."

I thought about what he'd just said. I'm certain his grandmother crocheted that blanket with all the love in her being for him, praying with each completed stitch that he would come home unscathed.

3:42 a.m. When was I going to have a person do that for me? Would I do that for my own kids? Absolutely, but would they choose work that put them far away, unable to discuss what they did for a living with anyone outside their workspace? I hoped not.

3:44. Time to regroup and focus on the pending tasks needed to complete this mission successfully.

"Radio one, copy." I grabbed the walkie-talkie that was placed between us and the driver.

"Everyone on board?" Mike asked.

"Roger."

"Excellent, you're two minutes out. We have something for you to change into," he said to me. He handed me a long skirt and berka to cover my exposed legs and hair.

The truck stopped. Mike stuck his face through the front partition separating us from the driver. "Time to play dress up."

He had two little girls at home and was no stranger to costumes and tea parties. But this morning he was all business, even though he still had a good sense of humor. We resumed moving and rode in silence.

"Are you nervous?" Jason asked, as he sat across from me, his duffel bag still between his feet.

"No. I don't get nervous," I replied. "I get calm inside my head."

"What do you think about that gets you into that calm space?"

"My boys."

As soon as the words came out of my mouth, the driver stopped the vehicle. It was still dark outside and time to get this mission executed.

"Jason, it's your first mission in the field, so just concentrate on what you must do. Okay?"

He stared at me, saying, "You look like a cross between one of them women here and a nun."

"Strange combo, huh?" I muffled my laugh and got ready for the call.

Mike stuck his head through the partition; pointing to Jason, he waved his hand saying, "Goodbye, or exit here."

I looked at Jason one more time and tried my best to smile. It was tough, though, as I had this nagging feeling that this was "Goodbye." He got the duffel to the edge of the truck by pushing it with both hands, putting his entire body weight behind him. He jumped out, grabbed the bag's handles and was gone.

Time for me to be dropped off. The truck started up again. Lookouts were placed on four surrounding roofs, locals who were paid handsomely to give our folks at headquarters the best real-time information they could. Trusting them and their intel was difficult for me. I liked getting my own information, but here there was no choice. No one had come this close to the bridge and the villages that surrounded either side.

The river was still; no sound of running water and no noise except for the random barking of a stray dog. The large canvas top of the truck felt like a weight on my head. I wanted to jump out and get to my spot. I could feel the beginning of my own adrenaline start to flow. My stomach tightened and my eyes narrowed. I was mortal and at risk.

The truck stopped. Mike gave me a huge smile. I could see his beautiful white teeth against the darkness of his skin. He had the best smile, warm, inviting, almost even cheerful, given what we were about to do. I smiled back, as big as I could, then pulled my long skirt up in front of me, trying carefully not to step on the fabric. It wasn't graceful, but I managed to make it to the ground without falling. Crouching down, I followed the local young woman guide, holding my outer skirt in my right hand. We had to move quickly. The longer we were outside, the greater the chance for someone to notice us, or me, and realize something wasn't right.

About a hundred feet to our right was the beginning of a fence that blocked people from going down the banks to the water's edge. On the other side were several concrete buildings, two-story with open-roof decks. We made our way into the second building, where a door had been left ajar. The guide took my hand. There were stairs; it was dark, no lights, and silent. She grasped my hand tightly so I would stay close to her and not trip.

We climbed the stairs, one foot following the other, touching each narrow step until we got to the top, which I figured was the roof. A hatch-like wood trapdoor was lifted above our heads. Whit was on the other side of the hatch. I held my arms up, and he grabbed them at each elbow. The young woman held her hands together and got underneath my right foot. I pushed off her palms, and up I went through the trapdoor and into a very small crawl space.

It was dark except for the natural light of daybreak coming from a single window cutout on the right wall. Not really a window, but an opening to the outside. Whit and I both crawled to the opening in the wall. My scope, ammunition, and long-range rifle lay there on the floor. We'd been trained to use night vision, but it made me dizzy. The images were fuzzy, so I opted not to put mine on. Whit loved the new technology. He claimed that his vision was crisper, clearer, when he wore the goggles. The heat-seeking technology was a precursor to video games.

I grabbed the scope and screwed it onto the makeshift bolt placed on top of the Springfield Krag-Jorgensen rifle. The effective firing range was approximately 900 yards. It had a five-round rotary magazine and a V-notched sight that now set a scope, less powerful than modern equipment.

"Hand signals," Whit whispered in my ear.

I knew all too well that I had maybe two shots before we would need to exit this crawlspace. The concrete floor felt cold but stable. Too many times I had to shift my body against old wood planks without making a sound, hoping that the wood wouldn't creak against my weight. This area felt solid. This space fit me, but Whit was taller than I, and he had to wedge his body against the floor and opening so he could look out and survey the outside of the building.

It was still early. No one, not even the donkey-driven carts of the local vendors were out and about. No locals on the street was perfect for us. The village children would still be sleeping. I was grateful for that, as the chance that we'd be seen decreased. There was no room for error. Soon the village would be awake. The sounds of explosives would rock the shacks and vibrate through the concrete buildings.

The waiting was the most difficult part. The rifle was loaded with two longer than standard bullets. This provided more impact, but I was concerned about the range. The army trainer at the base had assured me there was enough loft to reach my target. The calculations had been checked several times. Waiting. Silence. Then, while looking through his night vision, Whit signaled me to go to the ready position. I crouched down, raising the rifle barrel. He positioned it on the ledge of the opening. Two fingers up, then one finger, then a tight-clenched fist. I had movement through the scope. I squeezed the trigger slowly, waiting for the recoil of the Jorgensen. It was quick. I hit the mass. Before I could look again, a loud blast shook the building. That would be the explosives detonating, wiping out the middle of the bridge. We left the equipment behind. I wondered if it was the right thing to do, but we were wearing gloves so no one could trace the items to us.

By the time the building shook, Whit had already opened the hatch. He was down in no time. I backed up from the open space. He pulled me down feet first, from my ankles, then hips, holding on to my waist. I shot down the small opening and tried to adjust my eyes to the still-dark stairwell. Before entering the crawlspace, I counted seven stairs from the bottom to a turn in the stairwell, followed by five to the hatch.

Counting backward, I knew when we reached the bottom. Concrete dust was settling all around us. We bolted out to the street. Within seconds, a dark truck pulled up. We jumped into the truck bed and lay down. No Jason. The driver put a dirty tarp cloth over us. We lay in the dark space, quiet, feeling every bump, dip, and rock the truck rolled over. About twenty minutes passed. We stopped, and the tarp was lifted.

It was morning now, the sun was out, and we were exposed to the outside world. I jumped out of the truck, shedding my torn, dirty burka as quickly as possible. A military helicopter was fast approaching, come to extract us from this sun-worn landscape. As it landed, I grabbed Whit's hand, and we ran toward the chopper blades, ducking and shielding the top of our heads with our hands. We were hoisted into the bed of the helicopter and buckled in across from one another as it lifted off the ground. Whit manuvered his way to the front sitting next to the pilot. He rode shotgun. After a few minutes Whit gave me a thumbs up, and I knew the mission was a success. I could finally breathe as we began to leave Iraqi air space. Soon we would be in Jordan and aboard the army transport plane, ready to take us back home.

We never saw Jason again. I think he knew that when the bridge blew up, so would he. I hope he knew his sacrifice wasn't in vain, that he would have the gratitude of our team and that his grandmother would know just who he was. I debated writing to her, but never did, something I'll have to live with. I guess I was too selfish to take the time to complete one small gesture for him. Moving forward, I vowed to myself that I would contact the family if we ever lost a teammate. They deserved to know what their loved one did, how he died, and his value to the team and the mission.

27

Family

Los Angeles, California
2002-2009

I kept thinking that if something happened to me my son would be alone. Yes, he would have his father, but I wanted him to have a brother. Someone he would grow up with, be close to and always be there for him. A bond that I never had with my own brother, but because they would be close in age, from the same parents, and raised together since birth, maybe that would be a formula for them to always have each other's backs. Hopefully, too, Daniel and I could reconcile.

He and I had grown apart. He resented my going away for work, although he loved my steady paycheck and job benefits. They gave him the opportunity to be his own boss and to remodel or create new homes on his terms.

"Why don't you go into commercial as well as remodeling

homes?" I asked one sunny spring afternoon, while the three of us were at a neighborhood park close to our home. We now lived in Calabasas where the homes were surrounded by grassy parks, children's playgrounds, and community pools.

"I don't like designing buildings. It's boring."

"But it's good money with all the new warehouse development going on right outside Los Angeles. It could bring in consistent money and give you more freedom to choose the homes and clients you want to work with."

Our son, Evan, was sitting at the top of the park slide, ready to slide down to Daniel and me, when Daniel looked at me. "That's your job."

"What do you mean?" I didn't understand his comment.

He moved to the bottom of the slide to catch Evan at the end of the short metal tube. They were both laughing, happy as could be. Daniel lifted Evan on to his shoulders to help him back to the top of the slide, then said, loud enough for others to hear, "That's what you're for."

That comment stung. I knew we needed help if we were to stay together.

A few weeks later, we went to our first counseling session. Daniel had been to therapy before and had asked his former therapist for a referral to a marriage counselor. For three months, each Thursday after work, we met with the counselor. But only for three months.

"What do you want out of this relationship?" she asked me.

"I wish our son had a sibling."

"That's not what I asked you," she said, leaning forward in her worn brown-leather chair. Warm sun lit the window behind her. Daniel and I sat across from her on a small matching leather couch. I was uncomfortable with her staring directly at me.

"I asked what *you* want out of the relationship."

I knew she wanted me to say that I wished we could communicate differently, or that we would commit to spending more time together. But that's not what I wanted. I wanted our son to have a brother or a sister. We locked eyes before I answered her. "I told you what I want from this relationship."

Daniel said nothing. There was no movement from his side of the couch. Nothing to contribute or to help our relationship. We stopped counseling after that.

But my wish did come true that summer. Evan was going to have a sibling.

In March, just two months after the devastating Northridge earthquake, I delivered our second son, Eric. Different from our older son, who took everything in before he said a word, Eric was smiley, giggly, and all action all the time.

***

For the past four years, we'd joined our neighbors' family for a Labor Day weekend in Scottsdale, Arizona. It was becoming a tradition that helped cool things down between Daniel and me. But I didn't want to go this time. Eric was just six months old and Evan a toddler. And I was afraid of Daniel's having some outburst in front of our neighbors and their extended family.

But, after consulting the pediatrician who confirmed that Eric's most important shots had been administered, I reluctantly agreed to go on the trip. Maybe the change of scenery would help Daniel and me reconnect in some way.

Two days into our Scottsdale trip, my baby was happy, bouncing in my arms in the pool. Two days after we returned, he was lethargic, not eating, and just didn't look well in general. I remember looking at him, then at his babysitter, and then at my husband and saying, "He doesn't look right."

Had they given him something other than my frozen breast milk while I was at work? Oh, I should add here that my husband wasn't working full time. He'd been sued for a faulty cantilevered pool. The business wasn't properly incorporated. He was fighting his former client and contractors in court and was unable to keep his architectural business afloat.

Daniel was home, helping with taking our older son to preschool. And, so I thought, he was learning how to take care of our baby so we could let the nanny go by October. We'd be able to save a lot of money, which would help us keep our home while Daniel went through the ordeal of his business litigation. I knew he was depressed, but I couldn't help him out of his self-induced misery and become the man I once hoped he was. I had more important concerns to focus on.

I spent every night in the hospital watching as the MDs and nurses tried various medications to save my youngest son's life. As Eric lay sick, I prayed to God, bargaining that, if my son survived this mysterious infection, I would leave my marriage and raise my boys with all my love, giving them guidance, instilling in them a solid work ethic, and teaching them to respect women.

On the tenth night in the hospital, a nurse asked me to step outside the room and speak with the MD on duty. I could tell something was seriously wrong. Eric wasn't responding to the fourth IV drug concoction; the doctors were running out of ideas. He was near death.

"You should call your husband and have him come here

to say his goodbyes."

But there was no way I was going to give up without a fight. Fortunately, our pediatrician's partner had a colleague at the Centers for Disease Control and Prevention who provided an experimental treatment that saved Eric's life.

Twenty-four hours later, I called my boss to tell him the good news. The hospital was going to let me take Eric home. I knew Director Mike Smith had felt my pain. He'd lost a child early in his marriage. He also knew that, although I was happy to take my son home, my head wasn't in the right place to work. I'd taken two months off with my first child, three weeks with my second. It was time for me to be home for a while to establish a bond with my children.

We talked. He understood I had big decisions to make that would affect my sons for the rest of their lives. "Take some time to think everything through," he said, as if counseling me. "You've been focused on your child. Don't make any rash decisions about your marriage. Think it through." "

"Okay. I will."

Back home from the hospital, I spent nights sitting outside and listening to the solo hooting of an owl that liked to visit my neighbor's tree. Going back to a field assignment meant being away from my children. Just thinking about it, pangs of guilt created real pain throughout my body. How could I leave my two boys when I was the one who brought them into this world? Was I repeating a pattern from my own childhood, knowing how it felt not to have a mother to care for me daily?

The night sky was black, showing the stars at their most magnificent and reminding me of the night that Moshe and I spent in Jerusalem. Standing on his grandmother's balcony, admiring the night sky and the anticipation of feeling each other's bodies. I missed him. Another person I left, I thought. No wonder that, although he loved me, he ultimately chose to leave me, knowing that my work wouldn't provide the type of relationship conducive to raising a family.

The owl had moved on. The night was silent. My head hurt from all the unresolved feelings and questions I had about being a mother and a field agent. I could do both, but was it fair to my sons?

A month went by, and the same questions swirled around my head, making me half-present. The situation was bad between my husband and me. We barely spoke to each other. Daniel was stressed from his business collapsing and the lawsuits he faced. I knew there were money issues.

One afternoon the doorbell rang. I had my younger son in my arms as I opened the door to find a Los Angeles sheriff in my doorway. He asked me to verify my name and handed me a manila envelope. I shut the door, set my son down in his playpen, and opened the envelope. Our house was in foreclosure. I had no idea what was going on. Daniel had been paying the bills out of our joint checking account where both our paychecks went each month. Why hadn't he paid our mortgage?

A few hours later, Daniel came home. I left the letter on the kitchen table, knowing he would see it before coming outside where I was playing with the boys in our backyard.

"What have you done with our money?" I asked him, still in shock.

He told me he took money I earned for our family to pay his legal fees instead of paying our mortgage. When he started to have business problems, he should have told me. I shouldn't have found out about our house foreclosure from a sheriff coming to our front door. The last thing I wanted was to raise our sons in a home where there was no love or respect between the parents. Now we might lose our home.

And there was more. Daniel had been cheating on me with the young woman we'd hired to help with the children.

It was over between us. I had to leave. But, first, I needed to get back to work and plan for leaving my marriage. My annual salary was $48,000. Not much was left in our savings account. We needed to sell the house and go our separate ways. It would take me two years to save enough money for a lawyer, childcare plus six months' rent for an apartment.

When I did leave, I did so quickly. The night before—after the boys were asleep—I told Daniel that it was over. The next morning, I left with nothing more than a few pieces of my clothing, baby diapers, kids' clothes, blankets, and my two children, who were now six and three years old.

My kids were safe; we had a new apartment to live in next to Eric's preschool, and they would see their dad every Wednesday night for dinner and stay with him every other weekend. Life would be different, but that was all right.

A few days later, I felt excited as I drove to the West Los Angeles Federal Building. I no longer felt my old inhibitions about who I was. Yes, I was now a single mother. I was still connected to my job, never missing a briefing or an opportunity to connect with my past teammates. I was looking toward my new future and what my position would be. My intentions were good and my outlook positive.

When I arrived at the meeting, several people who had supported me on many of my bureau assignments greeted me. It felt good to be back in the building with folks I knew well and respected.

"Glad you're back! Happy to have you with us." Everyone seemed welcoming, and my heart beat faster as I rode the elevator to Director Mike's office.

Exiting onto the floor housing the Western Division leadership, I smelled the coffee brewing across the hallway from Mike's office. It was comforting. The Ramadi mission had left a major impact on me. All I wanted was a position here in the building where I could come home each night and put my sons to bed. Many women wanted these positions. You're connected to the field, but not in it. Instead, you were supporting agents with logistics, travel, contact information, and sometimes even driving them to and from certain local destinations or supplying clothing changes, wigs, makeup, and cash. I was prepared to move forward without my team. I had a new team: my family.

"Come on in," Director Mike said, with arms extended. We hugged, which was unusual. My big boss had never shown emotion to me in this way. It was like a father greeting his child after a long separation.

"You look good, but how are you?"

"What do you mean? You said I look good; I'm good."

He eyed me, looking down at my out-of-date flats, my scuffed, worn heals, my black slacks that were two sizes too big, and my black sweater and tweed jacket, which screamed late '80s and not mid-1990s style.

"How are your boys?"

"Everyone is healthy. Thank you. It's been good to be home."

I knew he was aware of my younger son's hospital stay, but I didn't know if he knew I was on my own now. Divorce, paperwork pending, was complete.

"You've had a rough go of it personally."

I looked directly at him without responding. Weakness wasn't a strength.

"First, your baby almost dying and then finding out your husband wasn't paying the mortgage and cheating on you while you were away on assignment."

He knew all the dirty details, but why were we rehashing the ugliness of my personal life and not talking about work?

"I wanted to have you here so we could talk through what's next for you." He sat back in his chair and calmly shot down my dream. "You'd probably like to come here every day and assist other agents or work in forensics. That's not going to happen. Your skills, no, let me correct myself, your talents are rare. There have been only two agents before you, many years ago, who could shoot with the accuracy you have using both hands. Your instructors may have downplayed this to you, but not to me. We know what your talents are."

"We?" I asked, not understanding who, besides he and I, and possibly the deputy general from my last mission in Ramadi, would know or care about my skills.

"My superiors. That's the 'we.' Collectively, we have decided to build on what's apparent to us. You have the mental capability, the intellect, to move into intelligence work. Not just mission work but gathering information.

"Your writing skills are excellent, thanks to UCLA having one of the toughest English literature programs in the US. The fact you graduated with honors confirms that. When we discuss what's needed for us to build proper courses of influence long term, whether here or abroad, we need information from trusted individuals. This is going to be your focus. For now, let's say it's the next evolution of your career."

I was in shock. How was this going to work for my family, my two sons? How could I be gone and raise them to be respectful, mindful young men? Then, before I could say anything negative, I realized that here was someone who had taken a chance on me when I was a college junior. How could I say no or question his plan for me?

"You took a chance on me before I knew anything of who I really was. Thank you, Sir. I won't let you down."

He could tell I was masking my apprehension; not questioning him was protocol. It still meant there were looming uncertainties that needed to be addressed. He leaned forward, out of the cozy reclining position he'd been in before. "I know you won't let me down. I also know you aren't going to let yourself down." I smiled and got up from the chair.

"Sir, I don't want to let my sons down."

He got up, and we shook hands. As I was about to leave his office, he said to me, "The best mothers have a balance between being present at home and being contributors outside of the home. It doesn't matter if that entails a job, volunteering, or helping others. The best mothers show their children what productive people do in a society. You're going to continue modeling this for your children."

I knew that if Director Mike Smith had confidence in me, I needed to let go of my fear.

***

"You can do this." That's what I kept saying to myself as the airplane rose higher into the clouds. A 5:00 a.m. departure to Las Vegas. I would switch planes there to O'Hare and then Newark. That evening I would leave with several selected off-duty soldiers to Erding Air Base outside of Munich, Germany. Then on to the next mission.

Looking at my hands, I reflected that I was entering into this assignment as a divorced woman. I had never worn my wedding band on assignment, but I knew I was married. This time was different. No husband, but the guilt was still there. I could hear Daniel's voice in my head telling me I was a horrible mother and wife.

"You can't mother from thousands of miles away. I don't get why you can't find a job that lets you be here in the morning to get them ready for daycare and be home after work to pick them up, make dinner, put them to sleep and, when they can't sleep, be here to comfort them."

I closed my eyes and thought about my children. The only thing I could do well was my job and make sure to come back to them as soon as I could. In the meantime, I would call, tell them I love them, and provide for them.

28

Fallujah: Back in the Action

Al Anbar Governorate, Central Iraq
2002

My sons were growing up quickly. Whenever I left the house, my older son asked where I was going and when I would be back. Although it had been almost two years since I'd left the country on a mission, Evan seemed to know I would be leaving again.

A few weeks later I got the call to get ready. Our core team—Big Mike, Whit, J.B., and I—would be coming together for another mission. I loved being home and watching my children grow. There was a part of me that never wanted to leave them, but in my heart, I knew being their mother was still not enough. I missed the action, knowing that what we could provide could save people from despotic rule, from having their freedoms stripped and even their lives taken. That's why when I got the call to Fallujah in 2002, I said yes without hesitation.

Starting in 2002 in Afghanistan, the US needed information about Russian and Saudi Arabian influence over the oil rights and provinces that were being controlled by the government leaders. Kaddafi was going insane, and Arafat was on a pilgrimage to overthrow the Israeli government. Each Arab nation had a separate channel for weapons, money, and intelligence required to 'shape' people to their way of thinking. The Chinese had money and wanted oil, but at a price they could negotiate, given they had their own transport. Chinese oil tankers would move Russian weapons and ammunition to where their buyers requested the drops be made. Whoever controlled the seas in that region had power. China and Russia had the seas locked up.

I was assigned to report to an army base in the middle of a struggle between the Iraqi government and our nation. Living on an army base wasn't my first choice of missions; Afghanistan had been eye-opening enough. At this point in my career, I didn't necessarily want to jump into a war zone, but my superiors felt differently. Fallujah was a hotbed of Iraqi protest. American forces patrolling Baghdad, Kabala, and other provinces were ordered to let the public demonstrate against the presence of the US. It was ground zero for the clash between the citizens and the soldiers. The army was not 'friendly' to the public for obvious reasons. To the outside world, the military commanders ordered (by rules of engagement) the infantry to stand down when confronted, only to tell them the Iraqis were dirt and deserved to be shot for running their mouths when the soldiers were back on base.

This was the atmosphere I entered in 2002. Newly divorced and raising two sons on my own since 1998, I really was in no position to decline any assignment. I went where I was told to go and executed my part of the mission. I was working with a US Special Operations team. Relations between the military and the intelligence community were not always cooperative. The army folks looked at everybody as an outsider, making a turbulent situation even more uncomfortable.

We generally passed through individually, usually a week or two, long enough to receive our orders, identify our targets and remove them. Although intelligence officers are a part of the army, most don't see combat, so they are minimally tolerated. This makes them less than welcome to their Department of Defense associates.

You can imagine how they feel: intelligence personnel showing up, asking them to put their lives on the line to protect us when we went into the villages seeking information. Now I was here, needing to befriend our soldiers as well as the Iraqis who were needed to inform our missions. This wasn't as easy as I thought it would be. The only way to win their respect was to shoot my target and then get out of their way. That first night was a precursor of what was to come.

As I approached the open-bed transport truck that would take us from First Battalion's base into the center of Fallujah, I reflected on the lessons my colleagues and I'd learned in Ramadi. Basically, stay under the radar and get out as soon as you can. And in my case, try to not act like a girl!

Just jumping into the truck bed, which was about five feet off the ground, was a challenge. There were handgrips on the sides above each of the four outer tires. Holding onto one grip and hoisting myself up without falling backward wasn't going to be pretty. It worked, although I banged my knee on the corner of the metal box toolbox that ran down the side of the open bed—the coveted side because you could sit on the bench-like box and hold onto the railing, stabilizing yourself when the truck hit a bumpy patch of road, which was inevitable.

We drove through a desert, with unpaved surfaces full of rocks, dirt, and potholes leading into narrow trails to the small villages along the way.

"Can I make room for you?" a tall young man asked me as he began to move over, knocking his fellow sniper teammate's thigh as if to push him out of the way.

"Thank you, but I'm good here." Rules of engagement: don't take a favor unless you can pay it back. A lesson I learned living on a base in the middle of nowhere, far from home.

We took off, starting to gain speed as each of us swayed back and forth with the wind in our faces, helmets pointed in the opposite direction of the bump we would next traverse. How long would I be here? I needed to work fast. My peripheral vision revealed that the soldiers, all ten of them, especially the five surrounding me in the truck bed, wanted to help me out. I couldn't see the three in the front cab, but the two lookouts were paying a great deal of attention to how I was sitting on the bare metal bench, my breasts bouncing to the cadence of the rocky terrain. I just looked down at the laces on the base-issued boots I'd been given. Wanting this ride to be over as soon as possible, my mind drifted in and out of the facial images that we'd been given to study.

I needed to find the contact, one of the villagers we paid who would connect me to the right people working for a catering company that supplied our military bases. The company was US based, but many of the workers came from the local villages, and, despite the fact we paid for their livelihood, believed we had no right to be there or to influence their government. These protesters would become the local insurgency.

The desert sun began to fade, which meant we had less than thirty minutes to get in and out of the area. There were three patrols per day, and none at night at the moment, so this would be the last patrol shift. I could tell these guys wanted to get out of here, which made me that much more unsettled. How was I going to get through to anyone in less than thirty minutes? What was the point of bringing me here on the last patrol that would soon end at nightfall?

The truck stopped. I had no weapon visible to these soldiers, no leg holster concealed under my khakis. What I did have was a knife. *If I have to use it, I will*, I thought as we offloaded from the truck bed.

My assignment was simple: obtain a description of the landscape of the small residential area comprised of five low-level apartment buildings. Each building was three or four stories high with a rooftop deck. Most concrete buildings kept their water cisterns on the top, anchored to the roof. Each rooftop would be accessible from the top-floor hallway. Most had only one access; some had two at opposite ends of the corridor.

The village was small. Eight buildings: five residential, one that resembled a warehouse, the other two, a school and a mosque. The first residential building to my right seemed still. Aromas of hot oil, chicken, lamb, onions, and peppers filled the air. Near the front door, children squatted, playing a game with shiny rocks. No other doors faced the front of the square.

I made my way behind the soldiers as they turned to enter

the building. I stayed behind, waiting for the "all clear" before approaching the entry. This apartment was active. Women cackled as they cooked. Children ran up and down the short hallway and staircase. These people knew the routine. They parted, making room for the soldiers to search each unit. Teenagers sat, more like lounging, halfway down the hallway. They concerned me.

The teenagers recruited the little ones to do their rifle and ammo runs. The children would be coaxed into doing the older guys' bidding, carrying whatever their small hands could hold. Candy went a long way, but recognition from the older siblings seemed to be the real reason so many of them did what they were told to do.

"Kush akin," the smart-mouthed teen at the end of the hallway yelled out to the young boy standing at the foot of the stairs. As the little boy ran up the stairs, the soldiers turned and fired. No warning. This is what happens in a contentious environment. The small boy rolled down the stairs and landed at my feet.

From out of nowhere, I felt the heat of a gun barrel pointed at my back.

The soldiers yelled at whoever was behind me, "Put down the gun!"

A shot rang out before I could move. Down went the body of the person behind me. If his finger had been on the trigger, he might have shot me from an impulse, a reaction to being shot. I would have been crippled or worse.

The teen at the end of the hall came charging toward me, racing at full speed—no weapons, just his hands in the air screaming at the top of his lungs. My knife was wedged into my back belt loop and underwear. I pulled it out just before he jumped on me. The only thing between the two of us was the sharp metal blade that pierced his heart. The dark red flow of his blood seeped onto my shirt and pants. He was still on top of me when the tall soldier who'd offered his seat on the truck, pulled me away from him. *He must think I'm bleeding,* I thought, as I tried to gather myself and stand, only to be told to sit and wait.

The building units upstairs had been cleared, the women leaving the food, some crying hysterically as they were carried or escorted out of the kitchen onto the street. The small boy and young teen now lay side by side. My knife handle protruded from the teen's body. He had been laid across the cold cement floor. Directly between us was the foot of the stairs.

***

I sat in the makeshift shower, crouched down, letting the lukewarm water splash on me, not wanting to move. Other than the sound of running water, silence surrounded me. The water grew cold, but my body didn't react. My mind was blank except for the vision of the hallway and the rose-colored light.

I don't know how long I sat in the shower. Time had stopped back in that building. I dried my hair and slipped on a fresh, white t-shirt and brown khaki pants. I looked at the cot opposite the bathroom and saw my knife on it. Clean, with the blade shining from the moonlight coming through the small window above the bed.

I lay down, wondering how we were going to approach entering the village again after the fatal incident with the boys. I still needed to connect with the designated contact and was resolute about needing to carry on so we could get out of there. I struggled into a kind of sleep.

When I woke up the next morning, my knife was still there. I'd wrapped it in toilet paper and placed it under the mattress and box spring within arm's length of my pillow. There was a knock on my door as I was getting dressed.

"Prep meeting in thirty minutes. Building eight."

"Thanks," I said, wondering who was on the other side of the door. "I'll be there."

While brushing my teeth and slicking my curly hair back into a makeshift ponytail, I couldn't shake the thought that the meeting was some type of court-martial for un-enlisted personnel. I'd taken a life. A young person, which made it that much worse.

I gazed at myself in the mirror. I hadn't been able to shake the images of the past day, and I looked pale. Heavy bags under my eyes revealed the little sleep I'd gotten the nights before and after the failed operation. It certainly wasn't my best look. The previous night I'd been nervous, having not been around the soldiers here, and I was on high alert after my last experience on a military base. The cries of the women haunted me. Would I ever be able to sleep well again?

What I did know was that I needed to be at Building 8 in ten minutes. I walked down the narrow aisle between buildings, past some soldiers who were outside smoking and staying among themselves. One smiled at me.

"How you doing, miss?" another said.

I couldn't help but think something was different. These guys were being nice to me. I entered the building.

"We should be starting the briefing shortly," said the CO of the base camp.

The soldier standing behind me said under his breath, "Let's get this underway."

I looked behind me. He had a confident look and tone.

Tall and strong, he appeared non-confrontational, but, clearly, someone who would have your back and could hold his own in a fight. He reminded me of what everyone wants in an older, protective brother.

"Coffee?" he asked, as he reached around my right side to present a strong, black steaming cup to me.

"Thank you," I said without turning around again. I was trying to be cool, but this sudden shift of attention toward me wasn't expected. At the same time, my gut told me that everything about the attention of this 'new friend' was about my sex. After all, I was female and a guest on the base. It turned out that that couldn't have been farther from the truth.

Apparently, my new friend's acknowledgment was about what happened in the village. I'd later learn that they recognized that I'd held my own. That I had done my part to protect the soldiers from the teenager. I had reacted instinctively, and my actions had, perhaps, saved another soldier from injury, maybe even death. I'd earned the unit's recognition and respect. Even though I was a guest, I was the one who had their backs, and now they would have mine.

During the briefing there was a definite air of aggression toward the villagers. Soldiers wanted either to see combat or go home, no in between. It's a scary time when soldiers want payback. I wanted to connect with my contact and then get out of here.

The CO began the briefing. There would be three teams. They would fan out to the remaining three villages that surrounded the main hub of the elite Muslim leadership. We needed to move fast, be vigilant, and narrow down where they were getting their arms, ammunition, and training. I thought I could help on two out of three. If I could get to my contact, she could provide the training facility location, as our intel believed her brother was involved. At a minimum, she could tell us where he was.

Our information indicated they were training with AK-47s, rocket launchers, and long-range missile targeting. The CO wanted that base located and neutralized. For me to contribute, I just needed to connect.

Later that afternoon, I was gearing up to load onto the truck carrying Group Three. My mind kept returning to the last village and the rose-colored walls that had haunted me the night before. I reached for my knife, but I knew I needed more than this to protect me and my contact. I decided to ask for a gun. Couldn't hurt. The worst they could say was no.

I saw the soldier handing out helmets and asked, "Could I get a weapon, so I can—"

He cut me off off mid-sentence. "We got you. Here, use this and keep it with you." He handed me a small .22-caliber pistol that resembled a Saturday night special. I thought this wasn't going to cut it, but he did give me something more than my knife, so I bit my tongue and simply replied, "Thanks."

I found it silly and maybe even sexist that this guy, like most men here, thought a woman couldn't shoot. The men generally have the larger weaponry. The bigger the gun, the bigger the soldier. I didn't agree with that, but I knew my place. Here you didn't ask questions. Hand-eye coordination, quick reflexes, and keen instinct as to when you had the right shot had nothing to do with being a man or woman. It was in a person's gut and mind. No one can give you that. No one can make you pull the trigger when you should take the shot that ultimately kills. It's within the shooter and his ability to react without hesitation.

"You'll ride with us just like last time," said my coffee-drinking soldier. I was happy to be with them again, as they now knew me, sort of. The other teams didn't really know me. We got to the last village before sundown.

"Thirty minutes max, back by 17:40," said the tank commander.

No one wants to be late or cause others to leave later than need be. This place smelled of death and anxious people. I studied every face, trying to determine how I was going to know which one was my contact. Working with such little information, I had to believe she'd come to me.

We started to go building to building, the soldiers leading through each broken doorway. A few soldiers climbed the outside ladders to the rooftops across the street from us, positioning for backup. From that vantage point, they could see exactly where we were and, hopefully, could protect all of us on the ground. No one was safe here. This village was last on the patrol list. If my contact wasn't there, what would I do?

My time here grated on me. The heat, the foul smell of stinky men, the fact I would have to deal with personal issues when I returned to the States, all made me anxious. Not sleeping well had started to take a toll on my overall wellbeing. Where was my contact?

Al Anbar is the major trade city in Iraq. Although we were in Fallujah, it wouldn't have surprised me if my contact traveled to and from there for her husband's family to do business. Considering how much money they would be making, 194 kilometers, or 120 miles, isn't that far. It would also make perfect sense to live out here in this rural, pedestrian village if you were trying to hide an illegal trading business.

Many of our contacts were women. I would suspect the main reason for this was to gain access to America. They wanted to get their children out of here. Clean air, no bombs, no gunfire—a chance to live the American dream. If they provided us with the information we needed, they could collect the "golden ticket," as we called it.

I thought back to the task at hand. If I were successful here, then the next mission would begin. If we could identify the arms trader, we would eliminate him, sending a message to his suppliers that a new leader oversaw this coveted supply route. That person would work for us, enabling information to flow freely back to our decision makers. Other missions would follow, but we needed to get to this person quickly. The longer this took, the more weapons would be distributed throughout the villages, making it that much harder to protect our soldiers as well as the Iraqi government.

Little pieces of candied gum, Chiclets, rattled around in the pockets of my cargo shorts. I remembered from my Israeli days that all kids love candy. Most mothers don't. Something about gum, though, makes it hard for a parent to say no.

It seemed each village had more kids than the next. I wanted to distract the children, getting them away from the building's entrances so the soldiers could do their job clearing each room. Before, they could play and live without cares or concerns, then we came, and their world was turned upside down, creating fear, caution, and anxiety. A little Chiclet would bring smiles from ear to ear.

When the soldiers and I approached the first building, the kids stopped what they were doing to run toward us. I waved the tiny, colorful boxes, shaking them so the pieces rattled. Before I knew it, I was surrounded by laughing, smiling faces grabbing the gum boxes from my hands. I could barely keep up with the demand!

"Thank you for being so kind," said a young woman. She had been blocked from view by all the children until they scattered after receiving their goodies. "I have something for you."

This was what I was waiting for, the signal that she was the person I was looking for. "Tea?"

"Yes, please," I said as she turned to lead me to their schoolhouse. She was a teacher; the children were her extended family. This small wood and concrete, one-story single structure was the village school. It could accommodate maybe thirty students. I marveled at how one teacher could teach all the different ages in one building.

I entered after her and smelled lavender and patchouli. We sat in the front of the room on carpets covering the floor. She'd prepared the tea beforehand, knowing I'd be looking for her. I didn't know how she'd received that information.

"My husband was a teacher at the university," she explained as we both sipped the sweet, orange-flavored tea. "I do not know how he got into this business. I want my two children to be safe, and he is not providing that for us."

I said nothing, just observed her mannerisms. I could tell she'd been waiting a long time to do this. She was calm, determined to fix the futures of her and her children, a path out of here to a stable, solid, safe environment.

"Here are the pictures I have of him." She fingered through the photos, knowing it was the last time they would be in her possession, and explained that part of his current address was handwritten on the back of the four pictures. "I broke up the address so if one picture was lost, the address would not be known."

She put the pictures into a small white envelope, then placed them on the old wooden tray that sat between us. "Please, tell me he will not suffer." I took the envelope and placed it in one of my pockets, now emptied of the gum boxes.

"I can't promise, but I will make a request on your behalf. Thank you. *Merci!*"

I got up and started toward the doorway, but stopped at the sound of gunshots being fired from outside. "Get down!" I screamed, so she could hear me over the noise.

I dropped to the wood floor, keeping my eyes focused on the street outside, and slid back out of the open doorway toward her. She held her hands over her ears. The shots grew louder, so I knew the people firing were coming closer. I didn't want to implicate her. She didn't deserve to be taken out in her own schoolhouse. She'd earned her golden ticket, and I didn't want her caught up in whatever was happening outside. I told her to stay put on the ground, not to move until she saw or heard the tanks leaving the village.

Ever so carefully, I peeked out the open window frame, trying not to make my head too visible. Reaching for my gun, I gave her a quick look and determined that the soldiers shooting must be coming from the main street to my left. The sound carried. I couldn't see anyone, but knew I had to get back to the truck. The window frame was open, no glass, and the drop below to the street was about three feet. Hurdling through it, I landed on the dirt, quickly crawling to the wall, pressing my back against the building, and moved away from the gunfire toward the back of the schoolhouse.

Bullets flew around me, piercing the school's stucco walls. When I got to the back of the building, it was quiet. I could see our transport about thirty feet east of where I was. *I've got to move now*, I thought, *before they leave without me*. To my left, the gunfire started up again. Now was the time.

I sprinted as fast as I could toward the open truck, praying I'd make it alive. The gunner did his job and protected me. Within seconds of jumping into the truck, we took off, barely escaping the village's attack.

Once again, I'd been in the thick of the action, as I'd wanted to be. Once again, I'd survived. Once again, I struggled with my role as a mother. Every time I thought I knew who I was or who I should or want to be, I struggled. Once again.

29

Damascus

Damascus, Syria
2011

16:14:00

This is the time designated for Whit and me to meet at the car we stashed across from where he should have already taken the shot. No one has followed me into the parking garage.

16:14:12

I wonder what's holding him up. The target should be dead, and Whit should have made it to the car by now.

16:14:16

Something's wrong. I feel exposed.

16:14:20

I hear tires screech around the corner. Two men jump out. A Glock 17 is pointed directly at my face. No warning. *Oh crap. Where's Whit?* I ask myself.

16:14:22

The second man ties my hands together and throws me into the open trunk. Seconds later I feel the prick of a hypodermic needle stuck into my upper arm. I see the trunk lid shutting. I scream, but the drug is too strong. Fighting to keep awake, I think to myself, *How in the hell did I get here?*

30

Duma

Duma, Syria: 10 km from Damascus

My memory is shot. I don't remember what happened to me after I passed out in the trunk of my captors' car, and I want so desperately to retrace my steps. I'd so stupidly trusted Whit to give me the all-clear sign without knowing he'd chosen the quickest route to the getaway car; and I hadn't checked who was in the parking garage before I ran down the concrete ramp from the fourth to the second floor.

Why was I hauled away in the back of a trunk without any of my teammates trying to save me? Where were the agents who supposedly backed us up? Surely the GPS coordinates of where I was captured, where these militants drove me, and where I was now being held had to be known and discussed, and a plan to rescue me being formulated.

Stay calm, breathe, and try to assess: am I hurt, bleeding, or unable to walk? What do I need to know and remember: where I am, who I am, who caused this, and who is keeping me here?

The transition from night to day is unclear. Stale air fills the concrete floor and stone walls of this four-foot by seven-foot cell. Very little room to stretch out horizontally, mostly vertically. If I was taller, it would be much worse. At 5'2" I have some room to move around. I can stand, sit, and lie down. I can walk. From the rusted metal bars to the back wall is nine steps, heel to toe.

No windows, no natural light fills the room, not until the door at the beginning of the hall is opened and the guards make their way down the narrow hallway counting those of us behind the bars. They don't count out loud. I try to determine where I am in relation to the number of cells. Am I at the end or near the middle?

When the door opens, I'm far enough away to see some light on the other side of the doorway, so I know I'm not near the entrance, but not too far. I can see an old gaslit lamp on the right and a wood chair up against the far wall of the hall. Once the door is closed, after the guard has done his counting, it becomes black again. No sounds or movement, just darkness.

I focus on the end of the hallway and eventually my sight adjusts ever so slightly, and I see a sliver of light around the door edge. Listening with all my concentration, I can faintly hear the guards' voices. It must be time to check on the prisoners, but it seems like the last time a guard counted us just happened. What is this? A new person, a change in routine, a new prisoner? The voice comes close, closer, filling up the darkness. No lights. Now the sounds of footsteps marching in two's down the old battered concrete floor.

"Yalla," the guard shouts. Time to get up!

Time to be shoved into another room, colder than this holding cell. They unlock the door as I cower in the far back corner of the pen. What's going to happen next? Will they hurt me? Will I survive it? I keep telling myself: *you will not die here. You can get through this.*

I feel their hesitation as they approach me. The guard closest to me pushes me; my back hits the stone wall. The other guard comes up to me and pins my shoulders back into the well-worn stones. What are they going to do to me now? Can I scream? Breathe? I can't move, but I want to run away, leave all of this behind like it never happened. I'm not here, never have been. I'm home with my sons. I'm not in a foreign dungeon, pinned to the back wall by two Assad-regime Syrian guards.

I'm wearing torn jeans under a shredded, dirty, long linen skirt. This is a surprise to them. One of the guards' grimy hands pats down the sides of my blue jeans, looking for something, then he stops. He reels back, yelling for the other guard to move away from me. They back out of the cell, never turning around. I can barely see them, but I feel the stare.

The old sliding metal-barred door clinks shut, and they both hurry down the walkway to the closed door leading to their desks. Why has the door been closed behind them? Usually it's open, shedding a dim light down the hallway. Why did they step away from me? What were they thinking? I crouch down, resting on the back of my heels, my hands still bloody from trying to punch the car trunk open. What's going to happen next? I fight the urge to cry. If I lose sight of what's happening, something worse than what I imagine now will take over. I just need to endure this until someone comes to rescue me. A team member, the Seals, the Special Forces, somebody back home knows something has gone wrong. I keep believing in the fact that this is not my end.

I stare into the black, unforgiving air around me, my thoughts jumbled from lack of water and food. Another door opens. I hear it, but it sounds different from the usual door separating us from the guards' quarters. Is this going to help or hurt me more than I already am? Will I be safe or will I be tortured? Will I be released? What will I have to sign to get out of here whole?

The two guards are now four. They speak Arabic, not a language I'm very fluent in. Two come up to the cell door and two stay back against the door opposite mine. The lock gives way, and they slide the door back. I can tell they're apprehensive. Could they really fear me? Why? Then it hits me.

Earlier, the guards must have finally realized I was a woman. No wonder their quick exit. I had to be right. Given their culture, they were probably confused. Women are 'hands off,' unless she's yours. It starts to make sense. None of them wants to be the one who gives me a bruise, or hurts, rapes, or kills me. I'm a true negotiation tool, to be kept untouched until the proper price is extracted.

Guards one and two approach me calmly; they take my arms and pull them together, while tying my wrists in front of my body. I walk in between them, two in front and two behind. Outside the cell, I stand in the dark, hands tied, my back facing where I'd been held. I want to look at that cell, but for all the strength in me, I can't turn around.

The guards behind me hold my shoulders, and the two in front place a cloth over my head. I can't see, but know it isn't to kill me. They didn't tie it or secure it in any way. The guards from behind me move to either side of me and hold my upper arms to keep me in place. With their guidance we walk toward the illuminated guard area. Now I can see the light that seemed so dim and far away when I was in that cell. I feel the warmth of a lamp through the glass globe of the fixture.

As we wait for who, I don't know, my heart beats faster. Perhaps they've made a mistake, and I'm to be let go. Maybe they've already negotiated my release, realizing this goes against their cultural norms. No possible way a male would want to jail a woman in this country. Women aren't held, tortured, beat as the men are, especially in a facility that holds men.

My instinct tells me this is some type of exchange. Being a woman here in Syria is a liability from the start. Surely, imprisoning me in what I believe to be a man's jail will put them at risk. My captors are in heated debate. My mind races. I wish I could see their faces if only to identify them once I'm out of harm's way. The lamplight starts flickering as their voices rise to the point, perhaps, that the argument will get physical.

I stand, head covered, looking down at my tattered skirt, wishing they would come to a compromise so the next step, whatever that is, will come. The saying "be careful what you wish for" never resonated with me. If you wish for something, why wouldn't you be excited when it materialized? Until now, most of my wishes had come true: leaving foster care to be adopted, having a sibling, going to school, getting into college, passing my Bureau tests, getting to work on some exciting and meaningful missions, all positive, all good life-changing events, until now. They push me from behind, this time far more aggressively than before. I feel in my gut that wherever they're taking me will be worse than my little cell.

The two guards are no longer beside me. Someone is in

front, pulling me by a rope that has been tied around my already bound wrists. Another is behind me, pushing me forward. We walk down the narrow hall, then down steps where I fall to my knees trying to navigate the stairs. The air is cold and damp. No light except the flashlight being held by the guard holding the rope connecting me to him. Turning right, I hit the wall. Stone or something old and worn. My forehead hurts.

This is not what I expected. No one is coming here to help me. At least not now. Apparently, no one cares where I am. The feeling of being alone, even though at least two or three men surround me, makes me feel just like I did as a child. All those people coming in and out of the home, no one seeing me, even though I was directly in front of them. Being passed up, as they walked continuously down the hallway to the next bed-lined room filled with nursery toys and cribs. Everyone wanted to adopt babies, not a young child, and here, these guards wanted to have captured a man, not a woman. Down we go, the air becoming damper and mustier.

My head throbs. It doesn't help that I'm being led by a makeshift leash tied to my already bound wrists and that my head is enclosed by some homemade shroud that smells like it was someone's dog blanket. The guard in front of me stops. I run into his back, not able to tell how close or far he is from the rope that binds us. I hear a door being unlocked, then get one last shove from the guard behind me.

My shroud is lifted. I'm now in another confined space, this time without bars. Though the bars in my old cell kept me contained, they did allow for some light to penetrate from the hallway. I see a woman, a large woman, her hands on her hips, staring at me.

The men are gone. The solid-wood door is closed, and,

I assume, locked. She points to my skirt, using her hands like we're playing a game of charades. She points her fingers downward, trying, I guess, to tell me to take it off. I wriggle out of it, first taking my bound hands and pushing the elastic waistband down as far as I can. It's difficult to do because I have little leverage.

Then I sit on the cold wood floor. It's wet and smells of fetid air mixed with animal stench, which makes me gag. I bend over, inching my skirt over my knees, trying not to upset her. She stands in front of me, not helping, but not harming me. The best I can do is get the fabric over my knees onto my shins. It's tough to figure out what I should do next, so I look up, needing direction.

She pulls the ragged cloth over my jeans and boots. Now what? She stares down at me. I can tell she's trying to figure something out, but what? Her hands grab onto my tied wrists, and she pulls me to my feet. Now she takes her stubby index finger and undoes the first of five buttons on my Levi's. She sees the white and blue women's briefs I'm wearing; the waistband peers out from the opening between the fourth and fifth buttons. Pulling the panel toward her, she scowls, squinting her eyes as if she's about to see something she would rather not.

I don't know how much she can truly see, given the small penlight she clutches between her teeth. Pulling my Hanes panty waistband toward her, she peers into my pants and quickly backs up. She's seen what she was afraid of. I'm a girl. She is only verifying what the male guards already know.

I laugh as she takes the penlight out of her mouth. It just happens. I have no real control over my emotions or the thoughts that stir around in my mixed-up head. She comes at me quick and hard. A right to the jaw. I stagger back, holding my cheek, trying not to fall.

***

I must have passed out. For how long? It's dark, this place, this somewhere with no light, no sound, no water, and no food. At least I wasn't strip-searched or had a male guard pull my panties down to verify my gender. *Be thankful no one has touched me* was my mantra, as it had been when I was in foster care.

Now, laughing out loud, I feel that I'm back in the system, just another jail, another no-name existence, where humans are numbers, not individuals. I have come this way fighting to figure out who I am, what self-worth is, and how I can find mine. When will I be out of here? I'm not finished by a longshot, and this certainly isn't going to be my end.

I crouch down in the dark, wet, boxy cell, my mind starting to flood with memories. My sons, my parents, my now ex-husband, my life moments of self-definition. Where do I feel most like me? What am I doing that makes me feel most like myself? I can envision myself at the range, training, shooting; laughing with my partner as we sit for endless hours in our unmarked car, waiting to scout someone or something that will break open a case; back in DC, testing for my Intelligence Agency transfer, riding the bus to school in Kansas City, hiding behind the thick-white curtains in the foster-care facility, listening to the nurses and aides earmark the 'weak' kids and the survivors. Is this going to be another point in my life where I need to dig deep and figure out how to take my situation, combined with who I am, and redefine myself again?

Yes. I'm going to live and that means getting out of here.

My hands still tied in front, I stand and feel for the door through the darkness. The wood is worn and smooth to my cold fingertips. I start pounding with the palms of my hands against the solid wood, trying to make noise. I can't get any leverage using my knuckles or the sides of my hands underneath my pinkies. I lift my arms as close to my face as possible, thinking at any moment the door will fly open and I can push my way out of the box into the hallway. But the door remains closed. No one comes.

I fall to the ground from sheer exhaustion combined with lack of food and water. My body starts shaking, and I can't stop. It's cold, it's wet, and I want to get out of here. I curl up and into an uneasy sleep. Drifting in and out of what seems to be a haze, hallucinating about lying on the warm sand of sunny Zuma Beach, thinking of nothing but what Jethro Tull song was playing on the boombox radio my high school friend Naomi used to cart along. My body is spent, almost numb.

Then I feel something close to me but can't make out what or who it is. Is it real or is my mind playing tricks on me? The brush of a tail across my wet cheek wakes me out of my haze. Yes! There is something crawling near me, on me. I try to scream, but no sound comes out. Batting my arms to my sides, kicking, twisting my best to shake whatever it is off me. Just when you feel it can't get worse, it does.

My skin crawls. I feel the bile rising in my throat as I back against the wall, knowing the floor is no longer welcoming. Something is crawling down there, and it's way too close to me. The swishing of a tail and talons scratching the solid-wood floor, I realize what it is. A rat! As disgusting as it is, it reminds me I'm not alone here. Something else lives here and has survived this place. *Focus on the goal,* I think, *and not on the pure foulness of it all.*

Still, I panic. The damn rat now has friends surrounding me. I can hear them squeaking at each other, circling me as I hold myself upright against the cold, wet stone wall. Kicking as hard as I can, my body goes into survival mode.

"No way are you getting me!" I yell at the top of my voice, trying to bat them away, and then, just as my foot connects with one and launches it into the old wood door, I feel a tail swishing across my neck, the clawed feet piercing my skull. As much as I try to shake back and forth, I can't get the horrid thing off my head. "God damn rats!"

I'm determined to get the rat off my head before its needlelike nails penetrate my scalp again. Filthy, I feel inhuman, my strength depleting. I try launching my body forward with the intent of hurling this vile thing off me. Instead, it clamps down harder than before and bites my ear. My screams don't end. I convulse and throw up whatever little water is left in me. Then the bile shoots up my throat and spews out of my mouth. All I know is the pulsing of my head, heart, and gut. Blood, torn flesh, the sound of survival for both human and rodent.

***

I wake up in an infirmary from a drug-induced sleep. Bandages surround my forehead, left ear, and a patch on my left side, neck to shoulder, blood splattered on my arms and legs. My head is in a vise so I can't move when the medic comes to check my vital signs. I am alive, but I feel nothing.

I don't want to see my face, so I lie in the hospital bed looking up at the timeworn acoustic-tiled ceiling. Shades of old water stains have made most of the tiles dull gray with a brown fringe around the corners where each meets up with the next to form perfect rows of ten across and twenty up and down. I concentrate on the watermarked tiles and try to forget the rats.

Closing my eyes brings it all back: the shrill shrieking of their communication to each other; the terrible pain I felt when my flesh was being bitten, scratched, pulled away from me; how I overcame them, only by spewing up the little bit of food that was left in my stomach. I need to stop thinking about the ordeal, but I can't.

When the nurse comes to check my bandaged head, she smiles faintly, not wanting me to see the sadness in her eyes. It's probably worse than I imagined, but I'm not going to look at myself, not today. The only thing I can think about is the present. This is what will help me get out of here.

"I need to use the bathroom," I say as nicely as I can. My voice is shaky. I can hardly get myself to be kind and pleasant, even though I should; this nurse is kind to me. My body doesn't want to move. She hands me a metal pan. I'm not going to use that lying here in this bed. I'm getting up and getting on with what I need to do. This isn't a pity party, and I'm way too young to use a bedpan.

"You rest," she says. I try lifting myself to a sitting position. How can I rest when I can't do a simple task that everybody does almost unconsciously? Using what little strength I had, I make it to an upright position. My head hurts; the blood rushes to my temples, making me feel weak and unsteady. I've got to get out of this place.

31

Flight

Duma, Syria
2011

As the days go by, I do get stronger. But any hopes of being rescued are gone. Nobody seems to be looking for me. Nobody.

"Time to shower," says a nurse as she waltzes into the room with several towels folded in her arms. She can barely see over the white, perfectly folded pile. "Oh," she stops in her tracks.

I'm trying to remain in a sitting position. I want to ask, *What's wrong? Haven't you ever seen a person who has been attacked by rats before?* Judging by her horrified expression, I probably look horrible.

"I must have made a wrong turn," she says, making an excuse for her reaction.

I don't believe her. When someone can't look you in the

eye, something isn't right.

Where once I'd been exceptionally strong, I feel extremely unsure of myself. I was a critical-mission team member, Bureau-trained field agent, and ambidextrous accurate weapons sniper. Now I look like a sideshow in the circus.

I hear her hurried steps as she sprints down the hallway.

I hoist myself out of bed, placing my blood-soaked bandaged leg over the bed's metal rail. I'm still me. No one is going to help me except me.

My muscles are weak. I try to step down and get my footing on the cold linoleum floor. All I can think about is one foot in front of the other. I grab the doorjamb that separates the small toilet and sink from the makeshift hospital bedroom. Steadying myself, I pray there's a mirror in the bathroom. I open my eyes, not able to contain myself. A small four-by-six picture-size piece of mirror is affixed to the right wall away from the toilet. Now is the time to face any fear I have about my appearance.

Supporting myself by holding onto the edges of the sink, I tilt my head so I can see my right ear. It's still there, just bright purple in color. Red spots dot my cheek and nose. *Must be dried blood.* I raise my eyes and lift my chin. I can make out horizontal scratch marks across my face and chest. My skin looks like a botched game of tic-tac-toe, where a small child has tried to draw the grid and then a parent draws over it to make it legible.

My legs seem fine: dirty, bruised, but no visible punctures or scratches, except for the big toe on my right foot. I remember kicking something with all the energy I had. "Damn. It bit me there," I say to myself.

At this point, I'm removed from myself. The idea of an animal trying to eat me seems so far from reality that the only way to deal with my situation is to remove all feeling.

I take inventory of myself. The dried blood, bit ear and toe, the deep scratches. None of this fazes me, until I look at my entire face. This is the most difficult part of it all: I look battered. For all the close calls in my life where something could've happened but didn't, something bad happened here. "Stop it." *These wounds will heal.*

I realize these guards aren't my true enemy. My anger isn't directed toward them. I sit down on the edge of my small cot and roll onto my left side. I need to face my feelings of betrayal, hurt, and rage toward my teammates who were supposed to protect me. But not now. For now, I need to set my questions aside. Once I'm back home with my sons I can deal with that. My entire focus needs to be on how to get out of here.

I adjust my sight. The sun is shining, and a glorious shadowing of light surrounds my empty hospital bed. Can I walk out now? There's no guard at my door, no bars on the windows. This can be the easiest way back to freedom. One problem. I can barely hold myself up or lower my body down on the toilet. How can I get the strength to get well enough so I can get out before they take me back to jail? Or will they? My body is bruised and bitten; my clothes are nowhere to be found. There's nothing here in this room except for the bed sheets and a small, worn towel to dry my hands and face. I could tie the strings at my neck and mid-back, but I have no shoes, socks, underwear, or bra. Can I just up and leave without being fully covered in this Muslim environment? Probably not a good idea.

My time in the infirmary is winding down. I've taken a liking to the tiny hospital bed and small efficient bathroom. Most of all, to the window. I could sit here most of the day, basking in the sunshine, adjusting to the rays as they filter through the small, thin pane of glass. Unfortunately, this is not helping to extend my convalescence. The sunshine gives me color, indicating I'm healthier than I want to look. Holding my body upright for hours on end leads to me recovering. Despite having over a dozen documented rat bites, I didn't get any kind of communicable or deadly disease. I'm not going back to that cell. If I must fight my way out of this place, I will, before going back to that hellhole.

Yesterday, the head nurse came in and ordered me to stand up. She gave me underwear and a bra. No socks or shoes, just those two articles of clothing. I put them on, maybe a little too fast, which was a mistake. Late that night the same nurse came back and towered over me.

"I know you are well. Soon you will leave."

I pretended to sleep, not showing that I knew she was there. An hour later she came in again and just stood there. She didn't touch me.

I can't sleep. Visions as real as my lying here in this bed come like tortured nightmares after watching a scary movie. I see myself back on that damp cell floor, my mind and body exhausted, trying to think back to why I was taken, why I was kidnapped.

What do I remember?

We'd been surveying the building across from the parking garage. Each day one of us took turns staring from the small crawlspace between the fifth and sixth ramps leading to the stairwell and emergency access doorway. Finally, right before Whit's shift was about to end, he radioed down for me to hold.

"Standby. Activity outside of entry. Could be our guy."

Sure enough, it was. He had bodyguards surrounding him, but Whit identified him from the height difference between him and those protecting him. Most men are taller than five foot eight; he wasn't. The guards shuffling him into a dark SUV did little to keep his identity secret. I was directly across from the parking garage, taking my time viewing the beautiful burkas in this tiny, woman-owned and operated boutique that shared the left wall of the building he publicly exited from.

Standby? He's getting away! There had to be a way to identify that SUV and get our 'friends' to help by picking up their coordinates. I left the safety of the shop and walked into the side entrance of the parking garage where the stairs were.

After climbing four flights, I flung open the door from the stairwell to the parking spots. This is where we were to meet our driver and exchange information. That's all I remember before being grabbed from behind, a pillowcase thrown over my head, hands secured behind me. I fought as hard as I could, using my legs and head-butting one foul-smelling, hard-headed captor. But where was Whit? Why had our plan gone wrong?

Noise interrupts my nightmarish remembering. Now, here in the infirmary, there's a commotion in the hallway. Two large men dressed in military uniforms rush in and grab me from my chair next to the window. They take me from my safe room and drag me down the cold hallway, my body trying to resist being hauled away like a bag of trash.

I'm thrown into a small containment room that looks familiar to me. We have these back home and throughout Syria. People enter them, but rarely leave. It's the one place even the hardest of detainees we captured talked about in fear. I know too well what happens next.

First, an official comes to tell me I broke a rule, committed a crime, or something else that has "offended the state." Then another less-official-looking guard, a 'thug,' enters with one or two backups. Then as I'm pushed onto the cold metal chair, my ankles are tied to the front chair posts, wrists are zip-tied to the cold, rigid metals rails, and then I'm bound in an 'x' configuration. One up, one diagonal, such that I can barely even move my fingers up and down because of how tightly I'm being held to the chair.

"Name?" More of a statement than an actual question.

I don't answer.

"Name!"

I will not answer.

The entrance is across from me. The door is shut. Inside are the four of us: two guards, interrogator, and me. No telling if this will be typical electroshock, drug-induced torture, or the latest intelligence craze, 'waterboarding.' I have no idea, but getting out of here alive will take some real effort. I've never been in this bad a situation. I'm the one doing the dirty work for my team, out here on my own with no protection. If I say anything, I'm disloyal. I'll be fired with cause: no pension, no reward for all the time I've put into the job. Missed family events, endless sleepless nights, all the things I sacrificed for my work will go unnoticed, unexplained, unanswered. My sons need to know why I wasn't there for every soccer game, school field trip and bedtime. They need to know what I've stood for. I need to get home to them. I sit, eyes closed, visualizing their beautiful happy faces, and wait for the pain to begin.

No one who hasn't been there can explain what it feels like to be kicked in the spleen, punched in the ribs, slapped upside your head until your ears ring in unison without ever hearing the questions. I just want to hear my sons' voices, their laughter and see their smiles. I recall every line on their faces, every perfect freckle on their small, perfect noses.

I endure the numerous blows until I am no longer present. My body is pulverized, but my mind is still strong, or, so I think, until the cold water rushes over my face. I am tipped upside down over a barrel that is tilted sideways. I am blasted with water from a long hose, then dunked under the surface with my head tilted backward. I can feel the shock of the freezing cold water on my open skin. I'm awake, but not completely conscious, just trying to breathe between the blasts from the hose and being dunked. I think of the old carnival rides that used to come to town, the dunk tank. Each shot of the makeshift firehose reminds me of the many times my brother and I missed as we tried to hit the target so the clown would fall into the water.

"Stay awake!"

Is my torturer telling me not to die? I'm drifting in and out of consciousness. I see my sons looking up at me, holding their arms out for me to pick them up. I can feel their small hands in mine. All I want is to feel their arms around my neck.

The guard is getting frustrated. I'm not capitulating. I'm now consciously holding my breath under the water. I am waking up, which means he will be ratcheting up the pain to break me. Do I give in?

Gasping for air, I'm jolted into consciousness, pulled out of the barrel, and dragged across the cold, wet cement floor, away from the improvised waterboard. Why? What's next? I lie on the wet cement, face down, hands bound to my ankles behind me. I turn my head to see who's near me. The two guards are blocking the doorway. I can't see who they're talking to. My vision is blurred, my head splitting from blows and the lack of oxygen. *Listen for the voices. Are they here or only in my head? Oh, my head hurts.*

I gasp for air, trying not to aspirate from all the water coming out of my stomach and lungs. I turn to face the voices and try to scream. Only cloudy water comes rushing out of my mouth.

Then, they stop. They don't want to stop. Someone made them stop. Who? Why?

I try to stay conscious. My ears are clogged from the dunkings; sounds are muffled. I strain to hear voices, to hear the words. I think I hear a voice repeating in Arabic, *"Quaslaqud esay tam!"* Stop!

I'm lying in my own blood, shivering from the cold water in which I have been repeatedly immersed.

The voice is not pleased. It comes closer. I can barely see the figure, the blur behind the voice. It looks down, sees me with my legs bound and my heels touching my behind, arms back, wrists tied together, my hands touching my toes.

That's all I can recall. I must have blacked out.

***

When I come to, I'm back in a cell. My eyes start to adjust to the dim light. This is a different cell. It has many vertical bars across a window high up and the front is a sliding-gate door, like a government holding lockup. Washed concrete floors, modern door handles and locks. It must be closer to a city or town. There'll be more people here than in the other rat-infested hellhole.

I've been untied. Progress. I can see down either side of the hallway. No rats, no stonewalls, no old beaten wood door. I feel surprisingly safe here, even if it is a jail. Fluorescent bulbs line the hallway, no dim single lightbulb at the end. Jail cells on one side, and from what I can see, there are two, maybe three, doors on the opposite wall.

Given the hole where I started, it must have taken a lot of political clout to get me to an official-looking place like this. No one knows I'm gone except my team members, and they've probably been told to write me off at this point.

My mind flashes back to the look on that female guard's face as she checked to confirm I was a woman. Did she have something to do with my being here now? Maybe she's behind one of those closed doors.

I try to remember how many days or months I've been locked up, but my mind draws a blank. All I can do is think of my two sons and what I can do to get out of here. For the first time since before I was pushed into the trunk of that car, I have hope. Is this the last stop before heading home?

The days blend into one another. It's hard not to scream out loud. I fantasize between wanting to tear apart these bars and jump through the metal-clad window or to just tackle the next guard who decides to stroll down the hallway before exiting through one of the three doors outside my cell.

Why can't somebody come get me out of here? Doesn't anyone care that I'm gone? Where are the people I trusted? Why doesn't anybody give a damn? My team ... the people who should have protected me—they're supposed to be the ones we trust with our lives. Not Jason, who was only involved in one mission, or Robby, who couldn't put the team before himself, but the core members like Big Mike, Whit, and J.B. Even Campbell would never have put me in a position of jeopardy without cover or backup. I need to figure this out myself. *Why* doesn't matter anymore; it is what it is.

At the end of this when I'm home and reconnected with my family, I'll seek answers. I'll figure out who did nothing and who tried to help me.

Today, when the guard enters my cell to deliver my meal and change my water supply, I need to see how to get past him and out one of those three doors. It's the only way out. I want to get out of here. *Please God, show me a way.*

I must really think this through, and it better work, as I doubt, I'll get a second chance. The times when the guards change, enter the hall, bring food then leave, and how many others are in this facility must be determined and charted for consistency.

I survey the cell, looking for any type of rock, stone, or something I can use to etch little tick marks at the base of the wall along my cot where they can be hidden from sight. Starting today, I'm going to keep track of how many days elapse. There doesn't seem to be anything on the cot, wash bowl, or bucket on the other side of the cell that's taken out each day and cleaned. I feel around the old, dilapidated wooden bowl—pieces of wood held together by metal bands. I feel a sharp metal edge poking out from the side of the bowl facing the wall. I pull it out. If I can bend the metal, maybe I can get the loose part to break off.

I spend each day trying to bend and move that small piece of metal back and forth so I can break it off. Finally, I get it! Now I can sharpen it against the metal door handle. Once it's sharp enough, I can use it to cut myself loose if I'm tied up again, or even use it as a weapon if need be. Most importantly, it gives me a boost of confidence, however small, that I'm in control of something. There will be a way out of here. I can make this happen.

Later, thinking of using this precious bit of metal to scratch a wall just to count the days seems idiotic. I now have far more important plans for it.

The next morning when the female guard comes to give

me food, I say, "Thank you." It's the first time I've said anything in her presence. She smiles—I don't think she understands English—but perhaps my smile conveys appreciation.

Time has stopped for me, or at least, been suspended, along with my life. If I can just hold on for the right time to overpower her, I think I can move more quickly than she can, since she favors her left leg and walks with a limp. It's unclear to me why I hadn't noticed this before. Had I not seen her until now? Have I been so self-absorbed with my own anguish of being here that I've not realized just how much of a gift she is to me?

As she makes her rounds back and forth, delivering and collecting trays, wash bins, and crap pots, I begin to figure out how many others are held here. One week it was six trays and another week it was three trays, until one day she brought my food and then walked directly across the first of the three hallway doors and was gone. My mind told me I didn't see what I just saw. How could I be the only one in here?

I'm here alone. I can get out. I grab my metal shank that I've made into a blade by painstakingly sharpening it against everything in my cell—metal, stone, the concrete floor. I'll only get one chance to overpower her. I must be ready to act.

She finally comes up to the cell and takes a key out of her apron pocket. Silently, she opens the locked bars. She stands inside the doorway and takes something else out of her pocket. I look at her confused. There is no tray, water, or waste bucket. She is standing in the opening. All I need to do is overpower her, stab the shank into her neck, and walk out. She just stands there, hand closed tight with her arms extended out toward me. I rise from the cot and take a step forward, toward her outstretched fist. She drops whatever she's holding and quickly takes a step back and closes the bars, locking me in.

As she scurries down the hall to the last door, I look at the wrapped two-by-two-inch paper package on the floor. I pick up the package. It's warm and smells like smoked meat mixed with oil and pepper. I begin to salivate before I can even get the wrapping off. I hold it close to my nose, soaking in the bouquet, wanting to tear into it, but also afraid it might be a trick designed to get me in trouble or to attract the attention of the guards if I drip it on my prison outfit.

Regardless, I can't help myself, and I tear open the paper and bite into the thick, red, sizzling hot meat. I am so hungry. I devour it within seconds. It isn't about enjoyment. It burns my mouth, but I don't care, as the barely chewed morsel slides down my throat and into my empty stomach. No time to sit and savor. I need to dispose of the paper before the guards come into the hallway.

The only real way to get rid of it is to eat it, but I can't get myself to swallow any more than the meat. For the time being, I end up wrapping my shank with the paper and hiding it under the mattress.

Lying on my cot, all I can think about is whether I'll get another visit from the kind 'attendant' and if it might present an opportunity to get out of here. I won't know until tomorrow whether she might come back. If the other guards suspect that she's sympathetic to me, they might replace her.

There must be a way to get through the door across from me. Realistically, I have only one shot; there's no turning back. I'll have to take it; there won't be another chance. I ask for help. *God, I don't want to die here. I don't want my life to be forgotten, my family wondering where I am and why I haven't contacted them. Please give me a sign that I'll leave here alive, and soon!*

Something stirs, then a bump wakes me up. Most nights I barely sleep, but tonight, after filling my belly with the cooked meat, I fell sound asleep. Now, I hear a man's voice, moaning in the darkness. Then laughter, coming from the same voice, I think. *"Haha, cuse ackta."* Damn.

He's slurring his words, cursing at himself. Maybe he's drunk; at the very least, he's been drinking. The voice grows louder, and I realize he's in front of my cell. Tensing up, I know there's going to be a moment when, if he opens the barred gate, I'll need to be ready to take advantage of it.

I grab my shank and lean into the mattress, making sure I don't drop it. Briefly, my thoughts turn to home, wanting to be with my children, wanting to watch them grow up. Is taking a life worth the chance to escape? For me the answer is yes. I've worked my whole life to build my self-worth, to become the best at what I do. I'm not going to die wasting away in some cell far away from home.

In the dark, I hear the cell door being unlocked and the barred gate sliding open. He is drunk. He mumbles as he leans against the wall and takes off his jacket. I suspect he has more in mind than a prisoner check. Holding the shank, I throw myself toward the wall where he has propped himself up. Darkness covers us as the metal punctures his neck. I press against him, holding him to the wall. I hear him gasp, one final breath, and then silence. Warm, wet moisture flows down onto my hand. I coil back, not knowing what's next. His body buckles. We meet on the floor, both of us crumpled up, with him on top of me. Time freezes.

I roll him off me. I need to move fast. After tearing off my bloody shirt, I replace it with his jacket, then undo his belt and carefully pull off his pants. I slip on his trousers and then his socks. The clothes are big on me, but not too much.

I cinch the belt tight. No sounds come from the hall. I take his cap and shove my dirty hair, or what's left of it, up into it. Then I take one final thing from his lifeless body: his gun.

I step over him, out of the cell, looking both ways, again trying to adjust to the dim lighting. Of the three doors on the opposite wall, I think the door on the far left goes to the front of the jail. I vaguely remember being brought in through there. I know the middle door must go to the kitchen, as that's the one they always come through with the food. People could be there, and I don't need any company now. I have no idea what's behind door number three, but my gut tells me it's the best option. My heart pounds as I approach the door. No one has come down the hallway. It's just me and the dead guard.

Now's the time to move. I've seen this door used to leave the hallway when the guards finish their patrol of the cells. I don't know what's in store for me, but I know this is my chance and I must act. Keeping my back to the wall next to the door, I straighten my new jacket, tighten the belt, and shove a few loose strands of my hair under the cap. I've also put on his boots, although they're a couple of sizes too big. I take a deep breath. *God, please don't let my face show the strain of what I'm about to do.* I turn the knob and walk through the door.

There's a loading dock with other doors into the building and a ramp with five carts, apparently used for moving supplies. No one is on the dock that's directly in front of me, four carts on one side and one at the top. I can hear some guards talking and smell their cigarette smoke wafting in from the far side of the building. They barely come into view. One looks up but returns to the conversation.

I grab the rusty handle of the cart in front of me, my mind racing as fast as my heart. *Stay calm, look ahead, don't rush, just breathe.* I push the empty cart across the walkway, down the ramp, turn a corner, and then slip out of the building.

It's dark and hot. I see no signs of people working at this time of night. I guess they all leave at the end of the day, all except the drunk, dead guard who, fortunately for me, decided to enter my cell in the middle of the night. I can't believe the quiet. My eyes need time to adjust to the one lamp lighting the loading dock, then the night. *Just walk, keep moving, don't make a sound, breathe easy.* My God, I'm outside. I'm going to walk out of here alive without having to kill anyone else. My world is in front of me, one carefully placed step at a time.

I go down the ramp to a dirt road that's fenced in on the left with some trees on the right. There are no lights, trucks, or cars. In front of me is nothing but dirt, a dirt road with no end in sight. Open, quiet, not gravel, just dirt. My steps make no noise. It's the dead of night, and I walk, recounting in my mind the number of shifts, the guards changing every six hours, then every eight hours. I looked into the eyes of that stupid, drunk gatekeeper as I removed his clothing, knowing I could pose as him and walk out, knowing that the shift wouldn't change for hours. He never saw it coming, his demise. I keep walking.

Soon I see a faint light ahead. I continue on the side of the dirt road. A vehicle slows down, almost to a crawl. I keep my head down, trying to shield my face as best I can. The headlights are weak and, as luck would have it, start to flicker. I can see the driver's trying to identify my uniform. He waves and picks up speed, passing me on the road. I nod back. The boots are big, so I am very careful, deliberately taking each step, trying not to fall or teeter, or look like a drunk. *Don't draw any attention to yourself.* The road extends further.

As I walk, I can't help but relive the last year, or what I think was, at least, a year. Me coming down the garage ramp to the team driver where Whit and Mike should have been waiting for me. The terrifying moment of fear when the unknown car pulled up, my captors jumping out, grabbing my arms, bagging my head, tying my hands together, injecting me, and throwing me into the trunk. All in seconds. The darkness of the trunk, not knowing where I was going or if I would be coherent when we got to wherever they were taking me. The chill of a damp cell, no food, little water, and the endless screeching of the house rats trying to assess me, their nails clicking on the stone floor, tearing the flesh on my back. The discovery that I was a woman by a female guard before I might have died. Being a woman changed my situation. Enduring the methodical torture as they tried to break me. It didn't matter to me what they did to my body; I had to keep my mind focused on staying alive. The water filling my lungs, and me passing out on the cold cement floor, wanting to scream but having only enough wind to breathe. The two guards throwing chemicals on my face trying to wake me, thinking they might have killed me. At the end, I guess they thought I had some value or else I'm sure I would have been killed. The realization that nobody was coming to rescue me. My own sense of purpose, to remember who I was when I was questioned by the silence that each day brought and the endless desire to make it back home to my sons. The tears that no longer flowed as I watched each night turn into day and then night again.

I just keep walking, trying to get as far away from the jail and to some city or town. Someplace with a phone. I walk for hours; the night sky is getting lighter. It is still dark, but I can tell the sun will be coming up soon. I need to get out of sight soon, as I'm sure they'll be looking for me when the shift changes and they find that I'm gone. I keep walking. Nobody is going to get in my way now. *Breathe slowly.* I decide to take off the large, black-soled boots and try to pick up the pace. The dirt feels cold under my bare feet. I feel a connection to it, the road and my freedom. *Just pace, walk with purpose, hold yourself up, you are going to make it.* I can't help but wonder why those guards outside paid no attention to me.

Another car approaches. I'm frozen with fear, but the driver pulls over and asks me in Arabic if I want a ride, to take a load off. Part of me wants to stop walking and take him up on his offer, but I'll have to talk, and he would then see I wasn't a guard.

"*Shuk run,*" I say, in a low voice, while coughing, trying to make it look like I'm sick. "*Yasheur bialmirad.*"

He waves me off, probably thinking I'm an ingrate. The dirt road comes to an end. The sky turns dark gray. I only have a couple of hours before the hot sun will start pounding down on me. A sign ahead says "Damascus. Eight Kilometers." I can make it there before sunrise. I walk. my emotions as raw as my feet. Funny how the driver who offered me a ride never said anything about my holding these boots rather than wearing them.

Why didn't they come after me? My anger begins to rise. I can't keep it in check. It fuels every step. How I want to scream at Whit, hit him, tell him, "This is why I don't trust people. You let me down. I'm the one person you're supposed to be there for no matter what. Why did you turn your back to me? Why?" I wonder if he and Mike have an excuse, a reason for not trying to find me. Whatever that might be, it won't be good enough. I continue to push my sore body one more step at a time toward the city.

Anger can replace logical thinking. It has its place. I now know why I hadn't dwelled on the why. I was captured, but the how of escape was up to me. The anger, hurt, and pain come when I need it most; it pushes me to keep moving.

I get to the beginning of what looks like a small community on the outskirts of Damascus. I am cold and dirty, and I know I look completely disheveled. A dim candle glows in a small, single-story, concrete box-like building that's probably a family's home. Dogs start to bark. I wonder if I smell like meat, maybe like the piece that the aide had snuck into my cell. Without her kindness, I might not have had the energy to walk for as long as I have. Morning approaches. I stay on the opposite side of the road from where the dogs bark, protecting their master's home.

Around the corner from the homes I find a small store next to a filling station. As I get closer, I see a telephone booth near the gas pumps. All operatives know one phone number that is etched in their brain like their name or birth date. No money is needed when calling that number. I step inside the booth and close the dusty door, leaving just me and the payphone. I pick up the receiver and hear the static of a dial tone, interrupted by beeps each time I press a number on the worn keypad. After a few seconds, the operator at the other end comes on the line.

"ID number?" she states more than asks.

"Seven-seven-eight-six," I reply.

"Repeat." Again, a statement, not a question.

"It's me. Seven-seven-eight-six."

"Can you stay where you are? Are you hurt?"

"I can stay outside the phone booth, but not long," I reply, without letting go of my emotions. "I'm all right."

Silence. I know she's stunned. By now, the system would

be showing that I'm gone. They must be thinking that this doesn't compute—how could someone be where she is, using her code?

The moments seem like hours as I wait for her reply. My patience is giving out; I'm on the verge of coming unglued. It's hard to remember much of anything after her next words to me.

"Coordinates confirmed. Stay close. We're coming for you."

"Copy that." I hang up the phone, and the tears start to run down my face. I know it won't take long; we always have personnel in Damascus, and they are on the way.

Looking down, I see a bloodstain on the guard's shirt I'm wearing. My tears have liquefied it into a vibrant, fresh, red color. *Hold it together,* I say softly to myself, as the thought of getting out of here safely, of going home, of being with my two sons again, is all too much for my brain to absorb.

Like a movie reel, I can vividly see my room in the orphanage, all the made beds, white sheets filling the space. Then the foster home, Loretta, Leo, the hot stove. I can see the look on my parents' faces when they came to pick me up once the adoption was completed. All the feelings of self-loathing, not belonging, being the mixed-race kid with White Jewish parents, wash over me as I sit and wait for my rescue ride out of this hellhole.

A few cars drive by. Two cars pull into the gas station and fill up their tanks. No one looks my way. I'm not visible to them. But this time I feel different: I am seeing me. I have survived until my stomach ached, but my head has remained clear. For what feels like the first time in my life, I am completely visible to myself. The realization that I am alive provides an adrenaline rush that propels each step I take. No one can count me out again. I am here. I do matter. Cautious of my surroundings, I hold back the tears. *Thank you, God, for this new life I'm being given. My gratitude to you will now be forever part of who I am.*

At that moment, a dark-colored SUV slows down and pulls into the station. My heart begins to race. I know they've come for me. My nightmare will be over. I look down and notice the blood still pooling on the ground under my feet. It's time to get up and move closer toward the vehicle. The car pulls up alongside me, and the passenger window is rolled down.

An operator in plain clothes and aviator shades looks at me and says, "7786?"

"Yes," I reply quietly.

"Get in! Now!" The back door opens, and I dive in headfirst. My entire body is shaking.

"Lie down and get out of that uniform. Clothes are on the floor."

I shed the uniform and quickly put on freshly laundered underwear, pants, and t-shirt over my dirty body. The cotton feels so smooth against my raw skin.

"Well, we certainly didn't expect to see you around here," he quips. I've not heard an American's voice for a very long time.

"Are we safe?" I ask, as the driver turns from the dirt road I'd just walked and on to the main highway.

He replies, "You're safe now. We're going home. Stay down out of sight and try to relax; you're in good hands."

Stretched out on the long back seat, I keep trying to hold my emotions in check, but I no longer can. The tears come, flow, staining the fresh white shirt that was just given to me. "Thank you," I say, almost inaudibly.

With the most reassuring, caring tone, he says, "You're one of us. Nothing's going to happen to you now. We got you. Try to rest."

I rest my head on the seat. I'm between worlds, somewhere between feeling safe and wondering if this is just a dream. I'm still fearful; I try to stay awake by watching the agent in the front seat. He looks invincible. I've seen this look of confidence before. I am safe. I drift in and out of sleep. I still have no sense of time.

When we stop, I hear voices, all American, speaking English. Now I know I'm getting out of here. A young man dressed in scrubs bends over, looking at my feet through the open car door.

"Hi. I'm Dr. Grant. Those feet could use some TLC."

"That's not the only thing," I reply.

They all laugh.

"A sense of humor after all you have been through. Don't worry. I'll attend to each wound, one at a time," he says in a direct doctorly voice. "But now we need to sedate you for the flight."

Two agents push me gently toward a gurney. One holds my ankles, while the other eases me forward by the shoulders. A young man dressed like a US paramedic wraps me in a foil-like blanket as I lie on a stretcher.

"I want to go home. Where are my sons? And ...?" Before I can finish my questions, I feel the pull of a needle as it's taken out of my arm. Colors start to form into shapes, morphing into something they are not. I see my bleeding toes. Then nothing.

The next few days are a blur. I barely remember anything about the flight. I recall instances of engine noise and people talking. Apparently, they kept me sedated for the four-hour flight from Damascus, Syria, to Frankfurt, Germany.

The sun streams through the high windows of the Landstuhl Regional Medical Center into my room. The high-powered light fixtures illuminate every spec of the room. I cover my eyes with my left hand. My right arm hurts, and my hand feels numb. The smell and feel of the freshly pressed linen sheets overwhelm my senses.

I look across my bed and see a row of neatly made cots lining the room and on either side of me. All neatly made up, but unoccupied. I'm the only patient in this spacious room. I remember my first real memories as a child. The long row of small beds in the orphanage. The image of a row of beds I'd kept stored somewhere in my child's mind. That image evokes pain. I don't belong there; I never did.

With the sun's bright cast streaming through me, and the smell of the clean sheets, I relax.

"Very good." That's what the volunteer at the orphanage told me when I read a new word.

"Good work," Director Smith encouraged me.

"Good," I've wanted to tell myself for so long.

This quiet, white, sundrenched room will stay imprinted in my brain forever. I close my eyes and think that soon I will be back home with them. Everyone is part of a "System." The key is to figure out what type you are in. Then understand your current place and next, how to move forward.

A Note from the Author

If you enjoyed this book, I would be very grateful if you would write a review and publish it at your point of purchase. Your review, even a brief one, will help other readers to decide whether to read this story. Thank you.
    With Gratitude,
    Sally